The Princeton Review®

AP® COMPUTER SCIENCE PRINCIPLES PREP

2023 Edition

The Staff of The Princeton Review

PrincetonReview.com

Penguin Random House

The Princeton Review
110 East 42nd St, 7th Floor
New York, NY 10017

Published in the United States by Penguin Random House LLC, New York, and in Canada by Random House of Canada, a division of Penguin Random House Ltd., Toronto.

ISBN: 978-0-593-45073-4
ISSN: 2767-1321

Editor: Chris Chimera
Production Editors: Emma Parker, Chris Stobart
Production Artist: Deborah Weber
Content Developer: Melissa Estremera

Printed in the United States of America.

10 9 8 7 6 5 4 3 2 1

2023 Edition

The Princeton Review Publishing Team
Rob Franek, Editor-in-Chief
David Soto, Senior Director, Data Operations
Stephen Koch, Senior Manager, Data Operations
Deborah Weber, Director of Production
Jason Ullmeyer, Production Design Manager
Jennifer Chapman, Senior Production Artist
Selena Coppock, Director of Editorial
Aaron Riccio, Senior Editor
Meave Shelton, Senior Editor
Chris Chimera, Editor
Orion McBean, Editor
Patricia Murphy, Editor
Laura Rose, Editor
Alexa Schmitt Bugler, Editorial Assistant

Random House Publishing Team
Tom Russell, VP, Publisher
Alison Stoltzfus, Senior Director, Publishing
Brett Wright, Senior Editor
Emily Hoffman, Assistant Managing Editor
Ellen Reed, Production Manager
Suzanne Lee, Designer
Eugenia Lo, Publishing Assistant

For customer service, please contact **editorialsupport@review.com**, and be sure to include:

- full title of the book
- ISBN
- page number

ACKNOWLEDGMENTS

Special thanks to Melissa Estremera for her content development work on the 2023 edition of this book. Additionally, The Princeton Review would like to thank Deborah Weber, Emma Parker, and Chris Stobart for their contributions to this title.

Contents

Get More (Free) Content

at **PrincetonReview.com/prep**

As easy as 1•2•3

1 Go to PrincetonReview.com/prep or scan the **QR code** and enter the following ISBN for your book: **9780593450734**

2 Answer a few simple questions to set up an exclusive Princeton Review account. *(If you already have one, you can just log in.)*

3 Enjoy access to your **FREE** content!

Once you've registered, you can...

- Take a full-length practice SAT and ACT
- Get valuable advice about the college application process, including tips for writing a great essay and where to apply for financial aid
- If you're still choosing between colleges, use our searchable rankings of *The Best 388 Colleges* to find out more information about your dream school

- Access comprehensive study guides and a variety of printable resources including AP Score Conversion charts, Key Terms lists, and the Glossary
- Check to see if there have been any corrections or updates to this edition
- Get our take on any recent or pending updates to the AP Computer Science Principles Exam

Need to report a potential **content** issue?

Contact **EditorialSupport@review.com** and include:

- full title of the book
- ISBN
- page number

Need to report a **technical** issue?

Contact **TPRStudentTech@review.com** and provide:

- your full name
- email address used to register the book
- full book title and ISBN
- Operating system (Mac/PC) and browser (Chrome, Firefox, Safari, etc.)

Look For These Icons Throughout The Book

 PROVEN TECHNIQUES

 OTHER REFERENCES

 ONLINE ARTICLES

Part I
Using This
Book to Improve
Your AP Score

- Preview: Your Knowledge, Your Expectations
- Your Guide to Using This Book
- How to Begin

PREVIEW: YOUR KNOWLEDGE, YOUR EXPECTATIONS

Your route to a high score on the AP Computer Science Principles Exam depends a lot on how you plan to use this book. Start thinking about your plan by responding to the following questions.

1. Rate your level of confidence in your knowledge of the content tested by the AP Computer Science Principles Exam:

   A. Very confident—I know it all
   B. I'm pretty confident, but there are topics for which I could use help
   C. Not confident—I need quite a bit of support
   D. I'm not sure.

2. If you have a goal score in mind, circle your goal score for the AP Computer Science Principles Exam:

   5   4   3   2   1   I'm not sure yet.

3. What do you expect to learn from this book? Circle all that apply to you.

   A. A general overview of the test and what to expect
   B. Strategies for how to approach the test
   C. The content tested by this exam
   D. I'm not sure yet.

It's Bubble Time
Bubble sheets for the tests in this book can be found in the back of the book and are available online—you can print them out from your online Student Tools. We highly recommend that you do so before taking a practice test, as learning how to transfer your answers to a bubble sheet is an important part of preparing for the test.

YOUR GUIDE TO USING THIS BOOK

This book is organized to provide as much—or as little—support as you need, so you can use this book in whatever way will be most helpful to improving your score on the AP Computer Science Principles Exam.

- The remainder of **Part I** will provide guidance on how to use this book and help you determine your strengths and weaknesses.

- **Part II** of this book contains Practice Test 1, the Diagnostic Answer Key, answers and explanations for each question, and a scoring guide. We recommend that you take this test before going any further in order to realistically determine:
  o your starting point right now
  o which question types you're ready for and which you might need to practice
  o which content topics you are familiar with and which you will want to carefully review

Note that the answer key for Practice Test 1 has been specifically designed to help you self-diagnose any potential areas of weakness so that you can best focus your test preparation and be efficient with your time.

- **Part III** of this book will:
  o provide information about the structure, scoring, and content of the AP Computer Science Principles Exam
  o help you to make a study plan
  o point you toward additional resources

- **Part IV** of this book will explore various strategies:
  o how to attack multiple-choice questions (MCQs)
  o how to manage your time to maximize the number of points available to you

- **Part V** of this book covers the content you need for the AP Computer Science Principles Exam.

- **Part VI** of this book contains Practice Tests 2 and 3, their answer and explanations, and a scoring guide. We recommend that you pepper in Practice Tests as you study for your exam. Don't take all Practice Tests in a row or even in rapid succession. Start with Practice Test 1 to get a sense of where you are. Then, as you complete your content review, take a Practice Test every so often to see how you are doing and if you are improving or need to review certain topics.

You may choose to use some parts of this book over others, or you may work through the entire book. Your approach will depend on your needs and how much time you have. Now let's look at how to make this determination.

HOW TO BEGIN

1. **Take Practice Test 1**

   Before you can decide how to use this book, you need to take a practice test. Doing so will give you insight into your strengths and weaknesses, and the test will also help you make an effective study plan. If you're feeling test-phobic, remind yourself that a practice test is a tool for diagnosing yourself—it's not how well you do that matters but how you use information gleaned from your performance to guide your preparation.

   So, before you read further, take Practice Test 1 starting on page 9 of this book. Be sure to finish it in one sitting, following the instructions that appear before the test.

2. **Check Your Answers**

Using the Diagnostic Answer Key on page 50, follow our three-step process to identify your strengths and weaknesses with regard to the tested topics. This will help you determine which content review chapters to prioritize when studying this book. Don't worry about the explanations for now, and don't worry about missed questions. We'll get to that soon.

3. **Reflect on the Test**

After you take your first test, respond to the following questions:

- How much time did you spend on the multiple-choice questions?

- How much time did you spend on each free-response question?

- How many multiple-choice questions did you miss?

- Do you feel you had the knowledge to address the subject matter of the free-response questions?

4. **Read Part III of This Book and Complete the Self-Evaluation**

Part III will provide information on how the test is structured and scored. It will also set out areas of content that are tested.

As you read Part III, re-evaluate your answers to the questions above. At the end of Part III, you will revisit and refine those questions. You will then be able to make a study plan, based on your needs and available time, that will allow you to use this book most effectively.

5. **Engage with Parts IV and V as Needed**

Notice the word *engage*. You'll get more out of this book if you use it intentionally than if you read it passively, hoping for an improved score through osmosis.

Strategy chapters will help you think about your approach to the question types on this exam. Part IV will open with a reminder to think about how you approach questions now and then close with a reflection section

The content chapters in Part V are designed to provide a review of the content tested on the AP Computer Science Principles Exam, including the level of detail you need to know and how the content is tested. In addition, the content chapters are broken up to reflect the 5 Big Ideas structure of the AP Computer Science Principles course, as outlined by the College Board. You will have the opportunity to assess your mastery of the content of each chapter through test-appropriate questions and a reflection section.

6. **Take Practice Tests 2 and 3 and Assess Your Performance**

Once you feel you have developed the strategies you need and gained the knowledge you lacked, you should take Practice Test 2, which starts on page 187 of this book. You should do so in one sitting, following the instructions at the beginning of the test.

When you are finished, check your answers to the multiple-choice sections. See if a teacher or friend will read your free-response answers and provide feedback, and go over them with you.

Once you have taken the test, reflect on the areas on which you still need work, and revisit the chapters in this book that address those deficiencies. Then go back and take Practice Test 3 and do the same. You've got 3 practice tests with this book—be sure to make use of all of them!

7. **Keep Working**

As mentioned earlier, there are other resources available to you, including a wealth of information on the AP Students website (apstudents.collegeboard. org/courses/ap-computer-science-principles). On this site, you can continue to explore areas that you could improve upon and engage in those areas right up until the day of the test. You should use a mix of web resources and book review to solidify your understanding of any question subjects that you keep getting wrong.

Need Some Guidance?
If you're looking for a way to get the most out of your studying, check out our free study guide for this exam, which you can access via your online Student Tools. See the "Get More (Free) Content" page for details on accessing this great resource and more.

Part II
Practice Test

Practice Test 1

AP® Computer Science Principles Exam

SECTION I: Multiple-Choice Questions

DO NOT OPEN THIS BOOKLET UNTIL YOU ARE TOLD TO DO SO.

At a Glance

Total Time
2 hours
Number of Questions
70
Percent of Total Score
70%
Writing Instrument
Pencil required

Instructions

Section I of this examination contains 70 multiple-choice questions. Fill in only the ovals for numbers 1 through 70 on your answer sheet.

Indicate all of your answers to the multiple-choice questions on the answer sheet. No credit will be given for anything written in this exam booklet, but you may use the booklet for notes or scratch work. After you have decided which of the suggested answers is best, completely fill in the corresponding oval on the answer sheet. Give only one answer to each question. If you change an answer, be sure that the previous mark is erased completely. Here is a sample question and answer.

Sample Question   Sample Answer

Chicago is a
(A) state
(B) city
(C) country
(D) continent

Use your time effectively, working as quickly as you can without losing accuracy. Do not spend too much time on any one question. Go on to other questions and come back to the ones you have not answered if you have time. It is not expected that everyone will know the answers to all the multiple-choice questions.

About Guessing

Many candidates wonder whether or not to guess the answers to questions about which they are not certain. Multiple-choice scores are based on the number of questions answered correctly. Points are not deducted for incorrect answers, and no points are awarded for unanswered questions. Because points are not deducted for incorrect answers, you are encouraged to answer all multiple-choice questions. On any questions you do not know the answer to, you should eliminate as many choices as you can, and then select the best answer among the remaining choices.

GO ON TO THE NEXT PAGE.

Quick Reference

Instruction	Explanation
Assignment, Display, and Input	

Text:
`a ← expression`
 	
Block:
`a ◀— expression`
	Evaluates `expression` and then assigns a copy of the result to the variable a.

Text:
`DISPLAY(expression)`
 	
Block:
`DISPLAY expression`
	Displays the value of `expression`, followed by a space.

Text:
`INPUT()`
 	
Block:
`INPUT`
	Accepts a value from the user and returns the input value.

Arithmetic Operators and Numeric Procedures	

Text and Block:
`a + b`
`a - b`
`a * b`
`a / b`
	The arithmetic operators +, -, *, and / are used to perform arithmetic on a and b.
	
	For example, `17 / 5` evaluates to `3.4`.
	
	The order of operations used in mathematics applies when evaluating expressions.

Text and Block: `a MOD b`	Evaluates to the remainder when a is divided by b. Assume that a is an integer greater than or equal to 0 and b is an integer greater than 0. For example, `17 MOD 5` evaluates to 2. The `MOD` operator has the same precedence as the * and / operators.

Text:
`RANDOM(a, b)`
 	
Block:
`RANDOM a, b`
	Generates and returns a random integer from a to b, including a and b. Each result is equally likely to occur.
	
	For example, `RANDOM(1, 3)` could return `1`, `2`, or `3`.

Instruction	Explanation
Relational and Boolean Operators	
Text and Block: a = b a ≠ b a > b a < b a ≥ b a ≤ b	The relational operators =, ≠, >, <, ≤, and ≥ are used to test the relationship between two variables, expressions, or values. A comparison using relational operators evaluates to a Boolean value. For example, a = b evaluates to true if a and b are equal; otherwise it evaluates to false.
Text: NOT condition Block: NOT (condition)	Evaluates to true if condition is false; otherwise evaluates to false.
Text: condition1 AND condition2 Block: (condition1) AND (condition2)	Evaluates to true if both condition1 and condition2 are true; otherwise evaluates to false.
Text: condition1 OR condition2 Block: (condition1) OR (condition2)	Evaluates to true if condition1 is true or if condition2 is true or if both condition1 and condition2 are true; otherwise evaluates to false.
Selection	

Text:
 	
IF(condition)
{
<block of statements>
}
 	
Block:
 	
IF (condition)
   (block of statements)
	The code in block of statements is executed if the Boolean expression condition evaluates to true; no action is taken if condition evaluates to false.

Instruction	Explanation
Selection—Continued	

Text:
 	
`IF(condition)`
`{`
`<first block of statements>`
`}`
`ELSE`
`{`
`<second block of statements>`
`}`
 	
Block:
 	
IF `condition`
 `first block of statements`
ELSE
 `second block of statements`
	The code in `first block of statements` is executed if the Boolean expression `condition` evaluates to `true`; otherwise the code in `second block of statements` is executed.

Iteration	

Text:
 	
`REPEAT n TIMES`
`{`
`<block of statements>`
`}`
 	
Block:
 	
REPEAT n TIMES
 `block of statements`
	The code in `block of statements` is executed n times.

Text:
 	
`REPEAT UNTIL(condition)`
`{`
`<block of statements>`
`}`
 	
Block:
 	
REPEAT UNTIL `condition`
 `block of statements`
	The code in `block of statements` is repeated until the Boolean expression `condition` evaluates to `true`.

Instruction	Explanation
List Operations	
For all list operations, if a list index is less than 1 or greater than the length of the list, an error message is produced and the program terminates.	
Text: aList ← [value1, value2, value3, ...] Block: aList ⟵ valuel, value2, value3	Creates a new list that contains the values value1, value2, value3, and ... at indices 1, 2, 3, and ... respectively and assigns it to aList.
Text: aList ← [] Block: aList ⟵ []	Creates an empty list and assigns it to aList.
Text: aList ← bList Block: aList ⟵ bList	Assigns a copy of the list bList to the list aList. For example, if bList contains [20, 40, 60], then aList will also contain [20, 40, 60] after the assignment.
Text: aList[i] Block: aList [i]	Accesses the element of aList at index i. The first element of aList is at index 1 and is accessed using the notation aList[1].
Text: x ← aList[i] Block: x ⟵ aList [i]	Assigns the value of aList[i] to the variable x.
Text: aList[i] ← x Block: aList [i] ⟵ x	Assigns the value of x to aList[i].
Text: aList[i] ← aList[j] Block: aList [i] ⟵ aList [j]	Assigns the value of aList[j] to aList[i].
Text: INSERT(aList, i, value) Block: INSERT aList, i, value	Any values in aList at indices greater than or equal to i are shifted one position to the right. The length of the list is increased by 1, and value is placed at index i in aList.

Instruction	Explanation
List Operations—Continued	

Text:
 	
`APPEND(aList, value)`
 	
Block:
 	
`APPEND` `aList, value`
	The length of `aList` is increased by 1, and `value` is placed at the end of `aList`.

Text:
 	
`REMOVE(aList, i)`
 	
Block:
 	
`REMOVE` `aList; i`
	Removes the item at index `i` in `aList` and shifts to the left any values at indices greater than `i`. The length of `aList` is decreased by 1.

Text:
 	
`LENGTH(aList)`
 	
Block:
 	
`LENGTH` `aList`
	Evaluates to the number of elements in `aList`.

Text:
 	
`FOR EACH item IN aList`
 	
`{`
 	
`<block of statements>`
 	
`}`
 	
Block:
 	
`FOR EACH item IN aList`
`block of statements`
	The variable `item` is assigned the value of each element of `aList` sequentially, in order, from the first element to the last element. The code in `block of statements` is executed once for each assignment of `item`.

Procedures and Procedure Calls	

Text:
 	
`PROCEDURE procName(parameter1,`
`                parameter2, ...)`
 	
`{`
 	
`<block of statements>`
 	
`}`
 	
Block:
 	
`PROCEDURE procName` `parameter1,`
`parameter2, ...`
`block of statements`
	Defines `procName` as a procedure that takes zero or more arguments. The procedure contains `block of statements`.
	
	The procedure `procName` can be called using the following notation, where `arg1` is assigned to `parameter1`, `arg2` is assigned to `parameter2`, etc.:
	`procName(arg1, arg2, ...)`

Instruction	Explanation
Procedures and Procedure Calls—Continued	

Text:
 	
`PROCEDURE procName(parameter1,`
` parameter2, ...)`
 	
`{`
`<block of statements>`
`RETURN(expression)`
`}`
 	
Block:
 	
PROCEDURE procName │parameter1,│
 │parameter2, ...│
 │ block of statements │
 │ RETURN expression │
	Defines `procName` as a procedure that takes zero or more arguments. The procedure contains `block of statements` and returns the value of `expression`. The RETURN statement may appear at any point inside the procedure and causes an immediate return from the procedure back to the calling statement.
	
	 The value returned by the procedure `procName` can be assigned to the variable `result` using the following notation:
	`result ← procName(arg1, arg2, ...)`

Text:
 	
`RETURN(expression)`
 	
Block:
 	
`RETURN │expression│`
	Returns the flow of control to the point where the procedure was called and returns the value of `expression`.

Robot	
If the robot attempts to move to a square that is not open or is beyond the edge of the grid, the robot will stay in its current location and the program will terminate.	

Text:
 	
`MOVE_FORWARD()`
 	
Block:
 	
`MOVE_FORWARD`
	The robot moves one square forward in the direction it is facing.

Text:
 	
`ROTATE_LEFT()`
 	
Block:
 	
`ROTATE_LEFT`
	The robot rotates in place 90 degrees counterclockwise (i.e., makes an in-place left turn).

Text:
 	
`ROTATE_RIGHT()`
 	
Block:
 	
`ROTATE_RIGHT`
	The robot rotates in place 90 degrees clockwise (i.e., makes an in-place right turn).

Text:
 	
`CAN_MOVE(direction)`
 	
Block:
 	
`CAN_MOVE │direction│`
	Evaluates to `true` if there is an open square one square in the direction relative to where the robot is facing; otherwise evaluates to `false`. The value of `direction` can be `left`, `right`, `forward`, or `backward`.

This page intentionally left blank.

GO ON TO THE NEXT PAGE.

COMPUTER SCIENCE PRINCIPLES

SECTION I

Time—2 hours

Number of Questions—70

Percent of total exam grade—70%

Directions: Choose one best answer for each question. Some questions at the end of the test will have more than one correct answer; for these, you will be instructed to choose two answer choices.

1. Consider the following procedure.

Procedure Call	Explanation
`drawRectangle(x1, y1, x2, y2)`	Draws a rectangle with the top left coordinate (x1,y1), and the bottom right coordinate (x2,y2)

The `drawRectangle` method will be used to draw the following on a coordinate grid.

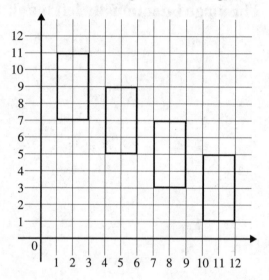

GO ON TO THE NEXT PAGE.

Which of the following code segments can be used to draw the rectangles?

(A)
```
x ← 1
y ← 11
REPEAT 4 TIMES
{
      drawRectangle(1, 11, 3, 7)
      x ← x + 3
      y ← y + 2
}
```

(C)
```
x ← 10
y ← 5
REPEAT 4 TIMES
{
      drawRectangle(x, y, x+2, y-4)
      x ← x - 3
      y ← y + 2
}
```

(B)
```
x ← 11
y ← 1
REPEAT 4 TIMES
{
      drawRectangle(x, y, x+3, y+7)
      x ← x + 3
      y ← y + 2
}
```

(D)
```
x ← 10
y ← 5
REPEAT 4 TIMES
{
      drawRectangle(x, y, x+2, y+4)
      x ← x - 3
      y ← y + 2
}
```

2. What would be stored at x upon completion of the following code segment?

```
x ← 10
y ← 20
IF (x < 15)
{
      IF (y < 20)
            x ← x - 10
      ELSE
            x ← x + 10
}
IF (x > 15)
      x ← x + 5
```

(A) 10

(B) 20

(C) 25

(D) 30

3. A concert is selling tickets online only for an upcoming show. The management is trying to use metadata from each sale to attempt to figure out what they should charge in the future for similar concerts. Here is the metadata taken from each sale.

- The time and the seat location of each ticket purchased
- The name and age of the purchaser
- The geolocation of the purchaser

Using the metadata given to us, which of the following CANNOT be analyzed to help determine future ticket prices?

(A) The seat locations of tickets that sold the fastest

(B) The financial status of each purchaser

(C) The amount of people who are most likely coming from out of town to see the concert

(D) The amount of time it took for the tickets to sell out

GO ON TO THE NEXT PAGE.

4. The following storyboard is used to create a password system.

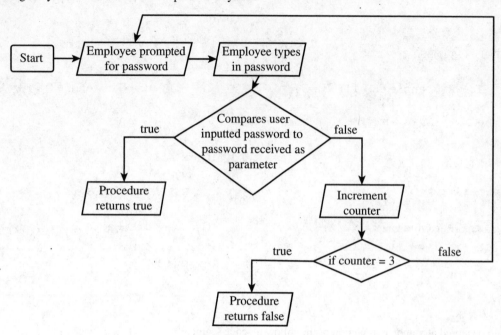

Which of the following code segments works correctly for this storyboard?

(A)
```
PROCEDURE correctPassword(password)
{
    counter ← 0
    REPEAT UNTIL (counter = 3)
    {
        DISPLAY("Enter the password:")
        pw ← INPUT
        IF (password = pw)
            RETURN(true)
    }
}
```

(B)
```
PROCEDURE correctPassword(password)
{
    correct = false
    REPEAT 3 TIMES
    {
        DISPLAY("Enter the password:")
        pw ← INPUT
        IF (password = pw)
            correct = true
        ELSE
            correct = false
    }
    RETURN(correct)
}
```

(C)
```
PROCEDURE correctPassword(password)
{
    counter ← 0
    REPEAT UNTIL (counter = 3)
    {
        DISPLAY("Enter the password:")
        pw ← INPUT
        IF (password = pw)
            RETURN(true)
        ELSE
            counter ← counter + 1
    }
    RETURN(false)
}
```

(D)
```
PROCEDURE correctPassword(password)
{
    REPEAT 3 TIMES
    {
        DISPLAY("Enter the password:")
        pw ← INPUT
        IF (password = pw)
            RETURN(true)
        ELSE
            RETURN(false)
    }
}
```

GO ON TO THE NEXT PAGE.

5. What is an appropriate way to prove that a problem is undecidable?

   (A) Create an algorithm that will solve one of the possible solutions, but will not solve all of the possible solutions.
   (B) Prove that there exists a solution to the problem that has no possible algorithm to solve it.
   (C) Create an algorithm that will solve the problem in a reasonable amount of time.
   (D) Prove that there exists an algorithm to solve the problem, but it cannot solve the problem in a reasonable amount of time.

6. Using a binary system with only 4 bits, if the decimal numbers 8 and 10 were added together, the sum would be 0010. What would be the reason for the incorrect answer?

   (A) A truncating error
   (B) A rounding error
   (C) An overflow error
   (D) An addition error

7. Consider the following procedure.

```
PROCEDURE someMath(num1, num2)
{
    IF (num1 > num2)
      RETURN(num1 - num2)
    ELSE
      RETURN(num2 * num1)
}
```

What would be output after the following calls to the procedure?

```
x ← someMath(10, 6)
y ← someMath(2, x)
z ← someMath(x, y)
DISPLAY(z)
```

   (A) 2
   (B) 4
   (C) 24
   (D) 32

GO ON TO THE NEXT PAGE.

8. Which of the following helps to explain the purpose of using comments in code?

   I. Using comments helps keep the documentation current when changes are made to the code.

   II. When using previous code segments, such as procedures, a coder can read the comments and know what to do without even looking at the code.

   III. When someone in the future needs to make changes to the code, they can look through the comments to find what changes need to be made instead of dissecting the entire code.

   (A) I only
   (B) I and II only
   (C) II and III only
   (D) I, II, and III

9. There is a disclaimer on a website that the information provided could be used for crowdsourcing. What would be an example of crowdsourcing using data that has been obtained by a website that collects health information and how a person feels daily?

   (A) Using the daily information to figure out if people with certain medical information feel ill more often than others
   (B) Creating an online fundraiser for people who are in need of financial assistance because of their medical situations
   (C) Not allowing any of the people's information to be used by any other institutions because of privacy concerns
   (D) Using the data to determine what people are losing their jobs and how to better reach these people

10. What would be the next three binary numbers after 10001101?

   (A) 10001111, 10010000, 10010001
   (B) 10001101, 10010011, 10010100
   (C) 10001110, 10001111, 10011111
   (D) 10001110, 10001111, 10010000

GO ON TO THE NEXT PAGE.

11. While at a library, a person logs into the public Wi-Fi network labeled "Library" with their private device. The person then uses their device to make a deposit into their bank account. That deposit never reaches the user's bank account, but is instead rerouted to another account. It turns out that the public Wi-Fi network was not from the library, but instead a cybercriminal installed an access point on the library's Wi-Fi without the library's permission and used that access point to reroute the money into the cybercriminal's account.

What type of attack would this be considered?

(A) Malware
(B) Keylogging
(C) Phishing
(D) Rogue Access Point

12. The following list `myList` contains all integers.

```
PROCEDURE changeList(myList)
    counter ← 1
    REPEAT UNTIL (counter > LENGTH(myList))
        IF (myList[counter] < 0)
            myList[counter] = 0
        counter ← counter + 1
    RETURN(myList)
```

Which of the following best describes how this code segment works?

(A) The code segment will replace all negative indexes in `myList` with 0 and return `mylist`.
(B) The code segment will have an error since it will go out of bounds on `myList`.
(C) The code segment will find all values in `myList` that are 0 and remove them, and then return `myList`.
(D) The code segment will count how many values in `myList` are negative, and return that value.

13. What would be the output from the following code segment?
```
a ← 28
b ← 5
c ← a MOD b
DISPLAY (c)
```
(A) 2
(B) 3
(C) 5
(D) 5.6

GO ON TO THE NEXT PAGE.

14. A large spreadsheet contains the following data about a company. Here is a small sample of what the data could look like. The top row is the header.

Name	Number of Years	Job Title	Revenue	Expenses
"Stanford"	25	"Manager"	1000	500
"Kathy"	22	"Manager"	1500	250
"Mike"	8	"Sales"	2000	1500
"Beth"	5	"Sales"	500	1750
"Brian"	3	"Sales"	1000	1200
"Jacob"	4	"Sales"	700	500

The company has to figure out which employees with the job title "Sales" need to be promoted to "Manager." In order to be promoted, an employee must fit the following criteria.

- Be an employee of 5 or more years
- Have a job title of "Sales"
- Have their revenue exceed their expenses

Which of the following would be the most efficient way to find all the employees that should be promoted?

(A) Filter out all employees with the Job Title "Manager"
Sort by Revenue
Sort by Number of Years

(B) Sort by Job Title
Sort by Number of Years
Create another column with the formula (Revenue – Expenses)
Filter out all employees with a value 0 or lower in the new column

(C) Manually remove all employees with the Job Title "Manager"
Manually remove all employees with Number of Years less than 5
Create another column with the formula (Revenue – Expenses)
Manually remove all numbers 0 or less from the new column

(D) Filter out all employees with the Job Title "Manager"
Filter out all employees with Number of Years less than 5
Create another column with the formula (Revenue – Expenses)
Sort the new column, and delete all that are less than or equal to 0

GO ON TO THE NEXT PAGE.

15. Computer A uses sequential computing, and has one processor. Computer B uses parallel computing, and has two identical processors that run in parallel. Each of these processors can only run one process at a time. No process can be split into two different processors.

    There are three processes that need to be run, and they can be run in any order. One of the processes takes 10 minutes, one of the processes takes 15 minutes, and the final process takes 22 minutes. How much longer will it take Computer A to run the three processes than it will take Computer B?

    (A) Same amount of time
    (B) 3 minutes
    (C) 22 minutes
    (D) 25 minutes

16. There are currently twenty employees at a store. The store is planning on opening up four new locations, each of which will have twenty employees. This means that the company will now have 100 employees.

    Currently each employee has an ID number that is only five bits long, and contains only 0s and 1s. How many more bits must the company add to its current five-bit employee ID system so it can have all 100 employees have a unique ID number of 0s and 1s, without wasting any extra bits?

    (A) 0
    (B) 1
    (C) 2
    (D) 3

17. A company will begin to use software through a third party that will allow them to log on to their servers more securely. Each employee will log on every day, and that login will give them access to their email and workspace. Which of the following would be an example of a phishing attack that could occur against the company?

    (A) An employee receives an email to change their password, but is instead sent to a fake website. This leads to them giving away their password, which the cybercriminal uses to steal important company information.
    (B) A hacker tries over and over to guess someone's password, using certain information about the person, such as birthday, address, child's name, etc., and then pretends to be that person.
    (C) A cybercriminal gets software downloaded onto an employee's computer in an attempt to damage or slow down the new login system.
    (D) An employee unintentionally downloads software to the system, and that software allows the cybercriminal to take over the computer to launch more attacks on the system.

GO ON TO THE NEXT PAGE.

18. Which of the code segments would produce the following output?

```
0 0
0 1
0 2
1 1
1 2
2 2
```

(A)
```
x ← 0
REPEAT UNTIL (x = 3)
{
    y ← x
    REPEAT UNTIL (y = 3)
    {
        DISPLAY (x + " " + y)
        y ← y + 1
    }
    x ← x + 1
}
```

(B)
```
x ← 0
REPEAT UNTIL (x = 3)
{
    y ← x
    REPEAT UNTIL (y = 3)
    {
        y ← y + 1
        DISPLAY (x + " " + y)
    }
    x ← x + 1
}
```

(C)
```
x ← 0
y ← 0
REPEAT UNTIL (x = 3)
{
    REPEAT UNTIL (y = 3)
    {
        y ← y + 1
        DISPLAY (x + " " + y)
    }
    x ← x + 1
}
```

(D)
```
x ← 0
REPEAT UNTIL (x = 3)
{
    y ← x
    REPEAT UNTIL (y = 3)
    {
        DISPLAY (x + " " + y)
        y ← y + 1
        x ← x + 1
    }
}
```

```
x ← 0
REPEAT UNTIL (x = 3)
{
    y ← x
    REPEAT UNTIL (y = 3)
    {
        DISPLAY (x + " " + y)
        y ← y + 1
    }
    x ← x + 1
}
```

GO ON TO THE NEXT PAGE.

19. The results of an online survey are automatically put into a spreadsheet. The survey is being used to find out the respondents' favorite candy by age group and state they live in. Here are the questions that are asked.

    Name (Open Field)
    Age (Dropdown menu)
    State (Dropdown menu)
    Favorite Candy (Open Field)

    Which of the following data pieces will most likely need to be cleaned the most?

    (A) Name
    (B) Age
    (C) State
    (D) Favorite Candy

20. Which of the following are NOT common protocols used on the Internet or the World Wide Web?

    (A) TCP
    (B) HTTP
    (C) UDP
    (D) IETF

21. Which of the following is an example of data mining being used to discriminate against a group of individuals?

    (A) Supermarkets use data mining from purchase history to determine what products they should group together at the store.
    (B) Medical professionals want to analyze large data sets of patient information to determine which patients would be the best candidates for different treatments.
    (C) Credit card companies use predictive analytics to determine what demographic of people will most likely have worse credit scores and need to be charged higher interest rates.
    (D) Social media sites use search history to help predict what websites someone will want to see.

22. A board game developer wants to see each player's chances of winning a game since the player who goes first might have an advantage. In order to do this, the developer must run over one thousand simulations.

    The game deals with a spinner that has 6 numbers on it, and all players will spin and move around the board. The players will not make any decisions, just move around the board the entire game. Which of the possible simulations will be the MOST efficient and cost-effective way to test out each player's chances of winning the game?

    (A) Have a person play the game by hand one thousand times, keeping track of which player wins each game.
    (B) Use a random number generator to have a person manually play the game, keeping track of which player wins each game.
    (C) Create an online simulator that runs through the game over a thousand times using random spins, keeping track of which player wins each game.
    (D) Hire 10 testers to play the game 100 times each, and track which player wins each game.

GO ON TO THE NEXT PAGE.

23. A group of students is allowing a researcher to track the amount of time they spend on their smartphones throughout the day. The goal is to prove that smartphone use does not correlate with student success. The following data sets have been received by the researcher about each student:

- Amount of time spent on their phones each day

- Current GPA

- Social media sites used

Which of the following information should also be requested by the researcher in order to attempt to disprove a causal relationship between smartphone use and student success?

(A) The student's geolocations throughout the day
(B) If the student is using their smartphone for academic purposes
(C) How much time during the weekends the student uses their phones
(D) The financial and scholarship records from each student

24. The following procedure is intended to return true if all the values in `myList` increase the entire time. For example, if `myList` contains [0, 1, 2, 3], the values are increasing. If `myList` contains [0, 4, 4, 6], they are not increasing the entire time.

```
PROCEDURE isIncreasing(myList)
{
    increasing ← false
    prev ← 0
    FOR EACH item IN myList
    {
        IF(prev < item)
            increasing = true
        ELSE
            increasing = false
        prev = item
    }
    RETURN(increasing)
}
```

Which of the following values for `myList` can be used to show that this code segment does not work as intended?

(A) [1, 2, 4, 6]
(B) [1, 4, 2, 6]
(C) [1, 2, 6, 4]
(D) [1, 2, 4, 4]

GO ON TO THE NEXT PAGE.

25. Every character has a corresponding ASCII key code. For example, the letter "K" has the corresponding ASCII key code of 75. Each letter is broken down into their ASCII key code in decimal (base 10) and then converted to binary (base 2). Here is a table of ASCII key codes:

Decimal	ASCII	Decimal	ASCII
65	A	78	N
66	B	79	O
67	C	80	P
68	D	81	Q
69	E	82	R
70	F	83	S
71	G	84	T
72	H	85	U
73	I	86	V
74	J	87	W
75	K	88	X
76	L	89	Y
77	M	90	Z

Which of the following would be the binary representation of "HEY"?

(A) 01001000 01000101 01011001
(B) 01101000 01100101 01111001
(C) 00010010 10100010 10011010
(D) 01001001 01000110 01011010

26. What is the relationship between the World Wide Web and the Internet?

(A) The Internet connects servers to devices, and the World Wide Web uses the Internet to transmit and receive HTML to those devices.
(B) The Internet creates web pages, while the World Wide Web sends those pages to and from devices.
(C) The Internet can log off and log on, while the World Wide Web is always on and connected.
(D) The World Wide Web was created first for data sharing, while the Internet came after to assist in sharing information.

GO ON TO THE NEXT PAGE.

27. Bradley wants to have a program that will determine what days he is supposed to work out and what days he is taking a day off. Bradley only wants to work out on odd numbered days of the month, and he takes weekends (Saturday and Sunday) off.

    There are two variables. One is an integer called day that stores the day of the month. The other variable is a string called week that stores the day of the week (e.g., "Friday," "Saturday").

    Which of the following code segments would NOT correctly output if Bradley should be working out or taking the day off?

(A)
```
var dayOdd = day MOD 2
IF (dayOdd = 0)
     DISPLAY("Day Off")
ELSE IF (week = "Saturday" OR week
  = "Sunday")
     DISPLAY ("Day Off")
ELSE
     DISPLAY ("Workout")
```

(C)
```
var dayOdd = day MOD 2
IF (dayODD = 0 OR week = "Saturday"
  OR week = "Sunday")
     DISPLAY ("Day Off")
ELSE
     DISPLAY ("Workout")
```

(B)
```
var dayOdd = day MOD 2
IF (dayOdd = 0 AND week =
  "Saturday" AND week = "Sunday")
     DISPLAY ("Day Off")
ELSE
     DISPLAY ("Workout")
```

(D)
```
var dayOdd = day MOD 2
IF (dayODD = 1 AND (week ≠
  "Saturday" AND week ≠ "Sunday"))
     DISPLAY ("Workout")
ELSE
     DISPLAY ("Day Off")
```

28. A bank needs to create a program to allow its customers to make deposits and withdrawals and print out a bank statement for each such transaction. Which of the following would be a good use of abstraction to manage the complexity of the program?

    (A) Subtracting a fee from the customer's account every time they withdraw money
    (B) Creating a loop that will continue until the customer is done depositing and withdrawing money
    (C) Creating a procedure that will print out the customers bank statement that can be used multiple times throughout the program
    (D) Checking to make sure the customers have enough money whenever they withdraw money, and then subtracting the amount withdrawn from their account

29. In order for drivers' education students to practice driving safely, a company created a driving simulation program. While the simulator does not have all of the typical controls of a car or move the driver physically around, it still simulates a driving situation around real streets. Which of the following would be the LEAST likely advantage to using this software?

    (A) A driving simulator can let the user know how it physically feels to get into an accident.
    (B) A driving simulator can help the user learn how to drive in traffic.
    (C) A driving simulator can show the user when to use turn signals.
    (D) A driving simulator can help the user learn how to follow all appropriate road signs.

GO ON TO THE NEXT PAGE.

30. Which of the following is NOT a benefit of parallel computing as opposed to using sequential computing?

(A) Parallel computing will solve larger problems that can be broken into smaller problems that do not need to be solved in a specific order significantly quicker than sequential computing.

(B) With problems that fluctuate between being small or large, parallel computing makes it much easier to scale no matter the size of the problem.

(C) If a problem can be broken into smaller problems, but those smaller problems have to be solved in order, you can still use parallel computing because it can solve the problem more quickly.

(D) Some problems may require algorithms that cannot be solved in a reasonable amount of time using sequential computing, but may be solved in a reasonable amount of time using parallel computing.

31. Which of the following would NOT be a harmful effect on society, culture, or economy caused by using solar panels that harness energy on a large scale?

(A) The amount of land being used by a large number of solar panels could degrade the environment and possibly the habitat of plants or animals living there.

(B) The renewable energy will create less of a need for energy from other sources that cause major environmental issues.

(C) A tremendous amount of water is needed to produce solar panels, so their manufacturers could drain local water resources.

(D) Solar panel production requires manufacturers and their workers to handle toxic chemicals.

32. Which of the following would do the LEAST to lessen the digital divide in a school?

(A) A school purchasing devices for all the students to use in and out of school

(B) Training all parents on how to use their child's devices to monitor their academic success

(C) Not assigning homework that would require an Internet connection at home

(D) Allowing students to bring in their own personal devices for their online schoolwork

33. A manager of a shop is trying to disseminate information about wait times for their customers. Each time a customer shows up, they sign in, get added to a queue, and wait to be helped. What would be the greatest advantage of using a list to store each customer's time they signed in and the time they were helped, as opposed to just using several independent variables?

(A) The ability to print out each user's sign in time and the time they were helped at the end of the day

(B) The ability to find the average wait time

(C) The ability to find the longest and shortest wait times

(D) The ability to print out the total number of customers that day

GO ON TO THE NEXT PAGE.

34. The following code segment is intended to store the maximum temperature of three days into the variable max. All three variables are integers. The code segment does not work for all cases.

```
max ← 0
IF (day1 > max)
        max = day1
IF (day2 > max)
        max = day2
IF (day3 > max)
        max = day3
```

Which of the following values for day1, day2, and day3 would this code segment not work correctly?

(A) day1 = 50, day2 = 70, day3 = 30
(B) day1 = 30, day2 = 30, day3 = 30
(C) day1 = –40, day2 = –20, day3 = –30
(D) day1 = 0, day2 = 20, day3 = 40

35. Which of the following lines of code should be turned into a procedure in order to reuse duplicated code to help manage the complexity of the program?

```
Line 1:    IF (CAN_MOVE(forward))
Line 2:    {
Line 3:            MOVE_FORWARD()
Line 4:            ROTATE_LEFT()
Line 5:            ROTATE_LEFT()
Line 6:    }
Line 7:    ELSE
Line 8:    {
Line 9:            ROTATE_LEFT()
Line 10:           ROTATE_LEFT()
Line 11:           MOVE_FORWARD()
Line 12:           MOVE_FORWARD()
Line 13:    }
Line 14:   ROTATE_LEFT()
```

(A) Create a procedure called turnLeftTwice(), and use it to replace lines 4 and 5, and to replace lines 9 and 10.
(B) Create a procedure called moving(), and use it to replace lines 3–5, and lines 9–12.
(C) Create a procedure called cantMove(), and use it to replace lines 9–12.
(D) Create a procedure called moveForwardTwice() and use it to replace lines 11 and 12.

36. Which of the following are some advantages of using a lossy compression algorithm?
   I. Using a lossy compression algorithm can greatly reduce the size of a file.
  II. Using a lossy compression algorithm can ensure that the quality will not be reduced.
 III. Using a lossy compression algorithm makes it quicker to send and store files.

(A) I only
(B) III only
(C) I and III only
(D) II and III only

GO ON TO THE NEXT PAGE.

37. The code segment is supposed to take the list `fullList` and add all the values that are larger than `largeNum` to the list `newList`. The numbers do not need to be removed from `fullList`. All we want is `newList` to contain all the numbers larger than `largeNum`.

For example, if `fullList` contains [10, 20, 5, 25, 30, 15], and `largeNum` = 13, then `newList` should contain [20, 25, 30, 15] after running the code.

```
1 ← index
FOR EACH item IN fullList
{
    <missing code>
}
```

Which of the following code segments would make the code work as wanted?

(A)
```
IF (item < largeNum)
{
    INSERT(newList,index,item)
    index ← index + 1
}
```

(B)
```
IF (item > largeNum)
{
    INSERT(newList,index,item)
    index ← index + 1
}
```

(C)
```
IF (item > largeNum)
{
    INSERT(newList,index,item)
}
```

(D)
```
IF (item > largeNum)
{
    index ← index + 1
    INSERT(newList,index,item)
}
```

GO ON TO THE NEXT PAGE.

38. The following grid contains a robot represented as a triangle. The robot is initially facing up, and the robot ends in the same location facing up.

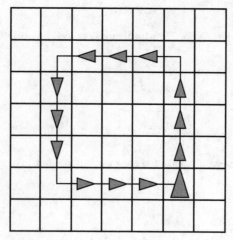

This example works for a robot that is moving three squares in each direction. We want to make it so the procedure takes one argument that will determine the number of squares in each direction the robot will go to make the square.

Which of the following code segments can be used to move the robot so it starts and finishes in the same location, facing the same direction, making a square the correct size?

(A)
```
PROCEDURE makeSquare(sideLength)
{
    REPEAT sideLength TIMES
    {
        REPEAT sideLength TIMES
        {
            MOVE_FORWARD()
        }
        ROTATE_LEFT()
    }
}
```

(B)
```
PROCEDURE makeSquare(sideLength)
{
    REPEAT 4 TIMES
    {
        MOVE_FORWARD()
        MOVE_FORWARD()
        MOVE_FORWARD()
        ROTATE_LEFT()
    }
}
```

(C)
```
PROCEDURE makeSquare(sideLength)
{
    REPEAT 4 TIMES
    {
        REPEAT sideLength TIMES
        {
            MOVE_FORWARD()
            ROTATE_LEFT()
        }
    }
}
```

(D)
```
PROCEDURE makeSquare(sideLength)
{
    REPEAT 4 TIMES
    {
        REPEAT sideLength TIMES
        {
            MOVE_FORWARD()
        }
        ROTATE_LEFT()
    }
}
```

GO ON TO THE NEXT PAGE.

Questions 39–40 refer to the information below.

Beth is writing a program that will create work groups in a class that she teaches. She wants to establish groups that work with an assignment about the digital divide. The students are going to write a paper on how the digital divide creates unfair disadvantages for different students. She wants each group to have students who can contribute their own personal experiences with the digital divide.

Once Beth enters every students' information into the program, it will create groups with even numbers of students.

39. Which of the following data input(s) are going to be necessary to complete this program?

    I.   Each student's list of friends in the class
   II.   Each student's socioeconomic status
  III.   Every student's access to the Internet at home

(A) II only
(B) I and II only
(C) II and III only
(D) I, II and III

40. Which of the following strategies would LEAST assist in creating a collaborative group environment for them to write a research paper on the digital divide?
(A) Have each student independently write a research paper, then combine their papers into one larger document.
(B) Have the students discuss their own experiences with the digital divide, and use that as a starting point to their research.
(C) Have each student research articles, then have everyone read the articles together and discuss.
(D) Have the group come up with an outline of the project together in a shared document.

GO ON TO THE NEXT PAGE.

41. The following grid contains a robot represented as a triangle. The robot is initially the black triangle in the bottom left corner facing up. The robot needs to end up as the other triangle in the top right corner facing down.

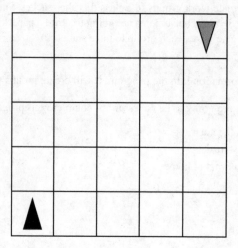

Which of the following changes needs to be made to fix the following code?

```
Line 1:   REPEAT 2 TIMES
Line 2:   {
Line 3:        REPEAT 4 TIMES
Line 4:        {
Line 5:             MOVE_FORWARD()
Line 6:             TURN_RIGHT()
Line 7:        }
Line 8:   }
```

(A) Change Line 1 to REPEAT 4 TIMES
(B) Move Line 6 after Line 7
(C) Switch Line 5 and Line 6
(D) Move Line 6 after Line 8

42. A group of high school students from the same school all have similar demographics. This group is asked to fill out a survey that has different types of poll questions. The group administering the survey is not sure of the number of students who will participate, so the data analyzation must be scalable for all sizes. The school cannot require the students to take the survey, so as few as five students may take the survey, or as many as 2,000 students may take the survey.

The survey consists of the following types of questions.

- Ten questions that have two options

- Ten questions that have four options

- Five questions where the students will write in answers to the poll questions

Which of the following is LEAST likely to cause an issue when trying to fairly analyze the data without bias or having to spend too much time cleaning the data.

(A) The data set from the questions with two and four options will be too large to analyze.
(B) The data will need to be cleaned too much, especially write-in answers.
(C) The data will have bias since everyone is from similar demographics.
(D) The data will be incomplete if there are too few students answering the poll.

GO ON TO THE NEXT PAGE.

43. Which of the following would be an example of a lossless compression?

   (A) A picture is compressed to a much smaller size, but when it is restored it does not have the same picture quality as the original file before it was compressed.
   (B) A file is compressed so it may be transmitted quicker, with no guarantees of being able to restore all the information.
   (C) A music file is compressed and loses some quality, but not any quality that makes a difference to the human ear.
   (D) A video is compressed since it was too large to be transmitted, but when it was restored back to its original size, it didn't lose anything.

44. A high school is holding an election for class president. There are two candidates running for office. Candidate A excels in all his classes and is in several clubs. Candidate B excels in athletics and music but struggles in academics. The entire school votes, and every student's vote is tracked in a data file.

   The school has a second data file that contains every student's GPA, attendance record, and demographics. In addition to that, the second data file also contains which clubs, athletics, and music programs each student is involved in.

   The stats class wants to combine both data sets and try to find as many correlations as they can between who the students voted for and information about the students. Using what we know about the two candidates, what filter would be LEAST important to use when trying to find a correlation?

   (A) Create a filter to compare the votes and each student's GPA to look for a correlation.
   (B) Create a filter to compare the students who are in the same clubs as candidate A and what percent of them voted for candidate A.
   (C) Create a filter to compare the students who are in the same athletics as candidate B and what percent of them voted for candidate B.
   (D) Create a filter that compares the attendance records of each student and who they voted for.

45. The following code segment is intended to store all the prime numbers that are between the numbers 1 and 20, inclusively, in the list `primeList`. The program currently has a procedure called `prime(number)`, which will receive a single parameter, and return true if that number is prime, false otherwise.

Procedure Call	Explanation
`prime(number)`	Returns `true` if the parameter (`number`) is a prime number, `false` otherwise

```
i ← 1
REPEAT 20 TIMES
{
    <missing code>
}
```

Which of the following can be used to replace `<missing code>` so that the code segment works as intended?

(A)
```
IF (prime(i))
    APPEND(primeList, i)
```

(C)
```
IF (prime(i))
{
    i ← i + 1
    APPEND(primeList, i)
}
```

(B)
```
IF (prime(i))
{
    APPEND(primeList, i)
    i ← i + 1
}
```

(D)
```
IF (prime(i))
{
    APPEND(primeList, i)
}
i ← i + 1
```

GO ON TO THE NEXT PAGE.

46. Upon completion of the following code segment, what would be printed out?

```
a ← 10
b ← 15
c ← a
a ← 20
c ← b

DISPLAY (a)
DISPLAY (c)
```

(A) 10 10

(B) 10 15

(C) 20 10

(D) 20 15

47. During an upcoming election, a social media site is accused of presenting bias toward one of the candidates. What adjustments can be made to the site that will be MOST effective for eliminating bias in their algorithms?

(A) Only show users news articles that may be favorable to whomever they are interested in voting for.

(B) Censor all information that might be questionable without checking the information, just to be sure that nothing gets posted that is untrue.

(C) Ensure that the search algorithms do not favor one candidate over another and show an equal amount of information about both candidates.

(D) Create an algorithm that will use the previously searched information to guide a user towards a candidate.

48. Which of the following will swap the values of `larger` and `smaller` only if `larger` is less than `smaller`?

For example, if `larger = 10` and `smaller = 20`, then the program should swap the two values since `smaller` is greater than `larger`. Therefore, `larger = 20` and `smaller = 10` at the end of the code segment.

(A)
```
IF (larger > smaller)
    larger = smaller
```

(B)
```
IF (larger < smaller)
    var temp = larger
    larger = smaller
    smaller = temp
```

(C)
```
IF (larger < smaller)
    larger = smaller
    smaller = larger
```

(D)
```
IF (larger < smaller)
    var temp = larger
    smaller = larger
    smaller = temp
```

GO ON TO THE NEXT PAGE.

49. An RGB triplet is a combination of three values that form a color, in the order of (red, green, blue). The decimal value of golden brown as an RGB triplet is (153, 101, 21). What would be the correct RGB value using binary?

    (A) (10011001, 01100101, 00010101)

    (B) (11011001, 11000101, 00001101)

    (C) (11011001, 01100101, 00001101)

    (D) (10011001, 11000101, 00010101)

50. The following procedure is supposed to return the number of items in `myList` that are between min and max, inclusively.

    ```
    1   PROCEDURE countBetween(myList, min, max)
    2   {
    3    counter ← 0
    4    FOR EACH item IN myList
    5    {
    6     IF(item ≥ min OR item ≤ max)
    7        counter ← counter + 1
    8    }
    9    RETURN(counter)
    10  }
    ```

    The procedure does not work as intended. What change needs to be made so the procedures will work as intended?

    (A) Switch Line 3 so it is inside the loop, right after line 5

    (B) Switch Line 9 into the loop, right after Line 7

    (C) Change Line 6 to `IF(item = min OR item = max)`

    (D) Change the `OR` in Line 6 to `AND`

51. Which of the following is a legal way to use materials you have found on the Internet?

    (A) The material does not have the © for copyright anywhere on it, so it is freely available for anyone to use.

    (B) When using only a smaller part of an online text, you do not have to ask permission, even if that small part is the most important part.

    (C) Any work on the Internet is automatically public domain and can be used in any way.

    (D) Anyone can use open source materials for which the rights for reproduction have been waived by the owner.

52. What is the LEAST concerning issue with putting your Personally Identifiable Information online?

    (A) Your geolocation can be used by someone to find you at any time.

    (B) Your browsing history can be used for targeted marking.

    (C) Your social security number online can be used to steal your identity.

    (D) Your geolocation can be used to commit a crime against someone if their location is always known.

GO ON TO THE NEXT PAGE.

53. Which of the following would properly perform a binary search, and what would be the maximum amount of searches needed to find an element on the list using a binary search?

(A) Searching for a name through a list of 50 names and ID numbers that are stored alphabetically. Using a binary search to find a name in this list would take a maximum of 6 searches.

(B) Searching for an ID number through a list of 50 names and ID numbers that are stored alphabetically. Using a binary search, this would take a maximum of 6 searches.

(C) Searching for an account number through a list of 100 account numbers that are stored from least to greatest. Using a binary search, this would take a maximum of 10 searches.

(D) Searching for an account number through an unsorted list of 100 account numbers. Using a binary search, this would take a maximum of 7 searches.

54. A list of names has n elements, indexed from 1 to n. A program needs to go through the entire list and find all the occurrences of the name "Jenny". The program would start by creating a variable called `counter`, and setting it to 0. Then it would create a variable called `position`, and set it to 1.

Which of the following algorithms would properly count all the occurrences of "Jenny" in the list, and print out the number of times it appears after the program is done counting?

(A) Step 1: If the value of index `position` in list equals "Jenny", increment `counter` by 1.
     Step 2: Repeat Step 1
     Step 3: Display `counter`

(B) Step 1: If the value of index `position` in list equals "Jenny", increment `position` by 1.
     Step 2: Increment `position` by 1.
     Step 3: Repeat Step 2
     Step 4: Display `position`

(C) Step 1: If the value of index `position` in list equals "Jenny", increment `counter` by 1.
     Step 2: Increment `position` by 1.
     Step 3: Repeat Step 1
     Step 4: Display `counter`

(D) Step 1: If the value of index `position` in list equals "Jenny", increment `counter` by 1.
     Step 2: Increment `position` by 1.
     Step 3: Display `counter`
     Step 4: Repeat Step 2

55. A company wants to run a website that stores pictures for users and hires a programmer to create it. The programmer is told that the website will be a low-cost alternative to more expensive websites, so they want the programmer to find the cheapest ways to upload, store, and download the images without losing quality.

Which of the following would be good examples of ways to keep the cost down?

 I.   Store all the pictures without any compression since that is the only way they will not lose any quality.
 II. Make all the images lossy since it will be quicker to download them from the site.
III. Make all the images lossy, but make sure you do not lose any quality that would be visible to the human eye when uploading and downloading them.

(A) I only
(B) II only
(C) I and II only
(D) II and III only

GO ON TO THE NEXT PAGE.

56. The figure below represents a network of physically linked devices. Any line that is drawn between two devices means they are connected. A device can communicate with any other device through these connections.

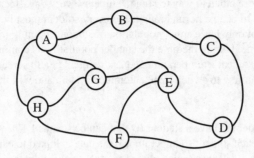

Which of the following statement(s) are true about this connection?

I. If devices B and D were to fail, then device C would not be able to receive any data from any other device.

II. If devices C and F were to fail, then device B could not connect to device D.

III. If devices G and E were to fail, no devices would be able to communicate with each other.

(A) I only

(B) III only

(C) I and II only

(D) I, II and III

57. Which of the following would be the MOST appropriate citizen science project, and why?

(A) Have non-scientists request people from different regions to track animals throughout the wild to see where they migrate during certain seasons

(B) A group of scientists requesting people from different regions take pictures of the sky at night, sending the pictures to them, and then having the scientists analyze light pollution from these regions

(C) Have people from different regions purchase science kits and analyze water samples in their kitchen, and then analyze their data individually

(D) A non-for-profit group having users download an app that tracks users as they go about their day. They use this data as open source to show where people frequently visit in different locations

GO ON TO THE NEXT PAGE.

Questions 58–62 refer to the information below.

A school is trying to figure out a more efficient way to sign in students every day. Because of a recent health crisis, every student's temperature must be verified to be in a normal range, and every student must be asked a series of questions about his or her recent health history. The school only has a small population of students coming in at this time, but soon all students will again be attending in-person full time. During the time the smaller population is coming in, the school has hired extra security members at each door to take each student's temperature and ask them all health screening questions. When the entire student population returns, the school is planning to switch to an automated system and will therefore not need security staff members at each door.

This new system requires every student to have a student ID that can be scanned. The school also purchased a walk-through temperature scanner that will take each student's temperature. This data is linked to each student's ID number, which is linked to all of the student's information in a database (name, class schedule, medical history, etc.). Before each student shows up to school each day, they must have answered a series of questions about their current health using devices such as a cell phone, laptop, etc. To do this, they must log in to a system that is linked to all their school information. Here is a flowchart of the system and the use of each block in the flowchart.

Block	Explanation
Oval	The start of the algorithm
Parallelogram	An input or output step
Diamond	A conditional or decision step, where execution proceeds to the side labeled "Yes" if the answer to the question is yes and to the side labeled "No" if the answer to the question is no
Rectangle	The result of the algorithm

GO ON TO THE NEXT PAGE.

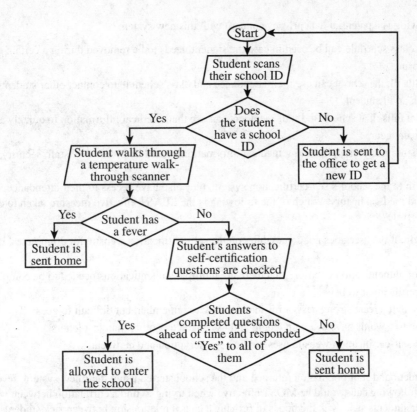

58. Which of the following has a potential harmful effect on society, culture, or economy when using the new system?

   (A) The entire process of students entering the building will be sped up, resulting in less lost time.
   (B) The need to hire more security personnel is eliminated, saving money, but resulting in job loss.
   (C) Having an automated attendance system will help track the spread of the health crisis within their school and community.
   (D) There will be less contact with the security staff since students' temperatures will be taken by a machine.

59. Which of the following actions would do the LEAST to address any problems that may occur due to a possible digital divide in this school's population?

   (A) Provide every student with a device and Internet connectivity so they are all able to answer the self-certification questions ahead of time.
   (B) Allow students to answer the self-certification questions on school devices when they get to school, instead of ahead of time.
   (C) Make sure that every student has an ID before they come to school, and if they do not have an ID, send them to the office to get one for free.
   (D) Ensure that every student has knowledge of how to use a device and how to use the self-certification system before starting to use the new system.

GO ON TO THE NEXT PAGE.

60. Which of the following is a potential data privacy concern with this new system?

   (A) The student's class schedule can be used in case the student needs to be removed during a certain class period because of a medical issue.

   (B) If a student falls ill, the school can use their attendance and class schedule to contact other students about them being in contact with an ill student.

   (C) When a student falls ill at school, the staff members can use their medical information to quickly assist with any major issues that can occur.

   (D) Access to student information, including medical information, would be given to all staff, security, and district personnel.

61. When students log in to the school's self-certification system, they also have access to their attendance, personal information, school schedule, and medical history. Which of the following is the LEAST effective measure taken to ensure that this information stays private?

   (A) After each login, if the user does not do anything on the self-certification website for 30 minutes, it automatically logs out.

   (B) Use multifactor authentication to ensure that there are multiple authentications needed to be completed before logging in to the self-certification website.

   (C) Require the users to create strong passwords that are easy to remember, but difficult to guess. This would include requiring the passwords have a certain length and use characters other than just letters.

   (D) Make sure the self-certification website uses public key encryption and certificates.

62. When the entire student and staff population returned and the school started using their new system, several students still got sick. Which of the following data would be MOST effective when trying to find a correlation between which students got sick, and if they got other students sick, with the hopes of proving a causal relationship between sick students getting other students sick due to proximity?

   (A) Comparing all the students who got sick to their medical history

   (B) Checking for overlap in each sick student's class schedules

   (C) Checking the time each student answers their self-certification questions in the morning

   (D) Comparing the students' temperatures each day with their medical history

63. Which of the following actions can help bridge the digital divide for people with disabilities?

   Select <u>two</u> answers.

   (A) Make sure that these devices are not covered by insurance because then only those with insurance will be able to afford them.

   (B) Making assistive technology less costly or free through the government so more people with disabilities can obtain them.

   (C) Create grants for more research into technologies.

   (D) Increase the cost of assistive technologies so there is more money available to enhance these technologies.

64. What are some examples that would make a system fault-tolerant?

   Select <u>two</u> answers.

   (A) A system is able to send packets as quickly as possible over the Internet.

   (B) The World Wide Web using HTML is able to read in website data sent over the Internet.

   (C) The Internet allows data to be rerouted in case a connection has failed, guaranteeing that it will find a path to its destination.

   (D) If there is a user error occurring somewhere within a system, it will be corrected automatically so there is no loss in production.

GO ON TO THE NEXT PAGE.

65. Which of the following tasks would require a heuristic approach to solving a problem?

Select <u>two</u> answers.

(A) A programmer is tasked with creating a program for a trucking company to have their drivers find the approximate quickest daily routes through a full day of multiple deliveries.

(B) Creating a better lossy compression algorithm for a company that will compress images better than the current compression algorithm that they are using.

(C) A programmer is given a list of names that are already sorted, and they must create a binary search of an already sorted database of names.

(D) Creating a linear search of a database of accounts that are not in alphabetical order.

66. Which of the following would produce the same result as

$$\texttt{num} \geq \texttt{10 AND num} \leq \texttt{20}$$

Select <u>two</u> answers.

(A) `NOT (num < 10 OR num > 20)`
(B) `num = 10 OR num = 20`
(C) `num  10 OR num ≥ 20`
(D) `num ≥ 10 AND (NOT (num > 20))`

67. What is true about Internet protocols?

Select <u>two</u> answers.

(A) Internet protocols are open and allow people to connect as many devices as they want to the Internet.

(B) Internet protocols are established so everyone has the same bandwidth when sending and receiving information.

(C) Internet protocols are set so that only users that are using the same devices can connect to each other.

(D) Internet protocols make it so data gets where it needs to go through routing and addressing packets.

GO ON TO THE NEXT PAGE.

68. A board game has a spinner that has 8 different, evenly spaced numbers on it. The spinner looks like the following.

The game is played in the following way:

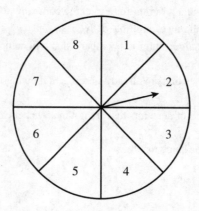

- A random number is chosen from 1 to 8 to simulate the spinner. The player gets the amount of points as the random number.
- If the first spin was an 8, the player gets another spin. Whatever the player gets on the second spin counts as 10 times the amount of that spin. The first spin does not count towards their score.

Example 1: If the player spins a 5 on their first spin, the score returned is 5.
Example 2: If the player spins an 8 on their first spin, the players gets a second spin. If the player spins a 3 on the second spin, the score returned is 3 times 10, which is 30.

The procedure game() was created to return the correct value from the spin(s).

```
PROCEDURE game()
{
        spin1 ← RANDOM(1,8)
        <missing code>
}
```

Which of the following can be used to replace <missing code> so that the code segment works as intended?

Select two answers.

(A)
```
IF (spin1 = 8)
        RETURN(RANDOM(1, 8) * 10)
ELSE
        RETURN(spin1)
```

(C)
```
IF (spin1 < 8)
        RETURN(spin1)
ELSE
{
        spin2 ← RANDOM(1,8)*10
        RETURN(spin2 * 10)
}
```

(B)
```
IF (spin1 = 8)
        RETURN(spin1)
ELSE
        RETURN(RANDOM(10, 80))
```

(D)
```
IF (spin1 < 8)
        RETURN(spin1)
ELSE
{
        spin2 ← RANDOM(1,8)
        RETURN(spin2 * 10)
}
```

GO ON TO THE NEXT PAGE.

69. The price of going to a local water park depends on a person's age and if they have a coupon or not. A person's age will be stored at the variable age and will be an integer. If the person has a coupon, it will be stored as a Boolean coupon, which is true if they have the coupon, false otherwise.

    If a person is under the age of 6, they do not pay to go to the water park. If they are 6 years old or older, they are charged $10. If they have a coupon, they are charged half.

    Which of the following code segments correctly sets the value of cost?

    Select <u>two</u> answers.

(A)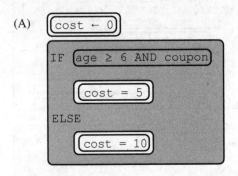

(C)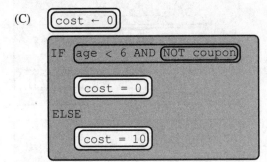

(B)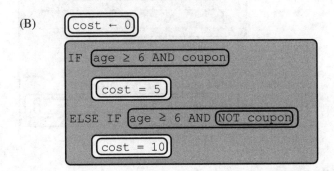

(D)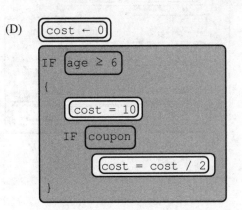

GO ON TO THE NEXT PAGE.

70. A teacher gives out three grades, "Exceeds" if a score is 90 or above, "Meets" if a score is greater than or equal to 70, but lower than 90, or "Does not meet" if a score is below 70. Which of the following would work for these specifications?

Select <u>two</u> answers.

(A)
```
IF score ≥ 90
    DISPLAY "Exceeds"
ELSE IF score ≥ 70
    DISPLAY "Meets"
ELSE
    DISPLAY "Does not meet"
```

(C)
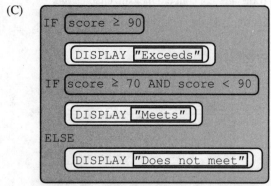
```
IF score ≥ 90
    DISPLAY "Exceeds"
IF score ≥ 70 AND score < 90
    DISPLAY "Meets"
ELSE
    DISPLAY "Does not meet"
```

(B)
```
IF score ≥ 90
    DISPLAY "Exceeds"
IF score ≥ 70
    DISPLAY "Meets"
IF score < 70
    DISPLAY "Does not meet"
```

(D)
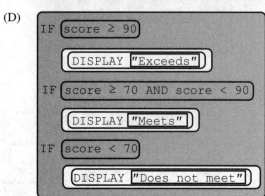
```
IF score ≥ 90
    DISPLAY "Exceeds"
IF score ≥ 70 AND score < 90
    DISPLAY "Meets"
IF score < 70
    DISPLAY "Does not meet"
```

STOP

END OF EXAM

Practice Test 1: Diagnostic Answer Key and Explanations

PRACTICE TEST 1: DIAGNOSTIC ANSWER KEY

Let's take a look at how you did on Practice Test 1. Follow the three-step process in the diagnostic answer key below and go read the explanations for any questions you got wrong or you struggled with but got correct. Once you finish working through the answer key and the explanations, go to the next chapter to make your study plan.

STEP 1 ≫ Check your answers and mark any correct answers with a ✔ in the appropriate column.

Q #	Ans.	✔	Chapter #, Section Title	Q #	Ans.	✔	Chapter #, Section Title
1	C		5, Iteration	28	C		5, Data Abstraction
2	C		5, Nested Conditionals	29	A		5, Simulations
3	B		4, Extracting Information from Data	30	C		6, Parallel and Distributed Computing
4	C		5, Calling Procedures, Developing Procedures, and Libraries	31	B		7, Beneficial and Harmful Effects
5	B		5, Undecidable Problems	32	D		7, Digital Divide
6	C		3, Identifying and Correcting Errors	33	A		5, Lists
7	D		5, Calling Procedures, Developing Procedures, and Libraries	34	C		5, Conditionals
8	D		3, Collaboration	35	A		5, Calling Procedures, Developing Procedures, and Libraries
9	A		7, Crowdsourcing	36	C		4, Data Compression
10	D		4, Binary Numbers	37	B		5, Lists
11	D		7, Safe Computing	38	D		5, Iteration
12	A		5, Lists	39	C		7, Digital Divide
13	B		5, Mathematical Expressions	40	A		3, Collaboration
14	D		4, Extracting Information from Data	41	B		5, Iteration
15	C		6, Parallel and Distributed Computing	42	A		7, Computing Bias
16	C		4, Binary Numbers	43	D		4, Data Compression
17	A		7, Safe Computing	44	D		4, Extracting Information from Data
18	A		5, Iteration	45	D		5, Lists
19	D		4, Using Programs with Data	46	D		5, Variables and Assignments
20	D		6, The Internet	47	C		7, Computing Bias
21	C		4, Extracting Information from Data	48	B		5, Conditionals
22	C		5, Simulations	49	A		4, Binary Numbers
23	B		4, Extracting Information from Data	50	D		3, Identifying and Correcting Errors
24	B		5, Lists	51	D		7, Legal and Ethical Concerns
25	A		4, Binary Numbers	52	B		7, Safe Computing
26	A		6, The Internet	53	A		5, Binary Search
27	B		5, Nested Conditionals	54	C		5, Lists

\#### Multiple Choice—Continued							
Q #	Ans.	✔	Chapter #, Section Title	Q #	Ans.	✔	Chapter #, Section Title
55	D		**4,** Data Compression	63	B, C		**7,** Digital Divide
56	A		**6,** Fault Tolerance	64	C, D		**6,** Fault Tolerance
57	B		**7,** Crowdsourcing	65	A, B		**5,** Algorithmic Efficiency
58	B		**7,** Beneficial and Harmful Effects	66	A, D		**5,** Boolean Expressions
59	C		**7,** Digital Divide	67	A, D		**6,** The Internet
60	D		**7,** Safe Computing	68	A, D		**5,** Conditionals
61	A		**7,** Safe Computing	69	B, D		**5,** Nested Conditionals
62	B		**4,** Extracting Information from Data	70	A, D		**5,** Nested Conditionals

 **Tally your correct answers from Step 1 by chapter. For each chapter, write the number of correct answers in the appropriate box. Then, divide your correct answers by the number of total questions (which we've provided) to get your percent correct.**

CHAPTER 3 TEST SCORE SELF-EVALUATION

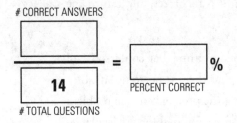

\# CORRECT ANSWERS

4

\# TOTAL QUESTIONS

= PERCENT CORRECT %

CHAPTER 4 TEST SCORE SELF-EVALUATION

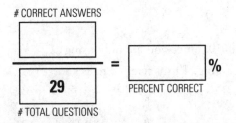

\# CORRECT ANSWERS

14

\# TOTAL QUESTIONS

= PERCENT CORRECT %

CHAPTER 5 TEST SCORE SELF-EVALUATION

\# CORRECT ANSWERS

29

\# TOTAL QUESTIONS

= PERCENT CORRECT %

CHAPTER 6 TEST SCORE SELF-EVALUATION

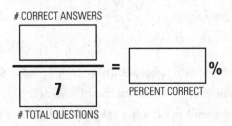

\# CORRECT ANSWERS

7

\# TOTAL QUESTIONS

= PERCENT CORRECT %

CHAPTER 7 TEST SCORE SELF-EVALUATION

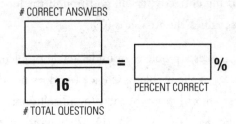

\# CORRECT ANSWERS

16

\# TOTAL QUESTIONS

= PERCENT CORRECT %

 **Use the results above to customize your study plan. You may want to start with, or give more attention to, the chapters with the lowest percents correct.**

PRACTICE TEST 1: ANSWERS AND EXPLANATIONS

1. **C** Choice (A) does not send the variables as parameters and will draw the top left rectangle each time. Choice (B) will not draw any of the rectangles correctly. The parameters of the first rectangle, when x = 11 and y = 1 will be `drawRectangle(11, 1, 14, 8)`, which is not correct. Choice (D) will draw the first rectangle at `drawRectangle(10, 5, 12, 9)`, which is incorrect. Choice (C) will draw the first rectangle at `drawRectangle(10, 5, 12, 1)`, which is correct. The second rectangle will be at (7, 7, 9, 3), which is correct. The next two follow the same trend. The answer is (C).

2. **C** At the beginning of the code segment, x = 10 and y = 20. The condition for the first IF statement is `x < 15` and, since that is true, it will enter the braces and do the next if-statement. The condition of the next IF statement is `y < 20` and, since that is false, it will do the ELSE which adds 10 to x. Now x = 20 and y = 20. You still need to check the final IF statement. The condition of that IF statement is `x > 15`, and since that is true the program will add 5 to x, resulting in x = 25. Note that the most frequently occurring error in this program is skipping the final IF statement, so make sure to do that one since it is an IF statement, and not an ELSE-IF statement. The answer is (C).

3. **B** The answer is not (A) since management will be getting the type of ticket sold from the metadata. The answer cannot be (C) since management will know the geolocation of each purchase. The answer cannot be (D) since management will know how fast the tickets are sold from the metadata. Management does not know the financial status of each purchaser from the metadata given, so (B) is correct. The answer is (B).

4. **C** Choice (A) will never return `false`, so it is incorrect. Choice (B) will go through the loop three times no matter what, and return whatever they entered last. Choice (D) will return `true` or `false` only depending on what they entered on the first time through the loop. The return statement will block the code segment from executing the repeats, causing an early return. Choice (C) does everything correctly; it will go through the loop only three times if it is incorrect, and return the correct value. The answer is (C).

5. **B** What makes a problem an undecidable problem is that there is no algorithm that could solve all instances of the problem. Choice (A) does not do enough to show that there is no solution, since another algorithm might solve for all solutions. Choice (C) is solving the problem, so the problem must be decidable. Choice (D) is showing that a heuristic solution exists, making it decidable. Choice (B) is the only answer that proves that there is no solution to the problem, making it undecidable. The answer is (B).

6. **C** Since 8 + 10 = 18 in decimal, the binary representation of 18 is 10010. Since you are only using four bits, you are not allowed the fifth bit that was added to the beginning. This is referred to as an overflow error. The answer is (C).

7. **D** The program starts by running `someMath(10, 6)`. The procedure `someMath` will receive 10 for `num1`, and 6 for `num2`. Since the IF statement is true, the procedure will return 10 minus 6, which is 4. Therefore, x will equal 4. Next, `someMath(2, x)` is called. Since x equals 4, `num1` will

equal 2 and `num2` will equal 4. This will cause the IF statement to be false, so the procedure will return 2 times 4, which is 8. This means that y will equal 8. Finally, the program will run `someMath(x, y)`, so `num1` will equal 4 and `num2` will equal 8. This will cause the IF statement to be false, so the procedure will return 4 times 8. This means that z will equal 32, so 32 will be the output. The answer is (D).

8. **D**   Comments are needed in all these cases. The answer is (D).

9. **A**   Crowdsourcing involves allowing widespread access to data to identify problems and develop solutions. Choice (B) will only be creating online fundraisers, not actually using the data. Choice (C) is against using the data publicly, so it can be eliminated. No information about the individual's job status is given, so (D) can be eliminated. Choice (A) can find a correlation between how a person feels and medical issues through the use of data, making it the correct use of crowdsourcing. The answer is (A).

10. **D**   When adding 1 to 10001101, the far-right digit when adding is 1 + 1 = 10, causing the far-right digit to become 0, and carry the one to the 2s digit to the left of it. The next addition just adds 0 + 1 = 1, causing the right digit to become 1. The last one starts with the far right, 1 + 1 = 10. This causes the far-right digit to become 0, and the 2s digit next to it to carry over a one. The 2s digit is 1 + 1 = 10, which causes the 2s digit to become 0 and another carry over. This continues until we get a carried over 1+0=1.

First number	Second number	Third number
10001101	10001110	10001111
+ 1	+ 1	+ 1
10001110	10001111	10010000

The answer is (D).

11. **D**   Malware is software that damages or takes over a system, so (A) can be eliminated. Choice (B) is not correct, since keylogging involves recording the keystrokes made by the user. Phishing is tricking a user into them giving up their personal information, so eliminate (C). A rogue access point is a wireless access point that will give a cybercriminal unauthorized access to a network. The answer is (D).

12. **A**   Choice (B) can be eliminated since the loop will iterate through `myList` the correct amount of times. Choice (C) can be eliminated since it will find every index of `myList` that are less than 0, not equal to 0, and instead of removing them, it makes them equal 0. Choice (D) also can be eliminated since it is incrementing `counter` each time through the loop, not just when the current index is less than 0. Choice (A) correctly explains that it will iterate the correct time through the loop, check to see if any of the indexes are less than 0, and replace the value at those indexes with 0. At the end it returns `myList`. The answer is (A).

13. **B** MOD will return the remainder of two numbers. 28 divided by 5 would be 5 remainder 3. MOD will ignore the full solution and only return the remainder. The answer is (B).

14. **D** Choice (A) will remove all the employees listed as "Manager," but then the spreadsheet will be sorted by the last sort, which is Number of Years, so (A) can be eliminated. Choice (B) never removes those listed as "Manager," so it can be eliminated. Choice (C) works correctly, but it is not as efficient as (D). Choice (D) will filter out all those listed as "Manager" and those without enough years. The extra column will make it easier to figure out who has a positive Revenue minus Expenses and, when sorted, it will list all of those with positive Revenue minus Expenses on top. This makes it easy to delete those who have a negative Revenue minus Expenses, and do so with much less manual work than (C), making (D) more efficient. The answer is (D).

15. **C** Computer A will have to complete all the processes separately, so you add up all the minutes, making it take 47 total minutes. Computer B can take the two shorter processes and complete them in 25 minutes (10 + 15) on one processor, and then can take the longer process and complete that on the other processor, so that will take 22 minutes. This means that it will take the longer of the two processors to complete the task, which is 25 minutes. Computer A takes 47 minutes, computer B takes 25 minutes, so when subtracted the answer is 22 minutes. The answer is (C).

16. **C** In order to have 100 unique ID numbers, the company must use a 7-bit system. Since $2^7 = 128$, the company will now have the ability to store 128 ID numbers. If the company only added 1 bit, it would have a 6-bit system, and $2^6 = 64$. Adding 3 bits would be a waste since the company doesn't need the extra bit if it only has 100 employees. This is why adding two bits, going from 5 to 7 bits, is the correct answer. The answer is (C).

17. **A** Trying to steal someone's password by guessing several different passwords is an example of brute force to steal the password, so eliminate (B). Downloading malicious software with an intent to harm is malware, so eliminate (C). Choice (D) is also a form of malware known as a bot. Email phishing occurs when a cybercriminal sends out a large number of emails hoping that someone will believe it and do whatever the cybercriminal wants, such as changing their email address unintentionally through a fake website. The answer is (A).

18. **A** Choice (B) will output 0 1, then 0 2, then 0 3 the first time through the inner loop. The variable y will start out equaling 0, but will be incremented to 1 before the first output. Choice (C) will start with y = 0, and the first time through the inner loop will print all the correct values for x = 0. The code will not reset y to 0 inside the loop, so it will stay as 3 and not enter the inner loop again. Choice (D) will increment x inside the inner loop, so when we are done with the first iteration of the outer loop x will already equal 3 and be done. Choice (A) will do the outer loop 3 times since it only increments at the end of the outer loop. It will reset y to x each time, and display before it increments y in the inner loop, matching the output exactly. The answer is (A).

19. **D** Name will not have to be cleaned since it is not part of what they are sorting, so (A) can be eliminated. Age and State are both drop-down menus, so they will not have to be cleaned, eliminated (B) and (C). Favorite candy might be written differently, using possible abbreviations, different spellings, capitalizations, etc. The answer is (D).

20. **D** TCP is an acronym for Transmission Control Protocol and works with the IP (Internet Protocol) to send packets, making it a common protocol of the Internet. UDP is an acronym for User Datagram Protocol, and is also an IP that is an alternative to the TCP. HTTP stands for Hypertext Transfer Protocol and is a protocol established by the World Wide Web to view web pages. IETF is the Internet Engineering Task Force promotes open standards for the Internet, but is not a protocol. Note, IETF is the only acronym that does not end in "P" for protocol. The answer is (D).

21. **C** Supermarkets grouping products at the store is not discriminatory, so eliminate (A). Predicting candidates for treatment is only helpful, so eliminate (B). Predicting searches is not discriminating against the user, so eliminate (D). Predicting who will have bad credit scores by demographic data and using that information to charge some people higher interest rates is discriminatory. The answer is (C).

22. **C** Any time that manual work is being done for a task that needs to be performed a large number of times, it will not be efficient, so (A) and (B) do not work. Even though (D) provides more efficiency, the cost will be increased. Choice (C) will be the most efficient since the results will be quicker than the other options. The answer is (C).

23. **B** The students geolocations in (A) does not have any use since you are concerned about how they use their smartphones, not where. For (C), the use of the smartphone on the weekend or weekday does not matter for this research, and neither does the financial and scholarship records from each student in (D). In (B), if the student is using their smartphone for a significant amount of time, but for academic purposes, it can prove that an excessive amount of time on the smartphone will not hinder the student's academic performance. The answer is (B).

24. **B** For (A), at the beginning of the program, item = 1. Since prev = 0, (prev < item) is true, making increasing = true. Then prev = item, making prev = 1. The next iteration, item = 2, and since (prev < item), increasing stays true. Since (prev < item) will be true the entire way, increasing will be true the entire time. Choice (C) has increasing = true until the very end. When prev = 6, and item = 4 in the last iteration, (prev < item) is false, making increasing = false. The Boolean false will get returned like it is supposed to. Choice (D) has increasing = true until the very end also. When prev = 4 and item = 4 in the last iteration, (prev < item) is false, so increasing = false, and that is what is returned. At the beginning of (B), prev = 0 and item = 1, so (prev < item), making increasing = true. Then prev = 1 and item = 4 in the second iteration, so increasing stays true. In the third iteration, prev = 4 and item = 2, which makes (prev < item) false, making increasing = false. The last iteration prev = 2, and item = 6, making (prev < item) true, making increase = true. Since this is the last iteration and increasing = true, Choice (B) will return true, when it is supposed to return false. The answer is (B).

25. **A** Binary starts with the smallest number on the far right, and double as the numbers go left. The farthest right digit is $2^0 = 1$, then the next digit to the left is $2^1 = 2$, then the next digit is $2^2 = 4$, and that continues left.

2^7	2^6	2^5	2^4	2^3	2^2	2^1	2^0	
128	64	32	16	8	4	2	1	
0	1	0	0	1	0	0	0	= 64 + 8 = 72 = H
0	1	0	0	0	1	0	1	= 64 + 4 + 1 = 69 = E
0	1	0	1	1	0	0	1	= 64 + 16 + 8 + 1 = 89 = Y

The answer is (A).

26. **A** Choice (B) is incorrect because the World Wide Web uses HTML to create pages, and the HTML is transmitted over the Internet. Eliminate (C) because the Internet is never off, there are protocols set up to prevent this. Choice (D) can also be eliminated because the Internet came first as a way to share information, the World Wide Web was then created to have a shared language to transmit information. The answer is (A).

27. **B** Choice (A) will display "Day Off" if it is an even day. The rest of the code deals with odd days, so if it is "Saturday" or "Sunday", it is a "Day Off". We have exhausted both possible cases in which Bradley gets a day off, so it displays "Workout" correctly. Choice (C) will display "Day Off" if any one of the three conditions is true, which is accurate, and if all three of the conditions are false it will display "Workout". Choice (D) will require both sides of the condition to be true using the AND statement. If the day is odd, the start of the condition is correctly true. If it is not "Saturday" OR it is not "Sunday", that means it is a weekday, making the end of the condition true. Choice (B) will not display correctly. The only way it will display "Day Off" is if all three of the conditions are true, when only one of them needs to be for a "Day Off". The answer is (B).

28. **C** In order to manage complexity, usually you want to create a procedure that will hide the unnecessary details from the user, or in this case, the programmer. Choice (A) and (D) will not hide any details; all the code will be there. A loop will not hide the complexity of a program, so (B) is not correct. Creating a procedure that can be used several times will help hide the complexity of what is printed out with their bank statements. The answer is (C).

29. **A** A driving simulator will not physically move the user at all, so it will not be able to show how it feels to get into an accident. The answer is (A).

30. **C** If order does not matter in which several smaller problems can be solved, parallel computing is an advantage, so (A) can be eliminated. Parallel computing does make it so solutions are easier to scale, so (B) can be eliminated. Parallel computing, if done correctly, does significantly reduce the amount of time a problem can be solved in, which means (D) can be eliminated. Choice (C) is not a benefit. If a problem has to be solved in order, sequential computing is the best way to find a solution. The answer is (C).

31. **B** Choice (A) is an unintended harmful effect since it will directly affect the land and habitat. Choices (C) and (D) are also unintended harmful effects that are created during the production of the solar panels. Choice (B) is not a harmful effect created by renewable energy; instead, it will prevent a harmful effect that is caused by other energy courses. Choice (B) ends up being a beneficial effect of solar panels. The answer is (B).

32. **D** Choice (A) would make everyone have an equal device in the school, reducing the digital divide. Choice (B) would ensure that all parents know how to access their kid's academics, eliminating the advantage that some parents who are more digitally literate have over others. Not all students are guaranteed Internet access at home, so (C) would eliminate the advantage that students with Internet access have over those who do not. Choice (D) makes it so students who do not come from families that can purchase expensive devices are at a disadvantage to those who can afford better devices. The answer is (D).

33. **A** Choice (B) could be handled using variables to keep track of the total wait time that day and the number of customers that day, and from those two variables you can find the average wait time without using a list. For (C), you can have variables that keep track of the longest and shortest wait times while the program is running, so a list is not needed. Choice (D) does not need a list because a variable can keep track of that while running the program. If you want to print out all the users' information at the end of the day, you must store that information in a list to have the ability to print it all out later. The answer is (A).

34. **C** For each day that the temperature is greater than `max`, the new day's temperature stores to `max`. However, `max` is originally set to 0. For (C), by the end of the code segment, `max` should equal –20, but instead it stores 0. Since `max` originally stores 0, and none of the three values are greater than 0, none of them will end up replacing the 0 at `max`. The answer is (C).

35. **A** The procedure created in (B) would not be correct since both those lines of code are doing different things. The procedures in (C) and (D) would not save any code since you are just moving the current code to a different section. The goal of this procedure is to replace code that is repeated. The program repeats lines 4 and 5 again in lines 9 and 10, so if we created a procedure to replace that code, we can call the procedure each time instead of writing both lines of code. The answer is (A).

36. **C** Statement I is an advantage since lossy compression does reduce the size of a file. Eliminate (B) and (D), which do not include Statement I. Statement II is not included in either remaining choice, so there is no need to consider Statement II. Statement III is an advantage since the smaller size will make it quicker to send and store the file. Eliminate (A), which does not include Statement III. Only one choice remains, so there is no need to continue. Note that Statement II is not an advantage because lossy compression algorithms reduce the size of a file, and the information that is compressed is lost permanently. This causes the quality to be reduced, even if that reduction in quality is not noticeable. The answer is (C).

37. **B** Choice (A) has the conditional set incorrectly. You only want the numbers that are greater than `largeNum`, not less than. Choice (C) will continually add the correct item, but to index 1 of `newList` each time since `index` is never incremented. Choice (D) will add 1 to `index` first, making it 2, so the first item greater than `largeNum` will be added to index 2, instead of index 1. Choice (B) will correctly add the indexes of `fullList` to `newList`, while we increment the index after adding to the `newList`. The answer is (B).

38. **D** Choice (A) does the inner loop correctly, but the outer loop should go through 4 times, not `sideLength` times. If `sideLength = 3`, it will only create 3 sides of the square. Choice (B) does not do the inner loop correctly; this square will always have a side length of 3. Choice (C) has the `ROTATE _ LEFT` in the wrong location. It will rotate every time it moves the robot one square. Choice (D) will do all 4 sides with the outer loop. Then it will `MOVE _ FORWARD` the amount of times that `sideLength` is equal to, and then `ROTATE _ LEFT` after moving that many times. The answer is (D).

39. **C** Statement I does not help with this program, since the list of friends in the class does not impact anything with the digital divide. Eliminate (B) and (D), which include statement I. Both remaining choices include statement II, so go straight to statement III. Statement III does help, since students without Internet access at home can help explain the digital divide to other students who might not be understanding. In order to get a good mix, we need different viewpoints in the group. Eliminate (A). Only one choice remains so there is no need to continue. Statement II works. In order to get unique viewpoints in each group, we must include students with different socioeconomic status. The answer is (C).

40. **A** Choice (B) would assist since students express their own unique perspectives on the digital divide, helping the collaborative process of the diverse student groups. Choice (C) would help. Although this does not start with collaboration, after the initial separation, the students will come back together to discuss what they have read. Choice (D) helps since they are collaborating on the outline together. Choice (A) does not encourage collaboration throughout the entirety of the project because the students will work independently the entire time until they just combine the paper at the end. The answer is (A).

41. **B** Since Line 6 is going to be done each time through the inner loop, which will be 8 times total, any choice that does not move Line 6 out of the inner loop is wrong, so (A) and (C) are not correct. Choice (D) has Line 6 moved out of both loops, meaning it will not turn twice like it needs to. Choice (B) moves Line 6 outside of the inner loop but keeps it in the outer loop. This will have the robot move forward 4 times, and then turn right, and when it does that twice it will end up in the correct location. The answer is (B).

42. **A** The answer is not (B) since cleaning a large data set poses challenges. The answer is not (C), since everyone has the same demographics, so bias will occur. The answer is not (D) since, if too few students answer, there will not be enough data for it to be meaningful data. For (A), as long as the data analyzation is scalable, it should be easy to analyze large amounts of data. The answer is (A).

43. **D** For (A), since the picture is losing quality, that would be a lossy compression. Lossless compression means that no information is lost from the original file, so if the quality was lost, it is not lossless. Choice (B) is not correct since we are not able to restore all the information from the original file, this would also be lossy compression. Even though the quality that is lost is not discernible to the human ear, anytime any quality or original information is lost, it is lossy compression. Choice (D) is the only option in which, after the file is compressed, it is able to be brought back to the original file. The answer is (D).

44. **D** Choice (A) would help since we know one of the students does well academically and the other struggles, so it is possible to find a correlation using the data given. Choice (B) would also be helpful since we know the clubs that Candidate A is in, and we know the clubs that all the students are in, so we can find a possible correlation between the students in the same club as the candidate. Choice (C) is helpful since we know the athletics that Candidate B is in, and the athletics that each student is in, so we can possibly find a correlation. Choice (D) does not help for finding a correlation since we do not know the attendance records for each candidate, so we cannot find a correlation. The answer is (D).

45. **D** Choice (A) will never go increment i, so it will continually run the procedure `prime` from 1. Choices (B) and (C) will only increment i when the IF statement is true, not every time through the loop. Choice (D) will increment i every time through the loop, and check each number 1 through 20 using the procedure prime and only append the correct values. The answer is (D).

46. **D** The first output is a, which is storing 20. The second output is c, which is storing 15. Remember, the last value stored at each is what will be printed. Since only a and c are output, the program will print out 20 15. The answer is (D).

47. **C** Choice (A) and (D) will both push users more towards certain candidates, creating even more political polarization and an echo chamber for the user. Choice (B) may overly filter information from one side, making it ineffective. Choice (C) will make sure that algorithms are not biased towards one candidate, making it an effective way to eliminate bias. The answer is (C).

48. **B** Eliminate (A) since the condition is written in the incorrect order, the swap is only completed if `larger` is less than `smaller`. Choice (C) will overwrite the value in `larger` with the value in `smaller`, so we lose the value and cannot retrieve it. Choice (D) starts by storing `larger` at `temp`, but then overwrites the value stored at `smaller` with the `larger`, so we lose that value. Choice (B) stores `larger` at `temp`, then overwrites the value in `larger` with `smaller`. Since the value that was initially at `larger` was stored in `temp`, that value can be assigned to `smaller`. The answer is (B).

49. **A** You would need to find the binary representation of 153, 101, and 21. Here are the breakdowns of each number.

2^7	2^6	2^5	2^4	2^3	2^2	2^1	2^0	
128	64	32	16	8	4	2	1	
1	0	0	1	1	0	0	1	= 128 + 16 + 8 + 1 = 153
0	1	1	0	0	1	0	1	= 64 + 32 + 4 + 1 = 101
0	0	0	1	0	1	0	1	= 16 + 4 + 1 = 21

The answer is (A).

50. **D** For (A), if `counter` is reset to 0 each time through the loop, it will never properly count each case. Choice (B) will cause an early return since the first time through the loop it will return `counter` and not do any further iterations. Choice (C) does not work since it is looking for numbers between `min` and `max`, not numbers equal to `min` or `max`. For Choice (D), if Line 6 is an OR statement, then it will always be true. As an OR statement, either `item` ≥ `min`, or `item` ≤ `max`. If `min` is less than `max`, then this statement is always true. As an AND statement, it will only be true if it is inclusively between the two values. The answer is (D).

51. **D** Just because materials are not copyrighted does not mean that the ideas in the materials are public domain, so (A) can be eliminated. This goes for (C) also; works and ideas do not have to be registered or copyrighted to still be owned by a person; therefore, they cannot be reproduced. If you use a smaller text online, sometimes it is okay, but if that smaller part is important, it cannot be stolen or reused without permission, so (B) can be eliminated. Open source materials that the owner specifically waives the rights for reproduction can be used by anyone, so (D) works. The answer is (D).

52. **B** Your geolocation online can be used to stalk or perform a crime against an individual, which is very concerning, so eliminate (A) and (D). Having your social security number online can lead to identity theft, which is also very concerning, so eliminate (C). As much as targeted marking can be annoying, it is the least concerning of everything on this list. The answer is (B).

53. **A** Choice (B) would not work since you are looking for an ID number on a list that is sorted by names. You cannot do a binary search with this list. Choice (C) works for a binary search, but $\log_2(100)$ = 6.64, which rounds up to 7 instead of 10. Choice (D) does not work since it is an unsorted list. Choice (A) is a binary search since it is sorted by names and you are searching for a name. Also, the maximum number of searches is correct: log2(50) = 5.64, which rounds up to 6. Note that without the use of a calculator that does logarithms, you can still do this problem. Start with 50, and count the number of times you can cut 50 in half until you reach 1. 50–25–13–7–4–2–1, it was cut in half 6 times. The answer is (A).

54. **C** Choice (A) will cause an infinite loop since `position` will never be incremented, so it will continually check index 1 and never exit the loop. Choice (B) is incrementing `position` whenever "`Jenny`" is found, and then incrementing position again in Step 3. This will cause some indexes to be skipped, and the count to be wrong. Choice (D) will count and go through the loop correctly and count the number of occurrences correctly, but it will print out the numbers of occurrences each time through the loop. The answer is (C).

55. **D** Statement I does not work. Even though the pictures are not losing any quality, they are still not any cheaper to upload, store, or download. Eliminate (A) and (C), which include Statement I. Statement II is included in both remaining choices, so ignore that statement. Statement III works since no quality is lost to the human eye when making the images lossy. Eliminate (B), which does not include Statement III. Only one choice remains, so there is no need to continue. Note that Statement II is correct since the lossy images will be smaller than the original, improving speed. The answer is (D).

56. **A** Statement III is not true. Even though devices G and E are central in this network, all the devices still have a connection to every other device if G and E are to fail. This eliminates (B) and (D) since they contain Statement III. Statement II is also false. Even with device C and F failing, a connection from B to D exists through B-A-G-E-D. This eliminates (C) since it contains Statement II, leaving only (A). Statement I is correct, since device C was set up with only two connections, and if those two connections are broken, then C cannot communicate with any other device. The answer is (A).

57. **B** Choice (B) would be the most appropriate citizens' science project since it is being overseen by scientists. Choice (A) is dealing with non-scientists as the leads of the projects. Choice (C) is more difficult because it is requiring people to purchase something and then analyze the data themselves. Choice (D) has privacy issues since it is releasing different people's locations during the day. The answer is (B).

58. **B** Choices (A), (C), and (D) are all beneficial effects since they are saving time, tracking the health crisis, and having less contact with other people. Although the school has the beneficial effect of saving money by hiring less personnel, there is the harmful effect on society by jobs being lost. The answer is (B).

59. **C** Choice (A) would enable all students to have access to the self-certification system from home, removing the digital divide dealing with access. Choice (B) would eliminate any issues that students might have if they do not have access to the Internet at home to complete the self-certification system. Choice (D) eliminates the issues that students might have who have not had access to computers or devices during their lifetime and will need assistance with tasks such as completing a self-certification system. Choice (C) will not do anything for the digital divide since ID's are a physical item. The answer is (C).

60. **D** Choices (A), (B), and (C) are all ways that the school can assist with medical issues since there is access to their medical history. Choice (D) is a concern. When there are too many people with access to private information, the chances of that information being stolen increases because of phishing attacks, etc. The answer is (D).

61. **A** Choice (B) would make it extremely difficult for someone to access someone else's login since he or she would have to know most of that person's personal information or various other pieces of information. Whenever a password becomes longer and uses more than just letters, the odds of cracking that password becomes significantly more difficult, so (C) can be eliminated. The use of public key encryption makes unauthorized access difficult, and certificates validate ownership and security with the keys, eliminating (D). While (A) does help security, the length of 30 minutes is long enough for someone to access a student's account if they forget to logout. The answer is (A).

62. **B** When looking for a causal relationship, you want to see if one data set will affect another and if the two are connected because of the data correlation. In this situation, you are trying to find if one student being infected will cause other students to become infected because of their proximity to already infected people. The medical history will most likely not affect other students, so (A) and (D) can be eliminated. What time a student self-certifies cannot be used to determine if that student infected other students, so (C) can be eliminated. When comparing infected students to other infected students, it can be determined whether they were around other students to make them infected, so the data can be useful in determining whether a causal relationship exists. The answer is (B).

63. **B, C** Choice (A) can be eliminated because if only people with insurance can get these devices, then they will still not be available for everyone. Increasing the cost of anything will not bridge the gap, so eliminate (D). Choice (B) is effective since the cost will be reduced or eliminated, and (C) will also be effective since the technologies can be enhanced through grants. The answers are (B) and (C).

64. **C, D** A fault-tolerant system is one that can have errors, or failures within the system, but will continue to work without any interruption. Choice (A) only deals with speed and not fault tolerance, so (A) can be eliminated. Choice (B) only discusses the fact that HTML reads in website data, which has nothing to do with fault tolerance, so it can be eliminated. Choice (C) does address the fact that connections can fail but information can still be guaranteed to make where it needs to go, so (C) is correct. Choice (D) also deals with uninterrupted work when errors occur, making it fault-tolerant. The answers are (C) and (D).

65. **A, B** A heuristic approach deals with finding the best possible solution or algorithm to solve problems when exact methods are not possible in a reasonable amount of time. A binary search and a linear search are both techniques that will give exact answers in a relatively short amount of time, so eliminate (C) and (D). Choice (A) will be a heuristic approach since you cannot give an exact solution, only an approximate is available. Choice (B) will be a heuristic approach since there is no guarantee that the algorithm you come up with will be the best possible compression algorithm available, even though it is the best you can come up with. The answers are (A) and (B).

66. **A, D** Another way to look at this problem is to use different sets of numbers. Since this is false for all numbers less than 10 and greater than 20, try a number in both of those ranges, such as 5. Since 5 makes the original statement false, eliminate (C), which makes 5 true. Since it is true for numbers between 10 and 20, inclusively, try a number between those numbers, such as 15. Eliminate (B), which 15 makes false. Here is the truth table for each number.

		5	10	15	20	25
Q)	num ≥ 10 AND num ≤ 20	F	T	T	T	F
A)	NOT (num < 10 OR num > 20)	F	T	T	T	F
B)	num = 10 OR num = 20	F	T	F	T	F
C)	num ≤ 10 OR num ≥ 20	T	T	F	T	T
D)	num ≥ 10 AND (NOT (num > 20))	F	T	T	T	F

The question has the same solution set as (A) and (D). The answers are (A) and (D).

67. **A, D** Eliminate (C) since Internet protocols are set so all devices can connect to other types of devices. Choice (B) can be eliminated since there is no guarantee that everyone has the same bandwidth. Choices (A) and (D) both describe two of the purposes of having established Internet protocols. The answers are (A) and (D).

68. **A, D** Choice (B) will correctly return spin1, but RANDOM(10,80) will return a number between 10 and 80, not a number between 1 and 8 that is multiplied by 10. Choice (C) will multiply spin2 by 10 twice, resulting in too large of a number. For (A), the IF statements are correct, and the RANDOM(1,8)×10 will first find the random from 1 to 8 and then multiple by 10, so this is a correct solution. Choice (D) will correctly do the IF statements, and then find a random number from 1 to 8. When it returns that random number, it will first multiple it by 10 to give a correct number. The answers are (A) and (D).

69. **B, D** Choice (A) will cause an incorrect value due to the ELSE statement. If age is less than 6, the IF statement is false, making cost = 10. Choice (C) would be incorrect since at no point could cost = 5. The answers are (B) and (D).

70. **A, D** Choice (B) will print out "Exceeds" and "Meets" for values greater than 90. For example, if score = 95, it will print out "Exceeds". Then it will do the second IF statement, and since score ≥ 70, it will print out "Meets". Choice (C) is also incorrect in the case of a number greater than or equal to 90. The first IF statement will be true, so it prints "Exceeds". The second IF statement is false, so it will do the ELSE statement instead and print "Does not meet". The answers are (A) and (D).

HOW TO SCORE PRACTICE TEST 1

Section I: Multiple Choice

$$\underline{\hspace{3cm}} \times 1.5000 = \underline{\hspace{3cm}}$$

Number Correct
(out of 70)

Weighted
Section I Score
(Do not round)

Section II: Create Performance Task

(This is completed and submitted outside of test time. See if you can find a teacher or classmate to score your Create Performance Task using the guidelines in Chapter 2.)

Task Score: $\underline{\hspace{2cm}} \times 7.5000 = \underline{\hspace{3cm}}$

(out of 6)

(Task Score
Do not round)

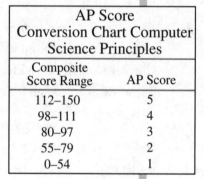

AP Score Conversion Chart Computer Science Principles	
Composite Score Range	AP Score
112–150	5
98–111	4
80–97	3
55–79	2
0–54	1

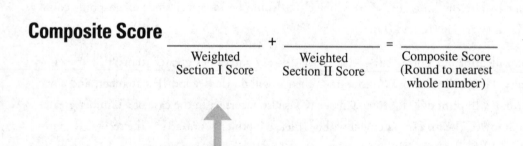

Composite Score

$$\underline{\hspace{3cm}} + \underline{\hspace{3cm}} = \underline{\hspace{3cm}}$$

Weighted
Section I Score

Weighted
Section II Score

Composite Score
(Round to nearest
whole number)

Part III
About the
AP Computer
Science
Principles Exam

- The Structure of the AP Computer Science Principles Exam
- How AP Exams Are Used
- Other Resources

THE STRUCTURE OF THE AP COMPUTER SCIENCE PRINCIPLES EXAM

The AP Computer Science Principles Exam is a two-part test. The chart below illustrates the test's structure:

Section	Question Type	Number of Questions	Time Allowed	Percent of Final Grade
I	Multiple Choice	70	2 hrs. of test time	70%
II	Create Performance Task	—	12 hrs. of class time	30%

The AP Computer Science Principles course and exam require that potential solutions of problems be written in any programming language. You should be able to perform the following tasks:

- design, implement, and analyze solutions to problems
- use and implement commonly used algorithms
- use standard data structures
- develop and select appropriate algorithms and data structures to solve new problems
- write solutions fluently in your chosen language
- write, run, test, and debug solutions in your chosen programming language
- read and understand a description of the design and development process leading to such a program (examples of such solutions can be found in the AP Computer Science Labs)
- understand the ethical and social implications of computer use

The following table shows the classification categories and how they are represented in the multiple-choice section of the exam. Because questions can be classified as being in more than one category, the total of the percentages is greater than 100%.

Big Ideas	Exam Weighting
Big Idea 1: Creative Development	10–13%
Big Idea 2: Data	17–22%
Big Idea 3: Algorithms and Programming	30–35%
Big Idea 4: Computer Systems and Networks	11–15%
Big Idea 5: Impact of Computing	21–26%

Have You Noticed?
You may notice that our Part V content chapters align exactly with these units. You're welcome :)

In addition to the multiple-choice questions, there is also a Create Performance Task, for which you are required to create your own program. You must submit a PDF file of your program code, a video of your app running, and a written response to given prompts. This is expected to take 12 hours of class time and must be submitted by a given deadline. Be sure to check the College Board site for the deadline.

The multiple-choice questions are scored by machine, while the Create Performance Task is scored by thousands of college faculty and expert AP teachers at the annual AP Reading. Scores on the free-response questions are weighted and combined with the weighted results of the multiple-choice questions. These composite, weighted raw scores are then converted into the reported AP Exam scores of 5, 4, 3, 2, and 1. Each row in the rubric is given either a 0 or a 1 score; there is no partial credit.

Score	2021 Percentage	Credit Recommendation	College Grade Equivalent
5	12.4%	Extremely Well Qualified	A
4	21.7%	Well Qualified	A–, B+, B
3	32.5%	Qualified	B–, C+, C
2	19.9%	Possibly Qualified	–
1	13.6%	No Recommendation	–

Scores taken from May 2021 test administration. Data taken from the College Board website.

Create Performance Task

The other portion of the AP Computer Science Principles Exam is the Create Performance Task. This is a student-created app, and the task includes coding, video, and written response. The Create Performance Task is scored from 0 to 6.

Unlike the multiple choice questions on the AP Computer Science Principles Exam or even the free response questions on other AP exams, the Create Performance Task doesn't change. You get to decide what task to complete, as long as it fits within the requirements laid out by College Board. Furthermore, College Board Provides a rubric to score your Create Performance Task, so it's possible to predict your score, even before you submit.

Row 1 (0–1 point)	Program Purpose and Function	Video: • Demonstrate input • Demonstrate program functionality • Demonstrate output Written Response: • Describe the overall purpose of the program • Describe what functionality of the program is demonstrated in the video • Describe the input and output of the program demonstrated in the video
Row 2 (0–1 point)	Data Abstraction	Written Response: • Include a program code segment showing how data has been stored in a collection • Include a program code segment showing the data in the same collection being used as part of fulfilling the program's purpose • Identify the name of the variable representing the list being used in the response • Describe what the data contained in this collection represents in the program
Row 3 (0–1 point)	Managing Complexity	Written Response: • Include a program code segment that shows a list being used to manage complexity in the program • Explain how the named, selected list manages complexity in the program code by explaining why the program code could not be written, or how it would be written differently, without using the list

Row 4 **(0–1 point)**	Procedural Abstraction	Written Response: • Include a program code segment showing a student-developed procedure with at least one parameter that has an effect on the functionality of the procedure • Include a program code segment showing where the student-developed procedure is being called • Describe what the identified procedure does and how it contributes to the overall functionality of the program
Row 5 **(0–1 point)**	Algorithm Implementation	Written Response: • Include a program code segment of a student-developed algorithm that includes sequencing, selection, and iteration • Identify the name of the variable representing the list being used in the response • Describe what the data contained in this collection represents in the program
Row 6 **(0–1 point)**	Testing	Written Response: • Describe two calls to the selected procedure from 3c. Each call must pass a different argument that causes a different segment of code in the algorithm to execute • Describe the condition(s) being tested by each call to the procedure • Identify the result of each call

How Will I Know?
Your dream college's website may explain how it uses the AP Exam scores, or you can contact the school's admissions department to verify AP Exam score acceptance information.

HOW AP EXAMS ARE USED

Different colleges use AP Exams in different ways, so it is important that you visit a particular college's website in order to determine how it accepts AP Exam scores. The three items below represent the main ways in which AP Exam scores can be used.

- **College Credit.** Some colleges will give you college credit if you receive a high score on an AP Exam. These credits count toward your graduation requirements, meaning that you can take fewer courses while in college. Given the cost of college, this could be quite a benefit, indeed.

- **Satisfy Requirements.** Some colleges will allow you to "place out" of certain requirements if you do well on an AP Exam, even if they do not give you actual college credits. For example, you might not need to take an introductory-level course, or perhaps you might not need to take a class in a certain discipline at all.

- **Admissions Plus.** Even if your AP Exam will not result in college credit or even allow you to place out of certain courses, most colleges will respect your decision to push yourself by taking an AP course. In addition, if you take an AP Exam outside of an AP course, they will likely respect that drive too. A high score on an AP Exam shows mastery of more difficult content than is typically taught in high school courses, and colleges may take that into account during the admissions process.

> Some people think that AP courses are reserved for high school seniors, but that is not the case. Don't be afraid to see about being placed into an AP course during your junior or even sophomore year. A good AP Exam score looks fantastic on a college application and can set you apart from other candidates.

OTHER RESOURCES

There are many resources available to help you improve your score on the AP Computer Science Principles Exam, not the least of which are your teachers. If you are taking an AP course, you may be able to get extra attention from your teacher, such as feedback on your essays. If you are not in an AP course, you can reach out to a teacher who teaches AP Computer Science Principles and ask if he or she will review your Create Performance Task or otherwise help you master the content.

Another wonderful resource is AP Students, the official website of the AP Exams (part of the College Board's website). The scope of information available on AP Central is quite broad and includes the following:

- course descriptions, which include further details on what content is covered by the exam
- sample questions from the AP Computer Science Principles Exam
- Create Performance Task sample responses and multiple-choice questions from previous years

The AP Students home page address is apstudents.collegeboard.org/what-is-ap.

For up-to-date information about the AP Computer Science Principles Exam, please visit apstudents.collegeboard.org/courses/ap-computer-science-principles.

Finally, The Princeton Review offers tutoring and small group instruction. Our expert instructors can help you refine your strategic approach and enhance your content knowledge. For more information, call 1-800-2REVIEW.

More Great Books
The Princeton Review writes tons of books to guide you through test preparation and college admissions. If you're thinking about college, check out our wildly popular book *The Best 388 Colleges* and visit our website PrincetonReview.com for gobs of college rankings and ratings.

Part IV
Test-Taking
Strategies
for the AP
Computer
Science
Principles Exam

PREVIEW

Review your Practice Test 1 results and then respond to the following questions:

- How many multiple-choice questions did you miss even though you knew the answer?

- On how many multiple-choice questions did you guess randomly?

- How many multiple-choice questions did you miss after eliminating some answers and guessing based on the remaining answers?

HOW TO USE THIS PART

Before reading the following strategy chapters, think about what you are doing now. As you read and engage in the directed practice, be sure to think critically about the ways you can change your approach.

Chapter 1
How to Approach
Multiple-Choice
Questions

THE BASICS

The directions for the multiple-choice section of the AP Computer Science Principles Exam are pretty simple. They read as follows:

Directions: Determine the answer to each of the following questions or incomplete statements, using the available space for any necessary scratchwork. Then decide which is the best of the choices given and fill in the corresponding oval on the answer sheet. No credit will be given for anything written in the examination booklet. Do not spend too much time on any one problem.

In short, you're being asked to do what you've done on many other multiple-choice exams: pick the best answer (or answers) and then fill in the corresponding bubble on a separate sheet of paper. You will not be given credit for answers you record in your test booklet (by circling them, for example) but do not fill in on your answer sheet. The section consists of 70 questions and you will be given 2 hours to complete it.

The College Board also provides a breakdown of the general subject matter covered on the exam. This breakdown will not appear in your test booklet; it comes from the preparatory material that the College Board publishes. Here again is the chart we showed you in Part III:

Big Ideas	Exam Weighting
Big Idea 1: Creative Development	10–13%
Big Idea 2: Data	17–22%
Big Idea 3: Algorithms and Programming	30–35%
Big Idea 4: Computer Systems and Networks	11–15%
Big Idea 5: Impact of Computing	21–26%

A few important notes about the AP Computer Science Principles Exam directly from the College Board:

- Students will be given the Exam Reference Sheet, which contains both block-based and text-based programming constructs and established a common way to communicate programming concepts for the purpose of the exam.
- Questions in Big Ideas 1, 2, and 3 can be represented as algorithms with no problem code or as program code using the Exam Reference Sheet.
- The program code questions will contain some graphical representations some of which use robots in a grid.

MULTIPLE-CHOICE STRATEGIES

Process of Elimination (POE)

As you work through the multiple-choice section, always keep in mind that you are not graded on your thinking process or scratchwork. All that ultimately matters is that you indicate the correct answer. Even if you aren't sure how to answer a question in a methodically "correct" way, see if you can eliminate any answers based on common sense and then take a guess.

Throughout the book, we will point out areas where you can use common sense to eliminate answers.

Although we all like to be able to solve problems the "correct" way, using Process of Elimination (POE) and guessing aggressively can help earn you a few more points. It may be these points that make the difference between a 3 and a 4 or push you from a 4 to a 5.

Don't Be Afraid to Guess

If you don't know the answer, guess! There is no penalty for a wrong answer, so there is no reason to leave an answer blank. Obviously, the more incorrect answers you can eliminate, the better your odds of guessing the correct answer.

Don't Turn a Question into a Crusade!

Most people don't run out of time on standardized tests because they work too slowly. Instead, they run out of time because they spend half of the test wrestling with two or three particular questions.

You should never spend more than a minute or two on any question. If a question doesn't involve calculation, then you either know the answer, can take an educated guess at the answer, or don't know the answer. Figure out where you stand on a question, make a decision, and move on.

Any question that requires more than two minutes' worth of calculations probably isn't worth doing. Remember, skipping a question early in the section is a good thing if it means that you'll have time to get two right later on.

Watch for < vs. ≤ and > vs. ≥

The difference between < and ≤ or between > and ≥ can be huge, especially in loops. You can bet that this discrepancy will appear in multiple-choice questions!

Know How to Use the AP Computer Science Principles Exam Reference Sheet

This chapter offers strategies that will help make you a better test-taker and, hopefully, a better scorer on the AP Computer Science Principles Exam. However, there are some things you just have to know. Although you'll be provided the AP Computer Science Principles Exam Reference Sheet as part of the exam, review it beforehand and understand the pseudocode language before the exam.

Trial and Error

If a question asks about the result of a code segment based on the value of variables, pick simple values for the variables, and determine the results based on those values. Eliminate any choice that is inconsistent with that result. This is often easier than determining the results in more general terms.

REFLECT

Respond to the following questions:

- How long will you spend on multiple-choice questions?

- How will you change your approach to multiple-choice questions?

- What is your multiple-choice guessing strategy?

- Will you seek further help outside of this book (such as a teacher, tutor, or the AP students' web page) on how to approach multiple-choice questions?

Chapter 2
How to Approach
Create Performance
Task

CREATE TASK SCAVENGER HUNT WORKSHEET

By the end of this chapter, you should be able to answer the following questions:

1. How many hours will you be given in class to complete the Create Performance Task?

2. Are you allowed to work with a partner for this task?

3. Are you allowed to get help from a teacher or anyone else for this task?

4. What are the three components that you'll have to submit for the Create Performance Task?

5. Which part of the 3 components must be done independently?

6. Can my entire program be collaborative?

7. Can you work on the entire task independently (Yes / No)? Explain your answer.

8. How large can your video file be?

9. What are the acceptable formats for the videos?

10. Are you allowed to have an audio narration in your video?

11. What information should your video contain?

12. What is the maximum number of words allowed for your response to prompts 3a–3d combined?

13. In what format should you turn in your program code?

14. What is the preferred way to give credit for code that you did not write in the Create Performance Task?

15. What other components of your submission should include appropriate acknowledgment?

WHAT IS THE CREATE PERFORMANCE TASK?

The Create Performance Task requires you to create your own computer program and then showcase this program with both a written response and a video showing the functionality of the program. The Create Task will constitute 30% of your final AP Computer Science score.

What you must turn in to College Board?

1. Final Program Code
2. A video of your program running and demonstrating functionality you created.
3. Written Response answers to all prompts provided by College Board

Required Elements in your Program Code:

1. Input from one of the following:
   - A file
   - The user
   - A device or sensor
   - A data stream
2. Output which is impacted by the following:
   - The input
   - The developed procedure/functionality
3. A list or collection data type that is important to the functionality of the program
4. Student Developed Procedure that includes the following:
   - A parameter that impacts functionality
   - Iteration
   - Selection
   - Sequencing

Video Requirements:

1. 60 seconds maximum
2. 30 MB max file size
3. Must be .mov, .mp4, .wmv or .avi
4. Cannot contain narration but captioning is optional
5. Must show input, output and functionality of code
6. Does not need to show code at all just program executing

BRIEF DESCRIPTION OF THE PROMPTS

The Written Response of the Create Performance Task will consist of responses to the following prompts.

3A

i. Describes the overall purpose of the program

Explain what the program is supposed to do. Describe the purpose of the program. The purpose is the why someone would use the program. For enjoyment or to learn a skill would be acceptable purposes of a program. It is important to be precise and stick to the point. Use technical terms to describe the functionality.

Ex: The Matching game will allow users to practice vocabulary terms which is both fun and educational.

ii. Describes what functionality of the program is demonstrated in the video

Describe the functionality, which is what you expect the program to do. The most important thing is to make sure that your video shows the exact same functionality that you describe here.

Ex: The Calculator program that I designed adds two numbers and displays the sum which is a whole number. This is also shown in the video in which the user enters 2 numbers of 5 and 3 and the program displays 8.

iii. Describes the input and output of the program demonstrated in the video

Input to a program as described is received in several formats, such as reading it from a text box, the terminal window, a drop-down menu, etc.

A data stream is a collection of data that is received from an external source. An example of a data stream is data read by a sensor.

Most programming languages provide input statements to read from any of these sources. Output is usually the monitor (a display statement) or could be a file.

Ex. The calculator program takes in two numbers from the user as input and then outputs the sum of the two numbers on the screen.

3B

i. The first program code segment must show how data has been stored in the list.

This should have program code snippets that access a list (array), set a size, and store values in the list. This may be several lines of code, if an empty list is created in a line and then values are added with other lines of code.

ii. The second program code segment must show the data in the SAME list being used, such as creating new data from the existing data or accessing multiple elements in the list, as part of fulfilling the program's purpose.

As for part (i), this should have program code snippets that access a list (array), set a size and store values in the list.

For both these prompts, the code snippets used should clearly demonstrate that they are useful in fulfilling the purpose of the program. The code snippets can be two clearly distinguishable pieces or two contiguous parts of the same code snippet. Both of the code segments have to use the same list/array/collection.

Be careful to only provide a single example of a list being created and then utilized. If more than one list is shown in code. Only the list that is shown first will be considered in grading.

Provide a written response that does <u>all three</u> of the following:

iii. Identifies the name of the list being used in this response

Clearly name the list or array, and make sure that the list name is the same as one you have used in the code snippet.

iv. Describes what the data contained in the list represents in your program

Explain the data that the list represents within the program, make sure to include the type of data that is contained in the list.

For example, the list `grades[]` is a list of integers that stores the grades of the students in the course.

v. Explains how the selected list manages complexity in your program code by explaining why your program code could not be written, or how it would be written differently, if you did not use the list

A list is a data abstraction. By using a list instead of multiple variables of the same data type, the code is concise and easy to read. This also reduces the chances of errors creeping into the code since the program now must manipulate the list.

Use this idea (or similar ideas) to explain how the list you have used in your program will reduce complexity. Be sure to use the list example that is illustrated in the code. Your explanation should be valid and relevant to your program code to score points in this section. At no point is a valid to say that the code cannot be written without a list.

3C

i. The first program code segment must be a student-developed procedure that:

- defines the procedure's name and return type (if necessary)
- contains and uses one or more parameters that have an effect on the functionality of the procedure
- implements an algorithm that includes sequencing, selection, and iteration

Provide a code snippet that meets the above specified requirements. There should be at least one parameter being passed and that parameter should add to the functionality of the program. The program should have loops, conditional statements, and program statements that implement an algorithm. The program code snippet selected should implement the algorithm described. The code snippet should not be the entire program. The procedure should be important to the functionality of the overall program.

This program should be developed by the student(s). It can be done collaboratively or independently.

ii. The second program code segment must show where your student-developed procedure is being called in your program.

The procedure from part (i) is called at a different part of the program.

iii. Describes in general what the identified procedure does and how it contributes to the overall functionality of the program

The response should describe what the code (selected for the response above) does and how the code functions. Explain how this procedure is important to how the overall game works.

iv. Explains in detailed steps how the algorithm implemented in the identified procedure works. Your explanation must be detailed enough for someone else to recreate it.

The description of the algorithm should match the code snippet provided. The selection or the iteration within the program should perform a useful function. As much as possible describe each line of code or blocks of code. Make sure to discuss how the loop and conditional statement are working.

3D

i. Describes two calls to the procedure identified in written response 3c. Each call must pass a different argument(s) that causes a different segment of code in the algorithm to execute.

First Call

Identify a code snippet that calls the procedure and passes parameters as arguments that are different from the second call. Describe the procedure call, the arguments that are passed, and the expected behavior.

Repeat for Second Call.

ii. Describes what condition(s) is being tested by each call to the procedure.

Condition(s) tested by the first call:

First Call

Describe the conditional statement that is tested by the parameter.

Repeat for Second Call.

iii. Identifies the result of each call

First Call

Describe what the result is from the first call. This could be a value returned from the procedure, something printed to the screen, etc. This response should describe the functionality that is executed.

Repeat for Second Call.

The arguments passed for the second call must be different from the first call. Neither call has to be shown in the program code. Both calls can be hypothetical.

Guidance on How to Respond to the Prompts to Get a High Score Using the Rubrics

- All criteria in each row should be met to get a full score. There is no partial scoring.
- Be sure to provide program code whenever asked. Otherwise, you may lose points for certain rows.
- All criteria required for the rubric should be clearly stated as response to that prompt. (For example, score for Row 2 will be evaluated by the response provided by Prompt 3b.)

CREATE TASK CHECKLIST

Row 1	Video	• Shows input • Shows output • Shows functionality
	Written Response	• Describes the overall purpose of program **Purpose:** The purpose of your program is the intended goal or objective of the program. It is WHY you designed the program. **Example:** A matching game was created with my program the purpose of the program is that I could use it study vocabulary for English. • Describes the functionality of program making sure to describe what is shown in the video **Function:** How it accomplishes the purpose **Example:** A matching game shows a series of cards and when I click on the top right card I need to match it with its definition shown in the bottom of the screen. When I match them correctly it prints out a message telling me I am correct and increases my score. When I incorrectly match them it shows a message telling me I am incorrect and decreases my score. • Describes the input demonstrated in the video • Describes the output demonstrated in the video

Row 2	Programming Code Segments	• Code Segment showing data being stored in a list • Code Segment showing same list being used to fulfill the functionality of the program • Ensure both code segments show the SAME list • Ensure list is NOT trivial and is needed for the program to function effectively • If multiple lists are shown in code segments only the first list will be considered for written response and all grading

	Written Response	• States the name of the list shown in the code segments
		• Describes the data contained in the list shown in the code segments
		    Should again state the name of the list
		    Should state what type of data (integers, strings, etc.) AND describe the purpose of the data
		    Example: the list, colors, contains strings of the different colors which can be used as possible hidden hangman words if the user chooses this category

Row 3	Written Response	• Describes how the list, selected list manages complexity in the program code by explaining how it would be written differently, without using this list
		    Make sure the same list is discussed
		    A valid answer is NOT that there is no way to write it without the list without a detailed explanation of the unknown number of variables needed, or inability to use a loop, or control structure, etc.
		    If list is not vital to functionality or doesn't lessen complexity student will not receive this point

Row 4	Programming Code Segments	• Code Segment showing data shows a student developed procedure that meets all requirements
		Procedure must have a parameter
		Parameter should influence the functionality of the code, so depending on the parameter different parts of the code should be executed
		• Code Segment showing same procedure being called or used
		• Ensure that procedure is not the whole code of the program
		• Ensure the procedure is NOT trivial and is needed for the program to function effectively
		• If multiple procedures are shown in code segment only the first list will be considered for written response and all grading
	Written Response	• Describes what the identified procedure does
		• Describes how the procedure contributes to the overall functionality of the program
Row 5	Programming Code Segments	• Uses same Programming Code Segment referred to in Row 4 but has additional considerations
		• Code Segment additional procedure requirements:
		Must have selection (conditional statements, IF-ELSE statements, etc)
		Must have iteration (any type of loop or recursion)
		Must have sequencing
	Written Response	• Describes how the procedure's algorithm works
		Must have selection (conditional statements, IF-ELSE statements, etc)
		Should be detailed enough that someone could recreate the procedure from the description
		Should include a description of use of iteration and selection

Row 6	Written Response	• Describes 2 calls to the student developed procedure
		Either or both of these calls can be theoretically
		Each call should pass different arguments to the same procedure
		• Describes how the procedure tests the different arguments for each call
		Description of conditions tested may be close to identical
		• Describes the result of each argument from the procedure
		Results of each argument should cause different results and/or different portions of the code be executed within the procedure

For sample responses and scoring commentaries please visit:
https://apcentral.collegeboard.org/courses/ap-computer-science-principles/exam?course=ap-computer-science-principles

POSSIBLE CREATE TASK TIMELINE

Day 1	• Outline line ideas for Create Task • Ensure it will require a list that is critical to functionality • Will it contain procedure with a parameter?
Day 2	• Create a more detailed pseudocode • Determine what variables are needed • Decide how you will use iteration and selection in your procedure • Check to see whether the parameter affects which portion of the code will be executed
Day 3–4	• Program the list • Program the procedure and determine how it will be used in the main program code
Day 5–7	• Finalize all programming code, ensure your procedure is called and is required for program functionality • Debug code vs. adding features
Day 8	• Record video, possible software includes Screencastify, Quicktime, etc. • Ensure all video requirements are met • Write up Written Response 3a
Day 9	• Write up Written Response 3d
Day 10	• Write up Written Response 3c
Day 11	• Write up Written Response 3b
Day 12	• Proofread submission and confirm your submission meets all components of checklist • Submit submission to College Board via Digital Portfolio

COMMON QUESTIONS ABOUT THE CREATE TASK

Do I put my name on my Create Task project?

Your name should NOT appear on your submission in any place.

Is there a specific language that you need to use for the Create Task?

No, the Create Task is language agnostic. Any computer science language can be utilized that will allow you to create procedures and complete all other requirements of the task.

What parts of the Create Task can you work with your peers?

You can work independently or collaboratively on the program code, but all other parts (video and written response) must be completed independently.

Can your teacher help you with your Create Task project?

Your teacher cannot give you feedback or help troubleshoot your code.

How long will you have to complete your Create Task?

In class you will have 12 hours to complete the Create Task including the program code, written response, and video creation.

Can you work on it at home outside of the classroom?

You can utilize any time outside of class to complete the task also.

Can you submit an assignment you already created in class?

You cannot submit work that has been submitted for assignments or received feedback from your teacher or another student other than your collaborative partner.

Can you use libraries and other resources for your Create Task project?

Yes, any library or other resources you use should be documented. If your language allows commenting, using a comment to give credit or citation is preferred by the College Board.

CREATE TASK SCAVENGER HUNT WORKSHEET ANSWERS

1. 12 Hours

2. Yes

3. No—other than your collaborative partner (student from your class)

4. a. Video

    b. Written response

    c. PDF of the source code

5. The video and the written responses

6. Yes. This includes design and testing phases as well.

7. Yes. It is quite okay for the program to have been worked by one person with no collaboration at all.

8. 30 MB in size and not exceed 1 minute in length

9. .mp4, .wmv, .avi or .mov

10. No. However, text captions are encouraged.

11. Input to the program, one aspect of the functionality of the program, output of the program.

12. 750 words

13. PDF

14. Write comments in the program code citing references giving credit to the external sources. If the programming environment does not support comments, then it can be documented in the editor when the program code is captured for submission in the written responses. This includes APIs and open source code.

15. Any media or data sources that have not been created by you or your partner should be acknowledged (citation, attribution and/or references) to avoid plagiarism.

Another Course? Of Course!

If you can't get enough AP Computer Science Principles and want to review this material with an expert, we also offer an online Cram Course that you can sign up for here: PrincetonReview.com/college/ap-testprep.

Part V
Content Review for the AP Computer Science Principles Exam

Chapter 3
Creative
Development

This Big Idea is primarily to find a way to tap into a student's creative talents and bring them to the forefront. Creativity, by definition, is a way of transforming one's ideas into reality. A product created as a result of personal creativity is a form of personal expression.

Programs can help solve problems, enable innovations, or express personal interests.

COLLABORATION

Programming is a collaborative and creative process that brings ideas to life through the development of software. Software development processes used in the industry often require students to work together in teams. Collaboration can take place at various points and in various ways.

An important concept that is discussed throughout the entire course is the idea of computing innovations. A computing innovation uses a computer program to take in data, transform data and output data. Smart Assistants such as Siri or Alexa are good examples. These devices have software running inside them. In contrast, a T-shirt labeled "tech shirt" made up of material that absorbs sweat well or keeps a runner warm in winter cannot be considered a computing innovation despite a catchy name. A social media website, though non-physical, is a computing innovation because many computer programs run collectively to make the website work.

To develop functional, robust software, teams must work together collaboratively to produce effective, functional programs. Getting multiple perspectives allows for improvements in the software. Collaboration can occur in the planning, designing, or testing (debugging) part of the development process. Collaboration tools allow students and teachers to exchange resources in several different ways, depending on what suits a particular task.

Many tools help the collaborative process be effective. One such example is Google Docs, which allows multiple users to edit the document simultaneously. Discussion boards such as Piazza (https://piazza.com/) let team members collaborate in an online space to exchange ideas and discuss solutions to different problems.

Collaborative learning can occur peer-to-peer or in larger groups. Peer instruction involves students working in pairs or small groups to discuss concepts to find solutions to problems.

The idea that two or three heads are better than one facilitates students collaborating by addressing misunderstandings and clarifying misconceptions.

The benefits of collaborative learning include the development of thinking skills, increased student responsibility, exposure to other perspectives, and an increase in understanding of diverse perspectives. This can help eliminate bias. People with different backgrounds and experiences may be able to identify different flaws in algorithms. It helps prepare students for real-life situations. A popular collaborative style of programming is called pair programming. Pair or collaborative programming is where two programmers develop software side by side at one computer, on the same algorithm, design, or programming task. Pair programming leads to greater satisfaction when the project is complete, better designed, and both participants learn from each other. Research has shown even when pairing a novice programmer with an expert programmer, the novice programmer can contribute effectively to the project. Even collaboration with users can help the programmers understand that perspective in a project.

IDENTIFYING AND CORRECTING ERRORS

There are 4 main types of errors in programming:

- **Syntax Error:** A mistakes in which the rules of the programming language are not followed. For Example:

```
a ← expression
DISPLAY (A)
```

A syntax error in this example occurs because the second statement attempts to display the variable A, which is not the defined variable. Variable names are case sensitive. Therefore, while the variable with a lowercase a in lowercase is defined by the first statement, the variable with a capital A in the second not defined. Therefore, the rules of the programming language were violated

- **Runtime Error:** A mistake that occurs during the execution of a program that ceases the execution. For example:

```
DISPLAY (5/0)
```

In this example, there is no syntax error, because the language of the code is used correctly. However, this causes a runtime error because you cannot divide by zero. The execution of the program will halt at this line.

- **Logic Error:** A mistake in the algorithm or program that causes it to behave incorrectly or unexpectedly. For example:

```
a ← 95
IF (a > 90)
{
  DISPLAY("You got an A.")
}
IF (a > 80)
{
  DISPLAY("You got a B.")
}
IF (a > 70)
{
  DISPLAY("You got a C.")
}
```

The code in intended to correctly printout what grade the student got. Since this particular student's score was a 95, which is greater than 90, the program *should* display You got an A. However, the program actually prints out the following:

```
You got an A.
You got a B.
You got a C.
```

This logic error occurs because the students score is also greater than 80 and 70 with no restriction that prevents multiple grades from being printed.

- **Overflow Error:** A mistake that occurs when a computer attempts to handle a number that is outside of the defined range of values. For example:

```
x ←  2000 * 365
DISPLAY (x)
```

The result is of the multiplication is a large number. In many languages, this product would be large enough to be outside the range of certain data types. Therefore, if x is defined as a variable of one of those data type, this multiplication will cause an overflow error.

Debugging is the process of finding and fixing errors. You should use test cases, extra output statements, examination for syntax errors and other debugging tools to find and fix any errors.

Brainstorming

Whenever you create a program, you should start to brainstorm on a topic for designing the program in a way that accomplishes the goal of the program in an efficient way. Below is a sheet that you can use to aid the brainstorming process.

Preliminary Topic Selection Guide

Program Topic: _____

Program Requirement	No	Probably Not	Probably Yes	Yes
The program will take about 5 hours to complete.				
The program would make use of lists or collections.				
The program should have features that support the design of an algorithm that can be made into a procedure that can be called from the main program. The procedure must have at least one parameter that must be used in a meaning-ful way, preferably for selection inside the loop.				
The parameter should effect which portion of the code is run. In other words, different parameters should cause conditional statement or loop to run different code.				
The program needs to use decision statements. It should be part of the identified procedure.				
The program needs to use loops. The loop should be used inside the procedure to iterate the list or collection.				
The program needs to have user input and output. The user input should affect what is output by the program.				

Chapter 4
Data

BINARY NUMBERS

Any digital data has a numerical representation using binary numbers. A bit is the smallest unit of information stored or manipulated on a computer; it consists of either zero or one. Depending on meaning, it could instead be described as false/true, off/on, no/yes, or anything else that has two possible values. We can also call a bit a binary digit, especially when working with the 0 or 1 values. Everything in a computer is 0s and 1s. The **bit** stores just a 0 or 1: it is the smallest building block of storage. However, it can be said that a bit is also the largest unit of information a computer can manipulate.

A group of bits is combined so that the computer can use several bits simultaneously for calculating numbers. When a group has eight bits, it is called a byte. A bit can represent anything we want, perhaps yes and no, but it has only two possible values. So, to represent more things, we have always grouped bits into larger chunks.

A group of 8 bits has 256 (2^8) possible unique combinations, where each combination can have its predetermined meaning. The number of bits determines some maximum number of unique combinations of bits.

Base Conversion

Binary to Decimal Conversion

Of course, binary numbers are rarely used in real life. Therefore, programmers must be able to go back and forth between the binary numbers we use in computing and the decimal numbers that we use in everyday life. The key is to remember that the different binary digits represent different powers of 2. For example, let's use the binary number 1101.

Use this table:

2^7	2^6	2^5	2^4	2^3	2^2	2^1	2^0	
128	64	32	16	8	4	2	1	
0	0	0	0	1	1	0	1	
0	0	0	0	8×1	4×1	2×0	1×1	
0	0	0	0	8	+ 4	+ 0	+ 1	= 13

Therefore, $(1101)_2 = (13)_{10}$.

Decimal to Binary Conversion

Similarly, in order to make the numbers we use in our everyday lives processable by computers, we need to be able to convert decimal numbers into binary numbers. To do this, we reverse the process. We need to find the powers of 2 that add up to the given decimal number. Start by finding the largest power of 2 that is less than the number. Subtract that number from the original, and repeat until you're down to 0. Try the example of the decimal number 200.

Use this table:

2^8	2^7	2^6	2^5	2^4	2^3	2^2	2^1	2^0
256	128	64	32	16	8	4	2	1
0	1	1	0	0	1	0	0	0

```
  200
 −128
 ────
   72
 − 64
 ────
    8
 −  8
 ────
    0
```

Therefore, the decimal number 200 is equivalent to the binary number 1100 1000.

Using Bits

There are many things the same pattern of bits could represent, like part of one pixel in an image.

A computer representing data within the computer is different from data interpretation by the computer and representation to the user. Programs translate data into a representation more easily understood by people.

Digital Images as Bits

Images displayed on the screen are converted into binary formats and then processed by a computer displayed on our screen. Digital images are a collection of pixels, where each pixel consists of binary numbers. If we say that one is black (or on) and 0 is white (or off), then a simple black and white picture can be created using binary. Draw a grid and color the squares (1—black and 0—white) to create the picture. However, before creating the grid, the size of the grid needs to be known. This data is called metadata, and computers need metadata to know the size of an image. The metadata for the image to be created is 10 × 10; this means the picture will be 10 pixels across and 10 pixels down.

1	1	1	1	1	1
1		1	1		1
1	1	1	1	1	1
1		1	1		1
1					1
1	1	1	1	1	1

Binary and Color Representation

Images are not often just black and white. To represent colors computers also use binary numbers. Color is based on light. Any color can be created using red, green and blue light. The maximum value for any color in decimal 255, which is represented by 11111111 in binary. The minimum number is 0.

Here are some examples of color representation showing both the decimal values and the binary values:

White = [255, 255, 255]   [11111111,11111111,11111111]

Black = [0, 0, 0]   [0,0,0]

Blue = [0,0,255]   [0,0,11111111]

Red = [255, 0, 0]   [11111111,0,0]

Each color is 3 bytes of data. Often engineers, computer scientists and analysts need to understand larger amounts of data. The measurement of data is based on the byte.

Music as Bits

An analog signal exists throughout a continuous interval of time and takes on a continuous range of values. A digital signal is a sequence of discrete symbols. If these symbols are zeros and ones, we call them bits. As such, a digital signal is neither continuous in time nor continuous in its range of values. Furthermore, it cannot correctly represent arbitrary analog signals. Sampling is recording an analog signal at regular discrete moments and converting them to a digital signal. Digital signals are resilient against noise. A digital signal representing an analog signal at discrete moments is an abstraction since it hides the continuous analog data. Digital signals can be stored on digital media (like a compact disc) and manipulated on digital systems (like the integrated circuit in a CD player). Data abstraction is filtering out specific details to focus on the information needed to process the data. The lowest level of data abstraction is bits. Higher abstraction is with numbers, letters, symbols, video, sound, and audio.

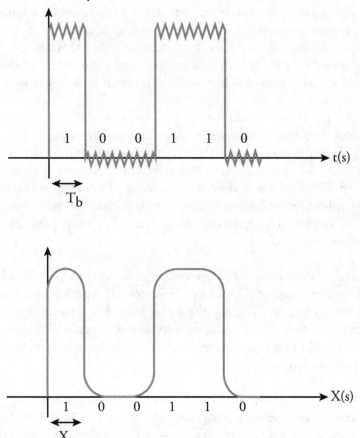

The above illustration is an example of an analog transmission of a digital signal. Consider a digital signal 100110 converted to an analog signal for radio transmission. The received signal suffers from noise, but it is still easy to read off the original sequence 100110 correctly given sufficient bit duration X_a.

DATA COMPRESSION

Data compression is used everywhere. Mp3, mp4, rar, zip, jpg, and png files (along with many others) all use compressed data. Without data compression, a 3-minute song would be over 100Mb and a 10-minute video would easily be over 1Gb. Data compression is a set of steps for packing data into a smaller space, while allowing for the original data to be seen again. Whether it's the music that we listen to through our music players, or the movies we watch (Netflix, Amazon Prime, etc.), digital data files are often compressed so that they can fit on your storage devices to stream from the Internet. Whether you're buying movies or music for downloading online, data compression is a particularly important concern, since it determines the quality and file size of the downloads. Compression is also an important consideration when it comes to backing up and archiving your important files, particularly for uploading over the Internet. Compression is a two-way process: a compression algorithm can be used to make a data package smaller, but it can also run the other way, to decompress the package into its original form. Data compression is useful in computing to save disk space, or to reduce the bandwidth used when sending data (e.g., over the Internet). Data compression deals with taking a string of bytes and compressing it down to a smaller set of bytes, whereby it takes either less bandwidth to transmit the string or to store it to disk.

Data compression condenses large files into much smaller ones. It does this by getting rid of data that isn't needed while retaining the information in the file. Thus, you could say, data compression involves the development of a compact representation of information. Most representations of information contain large amounts of redundancy. Compression algorithms exploit this redundancy in the data to get a compact representation of the data. This, when achieved, aids in accurate reconstruction of the data.

The task of compression consists of two components, an encoding algorithm that takes a message or image and generates a "compressed" representation (hopefully with fewer bits), and a decoding algorithm that reconstructs the original message or some approximation of it from the compressed representation. These two components are typically intricately tied together since they both must understand the shared compressed representation.

Lossless algorithms are those that can reconstruct the original message exactly from the compressed message, and lossy algorithms can only reconstruct an approximation of the original message. Lossless algorithms are typically used for text, and lossy algorithms for images and sound where a little bit of loss in resolution is often undetectable, or at least acceptable. Lossless compression packs data in such a way that the compressed package can be decompressed, and the data can be pulled out exactly the same as it went in. This is very important for computer programs and archives, since even a very small change in a computer program will make it unusable.

This type of compression works by reducing how much wasted space is in a piece of data. For example, consider this string which contains "XXXXXZZZZYYY". It can be compressed into "5X4Z3Y", which has the same meaning but takes up less space. This type of compression is called "run-length encoding," because you define how long the "run" of a character is. In the above example, there are two runs: a run of 5 A's, and another of 4 B's. This algorithm is an excellent example of a lossless compression working with a string of data.

Text compression is another important area for lossless compression. It is very important that the reconstruction is identical to the original text, as very small differences can result in statements with very different meanings. For example, in these two sentences, *"All is now well."* and *"All is not well."* the algorithm has to be very discerning as to what data it considers redundant.

Lossy compression is a technique that does not decompress digital data back to 100% of the original. Lossy methods can provide high degrees of compression and result in smaller compressed files, but some number of the original pixels, sound waves, or video frames are removed forever. Lossy is used in an abstract sense, however, and does not mean random lost pixels, but instead means loss of a quantity such as a frequency component, or perhaps loss of noise. For example, one might think that lossy text compression would be unacceptable because they are imagining missing or switched characters. However, consider the system high school students use to write college essays where sentences are reworded or words are replaced with synonyms so that the text is better compressed. Technically, the compression would be lossy since the text has changed, but the "meaning" and clarity of the message might be fully maintained, or even improved. However, text, and business data in general, does not use lossy compression, because this data requires perfect restoration of data. When the amount the compression increases, the size of the resulting file decreases. However, there is a greater amount of data that cannot be restored.

Images—a high image compression loss can be observed in photos when enlarged

Music—there is a difference between an MP3 music and a high-resolution audio file

Video—moving frames of video can handle a greater loss of pixels compared to an image

Lossy Compression with Images

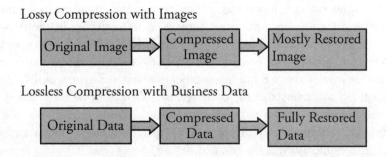

Lossless Compression with Business Data

Examples:

Lossy	Lossless
Images: JPEG	Archiving formats: Zip, GZip, bZip2, 7-Zip, etc.
Audio: MP3, Windows Media	Images/diagrams: GIF, PNG, PCX
Video: MPEG, DivX, Windows Video	Audio: ALAC, FLAC, WAV

EXTRACTING INFORMATION FROM DATA

Data science deals with extracting information from and visualizing the results of manipulating large data sets. In a digital world where social media apps collect data about our posts and our likes, online stores collect data about the products we view, and advertising agencies collect data about what we click, it seems like data is all-pervasive.

Each second, millions of data points are collected. Thousands of sensors installed across cities worldwide collect data about all sorts of topics: air quality, noise, the temperature, even about which parking spots on different streets are free or when specific gardens need watering. Users also generate data: everything they do on their smartphones, every interaction they have with any business can be stored. It is possible to process any text or image published online as data in order to extract information. Therefore, companies' big challenge is to give data meaning, transforming it so that it really and faithfully tells a good story about the business, its customers, or society in general.

The difference between data and information is that organized and structured data is information. Information is obtained by extracting useful information from vast amounts of data and creating correlations using this data. Depending on the data and the patterns, sometimes we can see that pattern in a simple tabular presentation of the data. It also helps to visualize the data in a chart, like a time series, line graph, or scatter plot.

Let's explore examples of patterns that we can find in the data around us.

Data analysis involves analyzing and thinking through the various processes and the data. It is sometimes difficult to separate the processes involved in organizing geographic information from the procedures used in analyzing it; the two processes go on simultaneously in many cases. However, in other instances, analysis follows the manipulation of raw data into an easily understood and usable form. Both activities involve the use and development of students' spatial skills. Models can be analyzed to understand the correlations and to describe the relationships and patterns resulting from the overlay of multiple data sets (e.g., describe the relationship of earthquakes taking place with specific kinds of fauna and flora under specific temperatures). Models can be used to analyze data from multiple data sets. By comparing these models, it is possible to identify patterns or relationships between data sets. Data is also analyzed to explain changes through time. Graphs such as a scatter plot of data, histograms, etc., help identify possible relationships or trends in the data.

In information technology, the prefix meta means "an underlying definition or description." Metadata is data that describes other data. Metadata describes whatever data it is connected to, whether it is video, a photograph, or web pages, and summarizes necessary information about data such as author, date created, usage, file size, and more. Metadata is needed to classify and categorize data. Metadata is organized information that describes, locates, or otherwise makes it easier to retrieve information. When a digital product is created, information such as its origin, time, date, and format is stored. A good understanding of metadata helps identify useful data. Data is usually simply a piece of information or a collection of measurements, tables of observations, or a story. On the other hand, metadata provide the relevant information about the data, which helps in identifying the nature and feature of the data.

Summarizing

Data	Metadata
Data is simply the content that describes or reports anything such as a measurement or observation.	Metadata describes the relevant information about the data.
Some data is informative; some may not be, as data can be raw data like numbers or characters, which may not be informative.	Metadata is always informative as it is a reference to other data.
Data may or may not be processed as raw data is always unprocessed data.	Metadata is processed data.

The problem with unstructured data is that they are hard to sort, manage, and organize. Files stored on servers could have thousands of duplicate copies of data in many different formats, some of which may be invalid or incomplete. The unstructured data is also hard to search and process. There arises a need to add some structure to the data by cleaning it up. The process of adding structure to data is called data mining or data analytics. There are two main ways of adding structure. The first is by adding a storage format to the data. A consistent format helps eliminate the invalid data, making this process a right choice for cleaning data. Another way of cleaning data is using log files that help cluster data that are easier to manipulate, such as grouping data with the same timestamps. In doing this, the data is cleaned up by parsing/extracting through the log files and finding meaningful data. This data is now called unstructured data.

Consider the fact that there is no downtime as far as the World Wide Web is concerned; thereby, there may be a need for many data stores. Sometimes the data available is much higher than the model can effectively process. In such cases, the model responses to the data fed in have a bias in them. More data does not fix this problem. It may worsen the situation by adding to the noise in the data. The World Wide Web is used by everyone, from scientists and businesses to five-year-olds exchanging emojis. As a result, there is a need for scalability, which is the potential of a system, network, or process to be enlarged to accommodate that data growth. Before we scale a system, there needs to be an analysis done on the system's capacity. It is important to understand the extreme requirements such as highest and average transactions per second, the highest number of queries, payload size, expected throughput, and backup requirements. This helps with the data store scalability design in making decisions such as how many physical servers are needed, the hardware configuration of the data storage devices, memory footprint, disk size, CPU Cores, I/O throughput, etc.

USING PROGRAMS WITH DATA

The increase in digitization of information, mixed with multiple transactions, has resulted in a flood of data. The advancement in technology has promoted the rapid growth of data volume in recent years. By analyzing large data sets of data, it is possible to categorize connections from unconnected data sources and find specific patterns. Data extraction is the process of obtaining data from a database or software such as a social media website so that it can transport it to another software (such as spreadsheets) designed to support online analytical processing. Data extraction is the first step. The next step is to transform (either through filters or programs). The final step is to analyze using graphs and other data visualization tools.

The process of extracting involves finding entities such a name, email I.D., online profile names, and other such private data belonging to someone. This data is then classified and stored in a repository such as a database. The information extraction (IE) process extracts specific, prespecified, and useful information from text, such as attributes related to objects, events, etc. The extracted information is used to prepare data for analysis, and hence there is a need for efficient and accurate transformation. Different techniques are applied based on the type of data (such as text, image, audio, and video).

An excellent example is data mining that happens within email software. Some emails have data embedded, which is added to the email software calendar. The email software knows to identify the data in these emails and add it to the calendar.

Below are the steps to extract data and analyze them:

1. **Analyze the data sources.** Data sources are found in different forms like web pages, video files, audio files, text documents, customer emails, and chat messages.
2. **Know what will be done with the results of the analysis.** It is vital to understand what sort of outcome is required. Is it a trend, effect, cause, quantity, or something else that is needed?
3. **Decide the tools needed to read the data, and the repositories such as databases needed to store the data.** Clean the data of whitespace, symbols, duplicates, etc.
4. **Understand the data patterns and text flow.** This should be done using visualization tools.

This process is also known as data mining. Below is an illustration that shows the process.

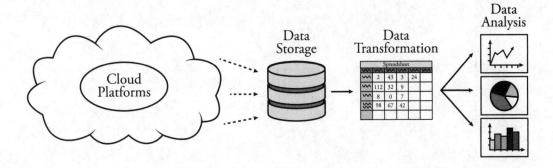

How to read and analyze graphs

A graph is a pictorial representation, a diagram used to represent data. It usually is used to depict a relationship. Graphs and charts represent data in points, lines, bars, pie charts, and scatter plots. Different types of graphs and charts display data in different ways. Some are better suited than others for different uses.

Picture graphs use pictures to represent values.
Bar graphs use either vertical or horizontal bars to represent the values.
Line graphs use lines to represent the values.
Scatter plots represent the data with points, and then a best-fit line is drawn through some of the points.

While analyzing graphs, it is essential to determine what the graph displays and why such information is pertinent to the experiment or the question's context. Read the graph first. Next, read the title and axes of the graph to determine the type of data represented. The *x*-axis is the independent variable, or that which can be changed. The *y*-axis is the dependent variable, or that which depends on the independent variable.

In a picture graph, look for the line with the highest number of pictures. For a bar graph, look for the highest bar. For a line graph or a scatter plot, look at the slope of the line. If the line is pointing to the upper right corner, then the slope is positive. If the line is pointing to the lower right corner, then the slope is negative. Use the graph to make predictions about future sets of data. Next, study the graph to understand what it shows. To interpret a graph or chart, read the title, look at the key, and read the labels. Draw conclusions based on the data. It is possible to reach conclusions faster with graphs than with a data table or a written description of the data.

KEY TERMS

Data Abstraction
Decimal
Base Conversion
Precision
Information/Data
Trends
Graphs
Binary
Hexadecimal
Integer Overflow
Integer Roundoff
Metadata
Patterns
Cleaning Data
Scalability
Bias
Data Compression
Lossy Compression
Lossless Compression

CHAPTER 4 REVIEW DRILL

1. Which of the following are likely metadata collected for a music file?

   (A) Song name
   (B) Size of song
   (C) Type of file (MP3, AVI, etc.)
   (D) Time at which the song was recorded

2. Binary to Decimal Conversion

Binary	Decimal
00110001_2	
11100000_2	
11000011_2	
11110010_2	
10010100_2	
10101110_2	
1101000_2	
01011100_2	
00001100_2	
10111111_2	

3. Decimal to Binary Conversion

Decimal	Binary
123_{10}	
210_{10}	
75_{10}	
103_{10}	
25_{10}	
77_{10}	
235_{10}	
102_{10}	
200_{10}	
45_{10}	

4. The biggest advantage of lossy compression algorithms over a lossless one is that while transmitting data

    (A) the loss of data is inconsequential

    (B) the packet transfer through the Internet is faster

    (C) the number of bits stored or transmitted is reduced

    (D) the algorithm is designed for efficient transmission

5. Lossless compression is most suitable for transfer of

    (A) images

    (B) music files

    (C) text files

    (D) computer programs

Summary

o The way a computer represents data internally is different from the way the data is interpreted and displayed for the user. Programs are used to translate data into a representation more easily understood by people.

o Data values can be stored in variables, lists of items, or stand-alone constants and can be passed as input to (or output from) procedures.

o Abstraction is the process of reducing complexity by focusing on the main idea. By hiding details irrelevant to the question at hand and bringing together related and useful details, abstraction reduces complexity and allows one to focus on the big idea.

o Bits are grouped to represent abstractions. These abstractions include, but are not limited to, numbers, characters, and color.
  - *Bit* is shorthand for *binary digit* and is either 0 or 1.
  - A *byte* is 8 bits.

o Analog data such as pitch, color, and location can be closely approximated digitally using a *sampling technique*, which means measuring values of the analog signal at regular intervals called *samples*. The samples are measured to figure out the exact bits required to store each sample.

o In programming languages, the fixed number of bits used to represent real numbers limits the range and mathematical operations on these values; this limitation can result in round-off, overflow, and other errors. Some real numbers are represented as approximations in computer storage. *Specific range limitations for real numbers are outside the scope of this course and the AP Exam.*

o Number bases, including binary and decimal, are used to represent data.
  - Binary (base 2) uses only combinations of the digits zero and one.
  - Decimal (base 10) uses only combinations of the digits 0–9.

o *Data compression* can reduce the size (number of bits) of data transmitted or stored.

o *Lossless* data compression algorithms can usually reduce the number of bits stored or transmitted while guaranteeing complete reconstruction of the original data.
  - In situations where quality or ability to reconstruct the original is maximally important, lossless compression algorithms are typically chosen.

o   *Lossy* data compression algorithms can significantly reduce the number of bits stored or transmitted but only allow reconstruction of an approximation of the original data.
  •   Lossy data compression algorithms can usually reduce the number of bits stored or transmitted more than lossless compression algorithms.
  •   In situations where minimizing data size or transmission time is maximally important, lossy compression algorithms are typically chosen.

o   Digitally processed data may show correlation between variables. A correlation found in data does not necessarily indicate that a causal relationship exists. Additional research is needed to understand the exact nature of the relationship.

o   Often, a single source does not contain the data needed to draw a conclusion. It may be necessary to combine data from a variety of sources to formulate a conclusion.

o   *Metadata* is data about data. For example, the piece of *data* may be an image, while the *metadata* may include the date of creation or the file size of the image.

o   Changes and deletions made to metadata do not change the primary data.

o   Metadata is used for finding, organizing, and managing information.

o   Metadata can increase the effective use of data or data sets by providing additional information.

o   Metadata allow data to be structured and organized.

o   The ability to process data depends on the capabilities of the users and their tools.

o   Data sets pose challenges regardless of size, such as:
  •   the need to clean data
  •   incomplete data
  •   invalid data
  •   the need to combine data sources

o   *Cleaning data* is a process that makes the data uniform without changing its meaning (e.g., replacing all equivalent abbreviations, spellings, and capitalizations with the same word).

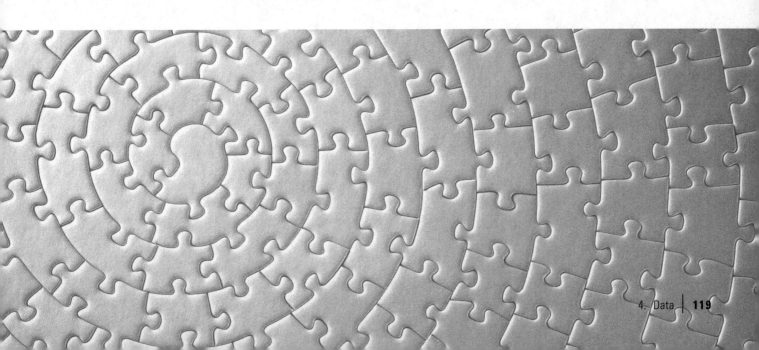

o   Problems of bias are often created by the type or source of data being collected. Bias is not eliminated by simply collecting more data.

o   Tables, diagrams, text, and other visual tools can be used to communicate insight and knowledge gained from data.

o   Programmers can use programs to filter and clean digital data, thereby gaining insight and knowledge.

o   Combining data sources, clustering data, and classifying data are parts of the process of using programs to gain insight and knowledge from data.

o   Patterns can emerge when data are transformed using programs.

Chapter 5
Algorithms and Programming

The AP Computer Science Principles Exam uses the Exam Reference Sheet (provided to students at exam time) with a specific pseudocode-like syntax for the different programming constructs. Students must get familiar with this pseudocode's syntax so that they can read code snippets written based on the reference sheet (found in this book on page 297).

The next few pages that discuss the Algorithms and Programming Big Idea use this reference sheet to explain the syntax and the concepts for each of the reference sheet constructs. Let us examine each learning objective in the Course and Exam Description individually.

VARIABLES AND ASSIGNMENTS

The primary purpose of a computer program is to manipulate information, and information is manipulated in many forms. A variable is a name for a location in memory used to hold a data value. A variable declaration instructs the compiler to reserve a portion of the main memory space large enough to hold a value and indicate the name we use to refer to that location. Most programming languages require that programmers be explicit about what kind of information needs manipulation. In turn, it guarantees that it is easy to manipulate the data.

Data Type	Description	Examples
int	Whole numbers	5, −2,
double	Real numbers	7.5, 3.78, −1.99
char	Characters—single letters	'a', 'p'
Boolean	Logical values	true, false

Many popular programming languages (probably including whatever language you have studied in this course) use standard type names such as int and double for numbers, char and string for letters and words, respectively, and Boolean for true or false, as shown in the table above. (We will examine Strings in another section.)

The College Board provided Exam Reference Sheet, however, does not specify the type of data that is stored in memory. Characters and numbers have a generic representation to assign a value to a variable, as shown below.

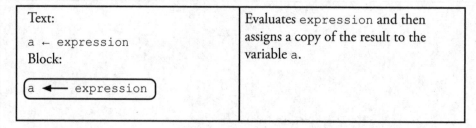

Text: a ← expression Block: a ⬅ expression	Evaluates expression and then assigns a copy of the result to the variable a.

A variable can store only one value as a result of an assignment statement. When a new value is assigned, an assignment statement overwrites the old one. An assignment statement is named as such and is intuitive because it assigns a value to a variable. The evaluation of the expression on the right-hand side happens when the expression executes. The variable on the left-hand side then stores the result (to be more precise, in the variable's memory location on the left-hand side).

You can assign a single number or word to a variable:

$a \leftarrow 5$ or $a \leftarrow$ "this"

You can also assign the result of an expression to a variable:

$a \leftarrow 5 + 4 - 3$

Here the value contained in a would be 6 since 5 + 4 is 9 and 9 − 3 is 2.

An input statement gets information from the user. An example below would ask the user for their name, store it in the variable name and then print out Hello and the data contained in the variable name:

```
DISPLAY("Please enter your name")
name ← INPUT()
DISPLAY("Hello" + name)
```

Text: DISPLAY(expression) Block: `DISPLAY [expression]`	Displays the value of expression, followed by a space.
Text: INPUT() Block: INPUT	Accepts a value from the user and returns the input value.

DATA ABSTRACTION

A popular way of defining abstraction is information hiding. Just as related program statements are bundled together, related program variables can be bundled together. Such abstractions allow us to think of the data within a program hierarchically. A list is an example of data abstraction. Let's dig deeper into this.

Look at this example:

Text:
 	
`aList ← [value1, value2, value3, ...]`
Block:
 	
`aList ← [value1, value2, value3]`
	Creates a new list that contains the values `value1`, `value2`, `value3`, and `...` at indices `1`, `2`, `3`, and `...` respectively.

A list is a data type that holds a collection of values. In the example shown above (as given in the exam reference sheet),

`aList ← [3, 7, 11]`

aList is described as a "list of integers."

Within a list, when accessing its parts using an integer index, `aList[1]` gives us the value 3, `aList[2]` `=` `7`, and so on. Lists allow for data abstraction in that we can give a name to a set of memory cells. For instance, in a colorList, a list that holds three colors [`'red'`, `'blue'`, `'green'`] instead of using three separate variables, `color1`, `color2`, etc., one variable colorList holds all the three variables. Each of the contents of the list is accessed by changing the index value.

> Note: List Index in the Exam Reference Sheet starts at 1. This concept is confusing because, in many programming languages, the index values start at 0.

Because the indexing on the Exam Reference Sheet is different from the language you likely used in your course, the conditions for an error message are different. On the AP Computer Science Principles Exam, a program will terminate and display an error message whenever a list index is less than 1 or greater than the length of the list.

MATHEMATICAL EXPRESSIONS

While writing programs, it is often necessary to include calculations. These are called expressions. An expression is a combination of one or more operators and operands that perform a calculation. The operations' operands might be literals, constants, variables, or other sources of data. This process of obtaining a value is called an evaluation. Evaluation of expressions is fundamental to having a good understanding of programming. For now, we will focus on mathematical expressions that use numeric operands and produce numeric results.

Below is a list of operations provided by the College Board in the Exam Reference Sheet.

Text and Block:
`a + b`
`a - b`
`a * b`
`a / b`
	The arithmetic operators +, -, *, and / are used to perform arithmetic on a and b.
	For example, `17 / 5` evaluates to `3.4`.
	The order of operations used in mathematics applies when evaluating expressions.

Text and Block: `a MOD b`	Evaluates to the remainder when a is divided by b. Assume that a is an integer greater than or equal to 0 and b is an integer greater than 0. For example, `17 MOD 5` evaluates to 2. The MOD operator has the same precedence as the * and / operators.

The operation MOD (short for modulus) is an important operation in computer science, but one you probably don't use a lot in math class. Modulus refers to remainder after division. For example, to find 5 MOD 3:

$$3\overline{)5} \quad \begin{array}{r} 1 \\ -3 \\ \hline ②\end{array}$$

Therefore 5 MOD 3 = 2. Notice that the resulting 1 isn't important. It's only the remainder that counts.

Most programming languages (as well as the AP Computer Science Principles Exam Reference Sheet) follow operations rules while establishing precedence.

- An operator with high precedence is evaluated first, followed by operators of lower precedence.
- Within a given precedence level, the operators are evaluated in one direction, usually left to right.
- There are two levels of precedence in arithmetic operations. The multiplicative operators (*, /, MOD) have a higher precedence level than the additive operators (+, -). Arithmetic operations with the same level of precedence are evaluated left to right.
- The final point to note: any operator precedence can be overridden with parenthesis.

For example, let's look at the expression 3 – 5 * 4 MOD 3. The operations with first precedence in this example are multiplication and MOD. Since multiplication is to the left of MOD, begin by executing multiplication:

$$3 – 5 * 4 \text{ MOD } 3 = 3 – 20 \text{ MOD } 3$$

Now, since MOD has precedence over subtraction, execute MOD:

$$3 - 20 \text{ MOD } 3 = 3 - 2$$

Finally, execute subtraction:

$$3 - 2 = 1$$

Therefore, $3 - 5 * 4 \text{ MOD } 3 = 1$.

Selection uses a Boolean condition to evaluate which of two parts of an algorithm to use.

Iteration is the process where a part (a set of instructions, a few lines of program code, etc.) of the algorithm repeats until it meets a condition or iterates for a fixed number of times either specified within the program or by the user.

Different algorithms can solve the same problem. A good example is Google Maps on a cellphone. Once the from and to locations get filled, the software frequently provides multiple routes as options—this is the algorithm within the software providing multiple solutions to the problem.

There are many ways to express algorithms. Some of them include natural language, pseudo code, and visual and textual programming languages. Natural language and pseudocode describe algorithms so that humans can understand them. Algorithms described in a programming language are compiled and run on a computer. The programming language used to express an algorithm can affect clarity or readability. It does not determine whether an algorithmic solution exists.

STRINGS

In computer science, a character is a symbol that appears on the keyboard, such as a letter, digit, or punctuation mark. A collection of these characters is usually surrounded with double quotes: "computer!" is called a string literal. A string can be a word or a sentence or even a single letter.

For example:

```
String mySentence = "CS Principles Rock!"
String myWord = "Principles"
String myLetter = "C"
```

The syntax for Strings depends on the programming language. The Exam Reference Sheet does not have a specific syntax for Strings.

Strings can be concatenated using the + sign:

```
String wordConcatenated = "black" + "board"
```

The + sign combines the two or more Strings together in end-to-end manner to make a single String. This is called concatenation.

Substrings are part of an existing string.

For example:

```
phrase ← "Computer Science"
```

"Science" and "Computer" are substrings of the variable phrase.

BOOLEAN EXPRESSIONS

An expression that evaluates true or false is called a Boolean expression, typically used in conditionals and iterative statements. Boolean expressions use relational operators and logical operators to make decisions.

The table below contains the list of relational operators. They are specific symbols given by the Exam Reference Sheet. While comparing two operands or expressions with a relational operator, the result is a Boolean value, a true or false.

Text and Block:	The relational operators $=$, $\neq$, $>$, $<$, $\leq$, and $\geq$ are used to test the relationship between two variables, expressions, or values. A comparison using relational operators evaluates to a Boolean value.
a = b	
a ≠ b	For example, a = b evaluates to true if a and b are
a > b	equal; otherwise it evaluates to false.
a < b	
a ≥ b	
a ≤ b	

It is important to note that the Exam Reference Sheet uses = as the equality operator to compare two operands, since the ← operator assigns a value to a variable.

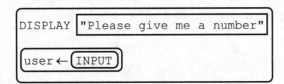

Below are the logical operators, which are useful for building complex Boolean expressions.

Text: `NOT condition` Block: `NOT` ⌜`condition`⌝	Evaluates to `true` if condition is `false`; otherwise evaluates to `false`.
Text: `condition1` AND `condition2` Block: ⌜`condition1`⌝ AND ⌜`condition2`⌝	Evaluates to `true` if both `condition1` and `condition2` are `true`; otherwise evaluates to `false`.
Text: `condition1` OR `condition2` Block: ⌜`condition1`⌝ OR ⌜`condition2`⌝	Evaluates to `true` if `condition1` is `true` or if `condition2` is `true` or if both `condition1` and `condition2` are `true`; otherwise evaluates to `false`.

Below are examples of Boolean expressions using logical operators.

Operator	Example	Result
AND	`(1 = 1) AND (6 < 7)`	`true`
OR	`(2 = 1) OR (6 < 7)`	`true`
NOT	`NOT (5 > 3)`	`false`

CONDITIONALS

An IF-ELSE statement is called a conditional statement. Sometimes while designing a program, one or more program statements will be executed when a condition is true. Some lines of code will not be executed when false. Conditional statements are also known as selection statements. The condition within an IF statement is usually a Boolean expression that returns a true or false.

The Exam Reference Sheet has the following syntax for IF-ELSE statements

Text:
`IF(condition)`
`{`
`<block of statements>`
`}`
Block:
 	
IF condition
 	
block of statements
	The code in `block of statements` is executed if the Boolean expression `condition` evaluates to `true`; no action is taken if `condition` evaluates to `false`.

Text:
`IF(condition)`
`{`
`<first block of statements>`
`}`
`ELSE`
`{`
`<second block of statements>`
`}`
Block:
 	
IF condition
 	
first block of statements
 	
ELSE
 	
second block of statements
	The code in `first block of statements` is executed if the Boolean expression `condition` evaluates to `true`; otherwise the code in `second block of statements` is executed.

Below is an illustration of a simple IF Statement

```
IF (number1 > number2)
{
    smallerNumber ← number1
}
ELSE
{
    smallerNumber ← number2
}
```

NESTED CONDITIONALS

In a program or code snippet where there is an IF statement within another set of IF statements, these are called nested IF statements. When the outer IF statement is executed, the inner IF statement may also get executed. This allows for the program solution to evaluate another expression after determining the results of a previous decision.

```
IF (number1 < number2)
{
    IF (number1 < number3)
    {
        smallerNumber ← number1
    }
    ELSE
    {
        smallerNumber ← number3
    }
}
ELSE
{
    IF (number1 < number3)
    {
        smallerNumber ← number2
    }
    ELSE
    {
        smallerNumber ← number3
    }

}
```

ITERATION

The loop construct is used in a computer program when the program requires a specific code statements to be repeated more than once. The Exam Reference Sheet syntax is as shown on the next page.

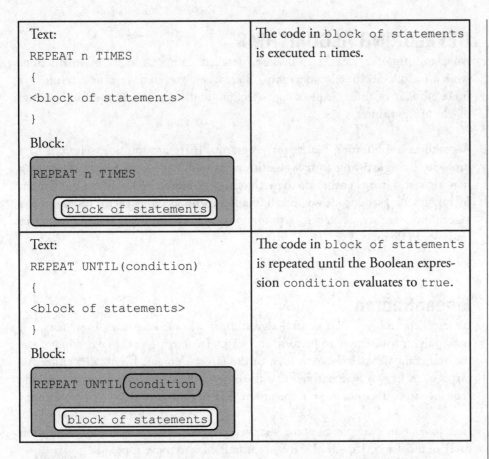

Text:
 	
``
REPEAT n TIMES
{
<block of statements>
}
``
 	
Block:
	The code in `block of statements` is executed n times.

Text:
 	
``
REPEAT UNTIL(condition)
{
<block of statements>
}
``
 	
Block:
	The code in `block of statements` is repeated until the Boolean expression `condition` evaluates to `true`.

The "REPEAT n TIMES" is a predetermined loop; that is, the loop will execute the program statements within the loop n number of times. The "repeat until *condition*" executes if the condition is true. The loop construct requires an exact ending condition that terminates the loop and exits the loop construct.

In summary, to have a clear functioning loop, every loop designed should have:

- a clear beginning condition
- a clear ending condition

This could be a program statement that leads the code towards the ending condition (a counter, a condition that is satisfied, or an input from the user that meets the condition the loop is looking for)

For example:

```
number ← 1
REPEAT UNTIL (number < 10)
{
    number++
}
```

The above loop will execute 9 times. When `number` is given the value 10, the loop will terminate.

DEVELOPING ALGORITHMS

An algorithm is a clear, step-by-step, detailed computable set of instructions (which include arithmetic operations) that, when executed, returns a result in a finite amount of time. Sequencing, selection, and iteration are the fundamental blocks of algorithms.

Algorithms are building blocks for programs. There are multiple solutions to a problem. Using existing correct algorithms as building blocks for constructing a new algorithm helps ensure the new algorithm is correct. Algorithms are written in English or pseudocode so that humans can understand them. Programs are algorithms that are written in a programming language so that computers can understand them.

Linear Search

An excellent example of a general algorithm is a linear search. A linear search is one straightforward way to perform the search by starting at the beginning of the list and compare each value in turn to the target element. Eventually, either the target element will be identified or will come to the end of the list and conclude that the target does not exist in the group. This approach is called a linear search.

Let's look at an example. Suppose you were to use a linear search for the location of 21 in the list [5, 16, –3, 21, 7]. Start at index 1 and move forward.

Target Value = 4

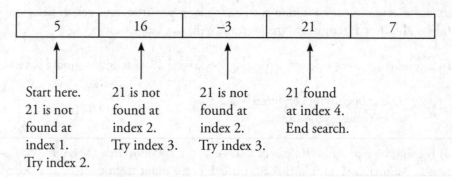

Therefore, algorithm will indicate that the element 21 is found at index 4.

This table (from the College Board-provided Course and Exam Description) describing all the shapes in a flow chart will be provided:

Block	Explanation
Oval	The start of the algorithm
Parallelogram	An input or output step
Diamond	A conditional or decision step, where execution proceeds to the side labeled "Yes" if the answer to the question is yes and to the side labeled "No" if the answer to the question is no
Rectangle	The result of the algorithm

LISTS

We have discussed lists as a data type and how lists are good examples of data abstraction. This section will revisit lists and discuss the various operations that use lists. We will discuss how list transversal works and examine the Exam Reference Sheet syntax for list operations.

In a list, each value is stored at a specific, numbered position in the array. The number corresponding to each position is called an index or a subscript. As stated on the Exam Reference Sheet, the index value begins at 1.

Below is the list of functions that use lists. The listing is provided to students as part of the Reference Sheet.

Text:
`aList ← [value1, value2, value3, ...]`
Block:
`aList ⬅ value1, value2, value3`
	Creates a new list that contains the values `value1, value2, value3`, and ... at indices `1, 2, 3`, and ... respectively and assigns it to `aList`.

Text:
`aList ← []`
Block:
`aList ⬅ ▯`
	Creates an empty list and assigns it to `aList`.

Text:
`aList ← bList`
Block:
`aList ⬅ bList`
	Assigns a copy of the list `bList` to the list `aList`. For example, if `bList` contains `[20, 40, 60]`, then `aList` will also contain `[20, 40, 60]` after the assignment.

Text:
 	
`aList[i]`
 	
Block:
 	
`aList` `i`
	Accesses the element of `aList` at index `i`. The first element of `aList` is at index 1 and is accessed using the notation `aList[1]`.

Text:
 	
`x ← aList[i]`
 	
Block:
 	
`x ⟵ aList i`
	Assigns the value of `aList[i]` to the variable `x`.

Text:
 	
`aList[i] ← x`
 	
Block:
 	
`aList i ⟵ x`
	Assigns the value of `x` to `aList[i]`.

Text:
 	
`aList[i] ← aList[j]`
 	
Block:
 	
`aList i ⟵ aList j`
	Assigns the value of `aList[j]` to `aList[i]`.

Text:
 	
`INSERT(aList, i, value)`
 	
Block:
 	
`INSERT aList, i, value`
	Any values in `aList` at indices greater than or equal to `i` are shifted one position to the right. The length of the list is increased by 1, and `value` is placed at index `i` in `aList`.

Text:
 	
`APPEND(aList, value)`
 	
Block:
 	
`APPEND aList, value`
	The length of `aList` is increased by 1, and `value` is placed at the end of `aList`.

Text:
 	
`REMOVE(aList, i)`
 	
Block:
 	
`REMOVE aList, i`
	Removes the item at index `i` in `aList` and shifts to the left any values at indices greater than `i`. The length of `aList` is decreased by 1.

Text:
 	
`LENGTH(aList)`
 	
Block:
 	
`LENGTH aList`
	Evaluates to the number of elements in `aList`.

The Exam Reference Sheet provides a loop construct that simplifies certain array loops. You can use it whenever you want to examine each value in an array.

Text:
 	
`FOR EACH item IN aList`
`{`
`<block of statements>`
`}`
 	
Block:
 	
`FOR EACH item IN aList`
   `block of statements`
	The variable `item` is assigned the value of each element of `aList` sequentially, in order, from the first element to the last element. The code in `block of statements` is executed once for each assignment of `item`.

An example of how the FOR-EACH loop can be used is shown in this snippet of code follows:

```
FOR EACH n IN temp
{
   if (n > 0)
     DISPLAY ("NUMBER IS POSITIVE")
}
```

BINARY SEARCH

In a binary search, the search algorithm requires sorted elements before applying the algorithm. Binary searches looks for an item by comparing the middlemost item of the collection. If a match occurs, then the index of the item is returned. If the middle item is greater than the item, then the item is searched in the sub-array to the middle item's left. Otherwise, the item is searched for in the sub-array to the right of the middle item. This process continues the sub-array as well until the size of the sub-array reduces to zero. Here's an example. The binary search in the diagram searches to the element 7 in the ordered list [2, 6, 7, 8, 9, 12, 15].

Target Value = 1

MID Value

1	2	3	4	5

1 is less than 3

MID Value

1	2	3

1 is less than 2

1

CALLING PROCEDURES, DEVELOPING PROCEDURES, AND LIBRARIES

One of the most basic building blocks of programming is procedures. Programmers break down problems into smaller and more manageable pieces. By creating procedures and leveraging parameters, programmers generalize processes that get reused. Procedures allow programmers to draw upon code that has already been tested, allowing them to write programs more quickly and more confidently. Even the simplest of programs usually uses procedures that are built-in within the programs. All programming procedures have input and output. The procedure contains instructions used to create the output from its input. A procedure call is a programming statement made by stating the procedure name, listing actual parameter names or values within parentheses.

A formal definition of a procedure is as follows: A programming procedure is a named group of program code that performs a specific task. Other languages call them methods, subroutines, or procedures.

After defining a procedure, programmers write code within it just like anywhere else in the program. Giving the function a name and defining parameters it should accept is called the header. The information the function needs gets passed as parameters. Finally, the function sometimes returns some result. Procedures are reusable. Once defined, the program calls it from other places.

The following are some of the advantages of writing procedures:

1. Procedures help abstract information. They are "black" boxes. A programmer calls a function; they do not care what exactly the code inside it does; they need the result. This is called procedural abstraction. Designing procedures in a program helps implement procedural abstraction. Furthermore, designing procedures helps separate the logic from the actual data. As long as it passes the procedure's parameters, it does not care what the data is. Each run of the procedure executes the code and returns a result.

2. Procedures help reuse code. Copying and pasting the same lines of code in multiple places adds complexity to the program. It introduces more places for something to go wrong. It becomes harder to maintain as well as isolate errors in the program. Creating a procedure eliminates these problems. They make it easy to reuse code anywhere else in the program. Once a procedure is defined, a programmer can call it anywhere in the program and know that it will behave the same way. All programming languages include procedures that a programmer can use without having to create them. These are called built-in functions or libraries. Consider the example: All programming languages have the built-in functions for displaying information on the screen. The built-in function for this as shown Reference Sheet is `DISPLAY()`. Application program interfaces (APIs) are specifications for using the library's procedures and understanding how they behave. Documentation for an API/library is necessary for understanding the library of procedures' behaviors.

Below is the syntax that the Exam Reference Sheet uses:

Text:
 	
`PROCEDURE procName(parameter1,`
`                parameter2, ...)`
 	
`{`
 	
`<block of statements>`
 	
`}`
 	
Block:
 	
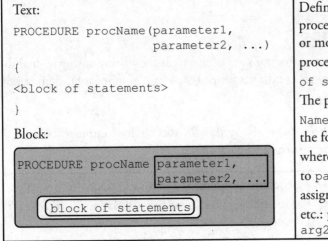
	Defines `procName` as a procedure that takes zero or more arguments. The procedure contains `block` `of statements`.
	The procedure `proc-Name` can be called using the following notation, where `arg1` is assigned to `parameter1`, `arg2` is assigned to `parameter2`, etc.: `procName(arg1,` `arg2, ...)`

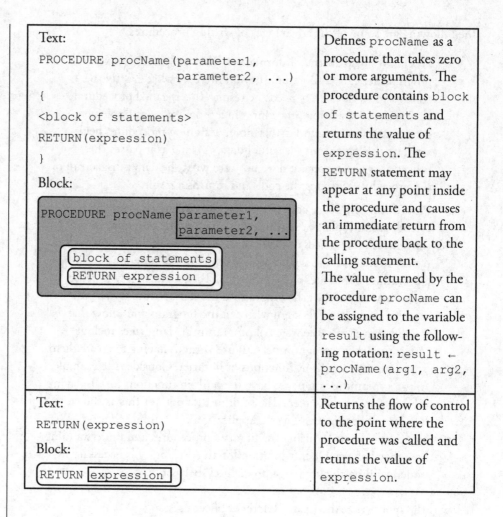

| Text:

`PROCEDURE procName(parameter1,`
`                 parameter2, ...)`
`{`
`<block of statements>`
`RETURN(expression)`
`}`

Block:

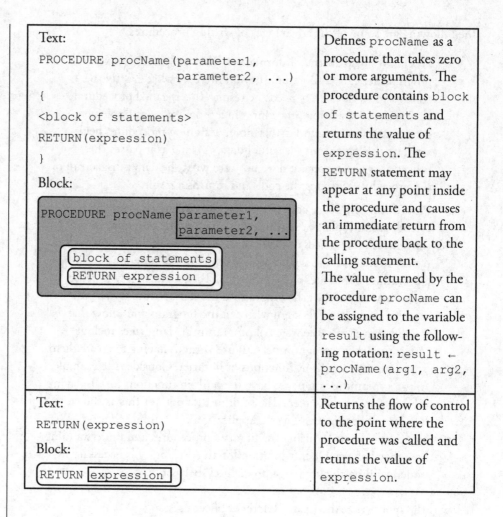 | Defines `procName` as a procedure that takes zero or more arguments. The procedure contains `block of statements` and returns the value of `expression`. The `RETURN` statement may appear at any point inside the procedure and causes an immediate return from the procedure back to the calling statement.

The value returned by the procedure `procName` can be assigned to the variable `result` using the following notation: `result ← procName(arg1, arg2, ...)` |
| Text:

`RETURN(expression)`

Block:

`RETURN expression` | Returns the flow of control to the point where the procedure was called and returns the value of `expression`. |

RANDOM VALUES

Random number generator programs are useful tools for writing software, mainly in designing games. A random number generator picks a number at random out of a range of values.

The Exam Reference Sheet shows the syntax for the random number. Note that the RANDOM function returns a whole number.

| Text:

`RANDOM(a, b)`
Block:

`RANDOM a, b` | Generates and returns a random integer from `a` to `b`, including `a` and `b`. Each result is equally likely to occur.

For example, `RANDOM(1, 3)` could return `1`, `2`, or `3`. |

Example:

```
value ← Random (2, 5)
//value could hold any value from 2 to 5, inclusive
```

SIMULATIONS

When real-world experiments would be dangerous to humans or to animals or would simply be too slow, computer simulations can be a very useful tool. Simulations are just a collection of computer software that responds to real-time input data to simulate a response that would resemble the real world. Often it is impractical to test the software in the real world. It is either too expensive or too inconvenient, and or sometimes can be a real danger to life.

Scientists build simulations for almost everything. Street Traffic Models and Solar Activity Models are two examples of simulations that we will take a closer look at in this section.

Street Traffic Models

Simulation, as a tool, is used when studying traffic systems when the system is too complicated. The advantage of simulation tools is that they provide visual demonstrations for different scenarios, both present and future. These models are necessary tools for planning and operating traffic systems, as they help to predict the behavior of vehicles in the traffic system.

The output from traffic simulation can be used to evaluate new infrastructure and to test forms of traffic control, e.g., maximum and minimum speed limits. Another advantage is the ability to use new technology that may not be available in real life such as use of autonomous cars. It is predicted that future traffic system will include a mix of partly and fully automated vehicles and human driven vehicles. Traffic simulation models have been found to be very useful in understanding traffic patterns and human behavior.

Solar Activity Models

All engineering disciplines use simulation tools that help them study phenomena specific to their field of expertise. Simulations are now part of the design process. Models require considerable time and effort to develop. Simulation models are used to study the solar system. Modeling and simulation is a powerful method to evaluate the design of a space system. Simulation models represent valuable knowledge that scientists use to build systems to explore space. New supercomputer simulations have successfully modeled a mysterious process believed to produce some of the hottest and most dangerous solar flares. The computer simulations demonstrate how certain phenomena could have occurred. All this is because of the development of sophisticated simulation models that are possible because of the availability of powerful computer systems that were previously not available.

ALGORITHMIC EFFICIENCY

Algorithmic efficiency is about determining how an algorithm performs with regards to both time and space. Often there are multiple solutions to a problem, and it is essential to understand that not all algorithmic solutions are optimal. Depending on the hardware used, the choice of algorithm can be different. Determining an algorithm's efficiency is mathematically done by implementing the algorithm and running it on different inputs. The correctness of an algorithm is determined by formal reasoning, not by writing an algorithm to implement a program. An algorithm may be correct but have a different efficiency from another algorithm. A more efficient algorithm could be more complicated by implementing, i.e., writing the algorithm's actual program.

One approach is what is called a heuristic technique, which is one that approximates a solution when typical methods fail to find an exact solution. Heuristics may help find an approximate solution more quickly when exact methods are too slow.

UNDECIDABLE PROBLEMS

In addition to problems that take a long time to compute, there are some problems that a computer can never solve, even the world's most powerful computer with infinite time: the undecidable problems. An undecidable problem may have instances that have an algorithmic solution. However, there is no algorithmic solution that solves all instances of the problem. A decidable problem is when the constructed algorithm answers "yes" or "no" for all inputs, such as "is the number even?" A problem where it is not possible to construct an algorithm is called an undecidable problem.

An example of this is the halting problem (Alan Turing). Algorithms exist that can correctly predict when some programs halt. These are simple programs that do not change based on different inputs. However, no algorithm exists that can analyze *any* program's code and determine whether it halts or not. Hence a halting problem is an undecidable problem.

KEY TERMS

Variables
Selection
Iteration
Boolean Expression
List
Strings
Abstraction
Application Program Interface (API)
Simulation Models
Algorithm Efficiency
Assignment
Sequencing
Loops
Data Types
Procedures
Pseudocode
Procedural Abstraction
Random Number Generator
Algorithm
Undecidable Problem
Heuristic
Libraries
Binary Search

CHAPTER 5 REVIEW DRILL

1. A Boolean is a data type that

    (A) holds numbers, including integers, floats, and doubles
    (B) holds characters, including special characters
    (C) holds only two values, true or false
    (D) holds letters, characters, and numbers

2. A variable (such as numbers, a list, etc.) is a good example of

    (A) data abstraction
    (B) modularity
    (C) procedural abstraction
    (D) algorithm

3. In the Exam Reference Sheet, the index value of a list starts at

    (A) 1
    (B) the length of the list
    (C) n
    (D) 0

4. An important property of an algorithm is that

    (A) it is a step-by-step process
    (B) it has abstraction built in
    (C) it is important to calculate efficiency
    (D) it is written using pseudocode

5. Combining two strings to make a new string is called

    (A) abstraction
    (B) adding
    (C) concatenation
    (D) manipulation

6. An example of a logical operator is

   (A) ←
   (B) OR
   (C) =
   (D) ≥

7. Which of the following are building blocks of an algorithm?

   (A) Sequencing, selection, and iteration
   (B) Variables, lists, and strings
   (C) Procedures, blocks, and modules
   (D) Recursion, selection, and iteration

8. While designing algorithms it is important to remember

   (A) all algorithms are efficient
   (B) it is possible to calculate the amount of memory an algorithm will use
   (C) there is more than one algorithmic solution to a problem
   (D) all algorithms have to be expressed in a specific format

9. Procedural abstraction is MOST useful because

   (A) of the ability to reuse code
   (B) it provides APIs
   (C) it helps with readability
   (D) it reduces complexity

10. Which of the following are true statements about simulations?

   (A) A simulation allows investigation of a real-world phenomenon without the constraints of the real world.
   (B) A simulation is an abstraction of a real-world object or phenomena.
   (C) The process of developing a simulation involves simplifying the functionality.
   (D) All of the above

Summary

- To find specific solutions to generalizable problems, programmers represent and organize data in multiple ways.

- A variable is an abstraction inside a program that can hold a value. Each variable has associated data storage that represents one value at a time, but that value can be a list or other collection that in turn contains multiple values.

- Using meaningful variable names helps with the readability of program code and the understanding of what values are represented by the variables.

- The assignment operator allows a program to change the value represented by a variable. The exam reference sheet provides the ← operator to use for assignment. For example, Text: `a ← expression` evaluates `expression` and then assigns a copy of the result to the variable a.

- To find specific solutions to generalizable problems, programmers represent and organize data in multiple ways.

- A list is an ordered sequence of elements. For example, [value1, value2, value3, ...] describes a list where value1 is the first element, value2 is the second element, value3 is the third element, and so on.

- An element is an individual value in a list that is assigned a unique index.

- An index is a common method for referencing the elements in a list or string using natural numbers.

- A string is an ordered sequence of characters.

- Data abstractions manage complexity in programs by giving a collection of data a name without referencing the specific details of the representation.

- Developing a data abstraction to implement in a program can result in a program that is easier to develop and maintain.

o   The exam reference sheet provides the notation [value1, value2, value3, ...] to create a list with those values as the first, second, third, and so on, items. For example, aList ← [value1, value2, value3, ...] creates a new list that contains the values value1, value2, value3, etc., at indices 1, 2, 3, etc., respectively, and assigns them to aList.

o   The command aList ← [] creates a new empty list and assigns it to aList.

o   The Exam Reference Sheet describes a list structure whose index values are 1 through the number of elements in the list, inclusive. For all list operations, if a list index is less than 1 or greater than the length of the list, an error message is produced, and the program will terminate.

o   The way statements are sequenced and combined in a program determines the computed result. Programs incorporate iteration and selection constructs to represent repetition and make decisions to handle varied input values.

o   To make a selection algorithm:
   • Write conditional statements.
   • Determine the result of conditional statements.
   • Write nested conditional statements.
   • Determine the result of nested conditional statements.

o   To make an iterative algorithms:
   • Write iteration statements.
   • Determine the result or side effect of iteration statements.
   • Compare multiple algorithms to determine whether they yield the same side effect or result.

o   To use list operations:
   • Write expressions that use list indexing and list procedures.
   • Evaluate expressions that use list indexing and list procedures.

o   To create algorithms involving elements of a list:
   • Write iteration statements to traverse a list
   • Determine the result of an algorithm that includes list traversal.

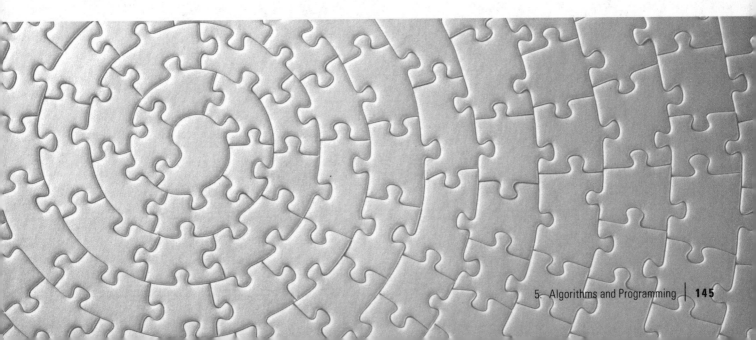

o To create binary search algorithms:
  - Determine the number of iterations required to find a value in a data set.
  - Explain the requirements necessary to complete a binary search.

o To use procedure calls:
  - Write a statement to call a procedure.
  - Determine the result or effect of a procedure call.
  - Select appropriate libraries or existing code segments to use in creating new programs.

o To generate random values:
  - Write expressions to generate possible values.
  - Evaluate expressions to determine the possible values.

o Computers can use simulations to represent real-life phenomena or outcomes.

o To determine the efficiency of an algorithm:
  - Explain the difference between algorithms that run in reasonable time and those that do not.
  - Identify situations where a heuristic solution may be more appropriate.

o There exist problems that computers cannot solve, and even when a computer can solve a problem, it may not be able to do so in a reasonable amount of time.

Chapter 6
Computer Systems
and Networks

THE INTERNET

The word networking almost immediately brings the word "Internet" to mind. While this idea is conceptually correct, the Internet is an example of a massive computer network. Computer networks make it possible for one device to communicate with another device. Another example of a computer network is the local area network, or LAN. The technology that lets us access all the desktops, laptops, wireless devices, and printers within a school, college, or home, is called a LAN.

Every computer in a network is called a "host." A network layer address identifies each host. To send information to a remote host, a host creates a packet that includes

- the network layer address of the destination host
- its network layer address
- the information to be sent to the network layer, which limits the maximum packet size. The information is divided into packets by the transport layer before being passed to the network layer.

Each computer in the network follows a protocol to exchange information between computers. The path that the data packets take from the host computer to the destination computer is called a route.

> **Routing** is the process of finding a path from sender to receiver.

> **Bandwidth** is the maximum amount of data that can be sent in a fixed amount of time (for digital data, it is measured in bits per second). Higher bandwidth is better because the data will travel more quickly.

The Internet and the World Wide Web are two terms that are often used interchangeably in casual conversation. Although they are certainly related, the terms refer to different ideas. The World Wide Web is a collection of interlinked website documents viewed with a web browser by typing in an address. Most web pages use HTML (HyperText Markup Language) to run on the browser. The web browser uses HTTP (HyperText Transfer Protocol) to interpret the web page.

The Internet is different, more general, and includes email, file transfers, and many other ways that computers communicate. The Internet has an enormous number of devices hooked to it. Realizing that the reality was that the system was likely to fail at unexpected times, designers and engineers designed the system to be reliable.

By building redundant connections into the Internet's physical systems, the designers ensured that data could be rerouted via a different path if part of the Internet fails. Furthermore, such changes to the path can happen in transit because routing on the Internet is dynamic. Creating such redundancy can require additional resources (such as additional computers and cables).

However, it also increases the Internet's fault tolerance (ability to work around problems) and helps the Internet scale (expand) to more devices and people.

While streaming data over the Internet, the stream is divided into *packets* that the IP sends individually. This process is what makes the Internet a *packet switching* network. Though the Internet is reliable, once in a while a packet will be lost. Devices on the Internet need to tolerate these faults. Sometimes the best solution is to decide that these faults aren't important. For example. if you lose one video frame, that lost frame will be imperceptible to the viewer, so that loss can be disregarded.

When the faults are more important, these faults can be tolerated using Transmission Control Protocol, better known as TCP. This protocol works by continuously sending packets until an acknowledgment of proper receipt is sent back. For applications that use TCP, it is TCP that divides the data into packets. Since packets can travel by different paths, they may arrive out of order. Despite the redundancy of the Internet, some data packets may not reach their destination. TCP guarantees reliable data transmission. It keeps track of which packets it receives successfully and resends any that have been lost or damaged. It also specifies the order for reassembling the data on the other end. The Internet is reliable, but data packets transmitted between computers within the network will sometimes be lost. Devices on the Internet need to tolerate these faults. The TCP protocol is used by computers on the Internet. The protocol's design is to keep sending packets while transmitting until a message is sent to the sending computers that the data was received successfully. The data split into packets travels by different paths. The packets may arrive out of order. Alternatively, some will not arrive at all. The receiving computer keeps track of the packets sent. It resends the lost or damaged data back (indicating that the damaged data packet needs resending). It also specifies the order for reassembling the data on the other end. All this happens to guarantee a reliable data transmission.

Internet Networking Layer	Protocol Name
Application Layer	HTTP, IMAP, SMTP
Transport Layer	TCP, UDP
Internet Layer	IP
Network Interface Hardware	Ethernet cable, Wi-Fi (Link Layer Protocols)

Scalability

Another critical design aspect of the Internet is that it is scalable. The scalability of a system is the system's capacity to change in size to meet new demands. A system is scalable when it can handle a significant amount of usage. A system may be scalable to handle only twice its designed amount, and some may handle a thousand times more. Because the Internet has global outreach, scalability will always need to be given attention.

FAULT TOLERANCE

One of the most significant features of the Internet is its fault-tolerant design. The engineers who designed the Internet made sure that it could continue to function even if some router within the system failed. The Internet has redundancy built in as part of its core design. As shown in the figure below, it allows it to have more than one path between any two connected devices if some part of the network fails.

If a device or connection on the Internet fails, it picks a different route to send the data. The problem that occurs with redundancy is that it often requires additional resources. However, it provides the benefit of fault tolerance. The redundancy of routing options between two points increases the Internet's reliability. It helps the system scale to more devices and more people.

Having understood the fault-tolerant nature of the Internet, we now examine the causes of network failure, particularly with respect to the Internet.

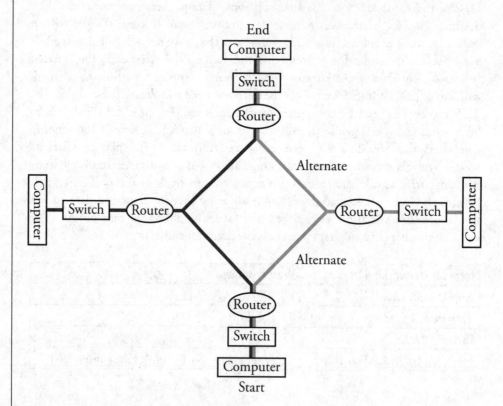

There are four broad categories of failure:

1. **Hardware Failure**

   This includes failure such as computers failing because of general wear and tear, misuse, etc., link failure because of cables getting worn out, power outages, incompatibility between devices, etc. Much of the network failures are attributed to router failure. Since there are many interconnected hardware elements in the network, even if one critical component fails, the network could crash. Failure could be a complete or partial failure of any one of these devices.

2. **Operational Failures**

Human errors in operating networking systems, mismanagement of equipment, device configuration changes, firmware/software upgrades all are causes that lead to failure within a network system.

3. **Weather**

The Internet has cables and wires spanning the world that connect computers. Natural disasters could cause the hardware to be destroyed, bringing the network activity to a halt. An example of this is a solar flare. A solar flare is an intense radiation that is released from the Sun. This happens because of the release of the magnetic energy from the sunspots. If something like this were to happen, it would melt down all the computer systems. This is a good example of how the Internet is subject to natural disasters that its fault-tolerant design cannot protect.

4. **Cyberattacks**

There are many malicious attacks that could cause the network to crash. One such example is a Distributed Denial of Service (DDoS). Unfortunately, a DDoS along with other such cyberattacks are quite easy to create and cause a lot of damage. Cybercriminals cause harm by bringing down networks hooked to the Internet. These bad actors can be surprisingly creative.

PARALLEL AND DISTRIBUTED COMPUTING

A computer program is a step-by-step, detailed set of sequential instructions. Traditionally, program instructions are processed one at a time, using a process called sequential computing. However, with increased demands of high processing speeds, engineers have had to rethink this process. At the heart of every computer that executes instructions is the microprocessor. These processors can run only so fast before the amount of heat generated results in the devices' malfunctioning.

Parallel computing is an alternate design of computers. Here, a program is broken into smaller sequential computing operations. Some of the small pieces (identified by the parallel computing software) use multiple processors. The design of both the hardware and software changes parallel computing when compared to sequential computing. Most modern computers use parallel computing systems, with anywhere from 4 to 24 processors running simultaneously.

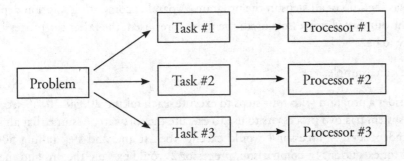

There are several advantages to parallel computing.

- Performing tasks at the same time saves time and money.
- Parallel computing solutions scale well because they can handle more instructions.
- Parallel computing may help save time and reduce heat and malfunctioning.

A problem in parallel computing is that the total time taken is as long as its longest parallel tasks.

Distributed computing is a model in which multiple devices run a program. Distributed computing can be within the same computer or different computers. They communicate by sending messages to each other. With distributed computing, the power of multiple computers working on the same problem is made available. Distributed computing allows different users or computers to share information. The system can allow an application on one machine to leverage processing power, memory, or storage on another machine. Distributed computing solves problems that otherwise would be hard to solve because of too little available storage or too much processing time.

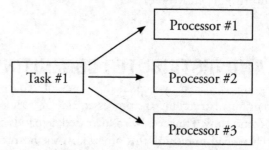

The most significant difference between distributed computing and parallel computing is that all processors may have access to shared memory to exchange information between processors in parallel computing. In distributed computing, each processor has its private memory and exchanges messages by passing messages between the processors.

Compared to sequential computing, parallel and distributed computing systems have increased capacities. Consequently, these systems can process large data sets or solve complex problems faster. Remember that a sequential solution takes as long as the sum of all steps in the program. A parallel computing solution depends on the number of processors used: the more cores used, the faster the processing is likely to be.

Here's an example.

Consider a program with four steps to execute, each taking 20, 30, 10, 50 seconds. The system has two processors to use to execute the software. Assume that all steps are independent. Processor 1 would execute the 1st and 2nd step taking 50 seconds for execution. In comparison, processor 2 would execute the 3rd and the 4th step taking 60 seconds for execution.

If the processes execute sequentially, executing all four processes would take 110 seconds. An important fact is that even though processor 1 only took 50 seconds, it still has to wait for processor 2 before the solution is complete. Moreover, the total execution time is 60 seconds.

This has two important conclusions.

- A parallel computing model is only as fast as the speed of its sequential portions.
- Adding parallel processors will not increase the efficiency of a solution by much. The speed up effect of adding more parallel processors gets impacted by either waiting for sequential steps to complete or other factors such as communication time.

An excellent example of this is when two students are working on a project. One team member is responsible for the drawings and sketches, and the other person does the writing. Even if the writing is complete, the project cannot be sent for publishing if the sketches are not complete. Adding another person to the team may not speed up the time it takes to complete the project. There is a limit to how many members to add and on how many additional members are to be utilized. Furthermore, the time needed to bring the new member up to speed must be taken into account.

KEY TERMS

Protocol
World Wide Web
Internet Protocol
Bandwidth
Redundancy
Distributed Computing
Route
HTTP
Transmission Control Protocol (TCP/IP)
Routing
Fault Tolerance
Parallel Computing
Sequential Computing

CHAPTER 6 REVIEW DRILL

1. Bandwidth is usually measured in

   (A) bits per second
   (B) bytes per second
   (C) KB per second
   (D) MB per second

2. A path in a computer network that can be found between a sender computer and receiver computer is called

   (A) network trace
   (B) a route
   (C) network configuration
   (D) packet trace

3. What does it mean when the protocols on the Internet are open?

   (A) The protocols are not owned by any company.
   (B) The protocols are not operating system dependent.
   (C) The protocols are designed using open source programming languages.
   (D) The protocols are not dependent on a specific hardware device.

4. One significant feature of the Internet that makes it reliable is

   (A) protocols
   (B) routing
   (C) redundancy
   (D) scalability

5. Which of the following is NOT a critical design aspect of the Internet?

   (A) Redundancy
   (B) Scalability
   (C) Fault tolerance design
   (D) Design of the World Wide Web

Summary

- Computer systems and networks facilitate the transfer of data. Some examples include computers, tablets, servers, routers, and smart sensors.

- A *computing system* is a group of computing devices and programs working together for a common purpose.

- A *computer network* is a group of interconnected computing devices capable of sending or receiving data.

- A computer network is a type of computing system.

- A *path* between two computing devices on a computer network (a sender and a receiver) is a sequence of directly connected computing devices that begins at the sender and ends at the receiver.

- *Routing* is the process of finding a path from sender to receiver.

- The *bandwidth* of a computer network is the maximum amount of data that can be sent in a fixed amount of time.

- Bandwidth is usually measured in bits per second.

- The Internet is a computer network consisting of interconnected networks that use standardized, open (nonproprietary) communication protocols.

- Access to the Internet depends on the ability to connect a computing device to an Internet connected device.

- A *protocol* is an agreed upon set of rules that specify the behavior of a system.

- The protocols used in the Internet are *open*, which allows users to easily connect additional computing devices to the Internet.

- IP, TCP, and UDP are common protocols used on the Internet.

- Routing on the Internet is usually dynamic; it is not specified in advance.

o	The *scalability* of a system is the capacity for the system to change in size and scale to meet new demands. The Internet was designed to be scalable.

o	Information is passed through the Internet as a *data stream*. Data streams contain chunks of data that are encapsulated in *packets*.

o	Packets contain a chunk of data and metadata used for routing the packet between the origin and the destination on the Internet, as well as for data reassembly.

o	Packets may arrive at the destination in order, out of order, or not at all.

o	The World Wide Web is a system of linked pages, programs, and files.

o	HTTP is a protocol used by the World Wide Web.

o	The World Wide Web uses the Internet.

o	Parallel and distributed computing leverage multiple computers to more quickly solve complex problems or process large data sets.

Chapter 7
Impact of
Computing

BENEFICIAL AND HARMFUL EFFECTS

Many people take up tasks and engineer products so that they can have an impact on society. Nevertheless, the reality is many ideas that people have never make it past the drawing board stage. Most modern-day ideas involve software, which requires programming to bring the concept to life. Technology has revolution-ized society in the 21st century through computing innovations. The ones that influence society these days almost always involve computing. Programming is a skill that is very important to know today. We recognize that algorithms rule the world.

> Know and understand that a computing innovation includes a program as an integral part of its function. A computing inno-vation takes in data, transforms data and outputs data in order to solve problems and/or show creative expression. A program is a collection of program statements that performs a specific task when run by a computer. A program is often referred to as software.

Computing Has Global Impacts

A world filled with computing innovations has changed the way people think, work, live, and play. Methods for communicating, collaborating, problem-solving, and doing business have changed. The primary reason they are changing is because of innovations enabled by computing. Advances in computing lead to innovations in other areas. Computational approaches lead to new understandings, discoveries, and a sea of change across disciplines. Students will become familiar with how computing enables innovation and analyze the potential benefits and harmful effects of computing in several contexts.

It is essential to recognize that computing and computing innovations have global effects—both beneficial and harmful—and are all-pervasive. Innovations enabled by computing raise legal and ethical concerns such as commercial access to music and movie downloads and streaming. Access to digital content via peer-to-peer networks such as bit torrent raise legal and ethical concerns. Both authenticated as well as anonymous access to digital information, open source and licensing of software, and censorship issues raise legal and ethical considerations.

Some other concerns that emerge from the development and use of computational systems and artifacts are privacy and security concerns. People now have instant access to vast amounts of information online. As a result of the Internet, data collection such as geolocation, cookies, and browsing history raises privacy and security concerns. Internet-based technology such as proxy servers and online ano-nymity software enable anonymity in online interactions. The curating of data can allow bad actors to possibly exploit the information available. The idea behind targeted advertising is to help individuals, but it can be misused. Digitized information being widely available has raised questions about intellectual property. The creation of digital audio, video, and textual content by combining existing content has given rise to copyright concerns.

DIGITAL DIVIDE

The digital divide describes the disparity between those who have access to technology and those who do not, including but not limited to access to a computer, the Internet, or other hardware and software. More broadly, it describes the uneven distribution of usage between groups by socioeconomic status, race, gender, and geographical location. However, the digital divide is not only seen in differences among such large-scale groups. Even within these groups, there can be massive difference between individuals in terms of access to technology. The reasons for the lack of access could be physical (geographical location), financial, or the existence of a disability. All these factors contribute to the digital divide.

Unfortunately, solutions for these problems are rarely addressed at scale because there are often more significant problems to be dealt with. Human needs such as food and health care take precedence over digital inclusion.

When we consider technological resources and solutions, we need to consider who has access. Who benefits from this technology? Furthermore, are these concerns that are occurring locally for a particular solution or globally? Ultimately, we as individuals and organizations, and governments have the power to improve or worsen this divide.

Research studies have found that people from the African American and Hispanic communities are less likely to say they own a computer or have high-speed Internet access. It is an encouraging trend to note that smartphones play a role in bridging these differences. Disabled Americans are about three times as likely as those without a disability to say they never go online (23% vs. 8%), according to a 2016 Pew Research Center survey. When compared with those who do not have a disability, disabled adults are roughly 20 percentage points less likely to say they subscribe to home broadband and own a traditional computer, a smartphone, or a tablet. Adults who report having a disability are also less likely to have multiple devices that enable them to go online. One in four disabled adults say they have high-speed Internet at home, a smartphone, a desktop or laptop computer, and a tablet.

As a result of COVID-19, millions of people in the United States feel isolated because of the lack of reliable broadband Internet at home. This problem is primarily because they cannot afford it or because it simply is not available where they live. The digital divide has always left many children and adults with fewer educational and economic opportunities. Especially during the coronavirus pandemic with schools, libraries, and workplaces closed, those without broadband struggled. Access to schoolwork, job listings, unemployment benefit applications, and video chat services that others use to keep in touch with friends and family are not available. For those on the wrong side of the digital divide, working from home is not an option.

A sobering fact is that the disabled population has a larger portion of seniors. In general, the senior members of our society (those 70 or more years of age) generally have lower digital adoption rates than the rest of the nation. Disabled Americans younger than 65 have much higher rates of home broadband services and owning digital devices. The explosion of Internet use, broadband adoption, and smartphone ownership have snowballed for all Americans—including those who are less well-off financially. Nevertheless, even as various factors that impact the digital divide have narrowed over time, lower- and higher-income Americans' digital lives remain markedly different. Rural Americans have made considerable gains in adopting digital technology over the past decade.

COMPUTING BIAS

When humans collect data to analyze, it is natural to assume some degree of bias. However, most people believe computers, specifically the software that runs these computers, are objective. It is essential to recognize that computers are only as objective as the algorithms they are running.

We will use a common scenario to describe how bias occurs in software systems. Say we want to design a machine learning algorithm that recommends candidates to employers. The first step is to have the algorithm learn what is desired from a candidate using a training set, which typically collects data based on what résumés resulted in getting hired for similar jobs. Unfortunately, this can lead to biases. If employers exhibited prejudice towards a particular gender, ethnicity, or group in the past positions, the algorithm would likely reflect a similar prejudice. This is only one way that bias can be embedded in an algorithm: bias can exist at every software development level. Phases of the software development cycle, such as gathering requirements for the software product, the system's design, or during testing and deployment, unconscious bias can creep in. This type of bias is commonly known as algorithmic bias. Often even the simplest of the algorithms cannot explain out exactly how systems might be susceptible to algorithmic bias. Frequently the programmers themselves do not know how a particular artificial intelligence-based algorithm responds to data fed into the algorithm. Machine learning-based systems train on data fed into software systems.

When thinking about "machine learning" tools, one idea is training the software. This involves exposing a computer to relevant data collections, and then that computer learns to make judgments, or predictions, about the information it processes based on the patterns it detects. While discussing data, we typically think of formal studies where researchers deliberate about the data's limitations and consider the demographics and representation details. The results are then peer reviewed. This is not true with AI-based systems. Consider the Internet. It is possible to teach an artificial intelligence system to crawl through the web and read what has been written. Several studies have found that building a system of this kind could produce prejudices against under-represented minorities and women.

Another possibility is that the foundational assumptions of engineers can also be biased. While the data used to build an algorithm and influences the decisions it makes, the programmers who design it and decide upon a deployment strategy are responsible for implicit bias that can creep into the systems. Moreover, even though this is clear, what is not clear is who is ultimately responsible for what is judged to be acceptable and ethical and what is not.

Algorithmic bias occurs in two primary ways: accuracy and impact. An AI can have different accuracy rates for different demographic groups. Similarly, an algorithm can make vastly different decisions when applied to different populations. This can potentially have a significant impact on the affected groups of people.

With that in mind, some people argue that such AI probably should not exist, or at least they should not come with such a high risk of abuse. Just because a technology makes accurate decisions, it does not mean that the decisions are fair or ethical. Several research institutes have made technical efforts to "de-bias" flawed artificial intelligence. It is also vital to keep in mind that technology alone does not have the entire solution. Ultimately, society and traditional systems that determine how society functions will need to be part of the process of making the fundamental challenges of fairness and discrimination presented by artificial intelligence-based algorithms.

CROWDSOURCING

Crowdsourcing is the practice of obtaining input or information from a large number of people via the Internet.

Crowdsourcing is a common practice that utilizes the collective knowledge of a group to accomplish something or achieve a common goal. The Internet is the most commonly used medium to achieve these goals. It is the process of obtaining needed services, ideas, or content by soliciting contributions from a large group of people, and especially from an online community, rather than from traditional employees or suppliers. The crowdsourcing process breaks up tedious work by combining numerous people (volunteers, part-time workers) where each contributor adds a small portion to a larger goal.

Crowdsourcing has become an essential tool for businesses in various areas, such as data collection and general problem-solving. The practice of crowdsourcing has been so revolutionary that companies have scaled quickly and, in some cases, revolutionized entire industries.

In crowdsourcing, a business breaks up a more extensive project into individual micro-tasks. The business picks workers who have the skill sets to complete the business's work. A business may use a digital space called a crowdsourcing platform to unite these workers into one place and allocate their micro-tasks. Some of these businesses require workers to have specific skill sets or knowledge of specialized platforms. For example, many software developers utilize GitHub for this purpose.

Some of the advantages of crowdsourcing are:

Scalability: Scaling is a difficult problem since often, while working on massive projects, businesses have inadequate resources. Crowdsourcing provides an easy solution for scaling out any workforce by allocating small portions of a project to be completed by workers anywhere and providing greater flexibility.

Faster Completion: When a project is split into a collection of smaller pieces, providing those pieces to a larger group of workers expedites project completion. As a result, crowdsourcing allows businesses to perform tasks.

Lower Costs: Crowdsourcing is an inexpensive way to complete projects. Since most crowdsourcing is online, the operational costs are minimal when people meet to complete a task. Moreover, when the projects get completed faster, the profit margins may be higher as well.

Customer Involvement: Some crowdsourcing efforts get the customer involved in the effort. This results in an extraordinary level of consumer engagement. By asking consumers to solve a specific problem, the business gains valuable information from their customers.

Below are two examples of projects that have significantly benefited from crowdsourcing.

Open Source Software: Open source development allows programmers and developers to access the source code and to modify and improve the code as they see fit. The most significant advantage of this is that it allows many eyes to analyze the code and utilize unique skill sets to make it better. Several different companies have used crowdsourcing in this way to create stellar software that is highly popular. Some examples of open source software include the Linux operating system, Firefox browsers, and others.

Amazon's Mechanical Turk: MTurk is a crowdsourcing model followed by businesses that aim for work to be done by qualified workers who look for work on the Mechanical Turk platform. Businesses get a diverse number of workers, and workers select what they want to work on. The skills of distributed workers are made available on a pay-per-task model. Businesses can lower costs while achieving significant results.

Citizen Science: Citizen science uses the collective strength of communities and the public to identify research questions, collect and analyze data, interpret results, make discoveries, and develop technologies and applications—all to understand and solve environmental problems. Citizen science is a specialized form of crowdsourcing. In crowdsourcing, organizations put out an open call for voluntary assistance from large groups of individuals for online, distributed problem-solving. In citizen science, the public participates voluntarily in the scientific process, addressing real-world problems that may include conducting scientific experiments, collecting and analyzing data, and solving complex problems. Citizen-science proponents have grand visions. They hope that citizen science if done correctly, can be a significant source of high-quality data and analysis in areas relevant to government officials as well as research institutions.

LEGAL AND ETHICAL CONCERNS

Intellectual property is a product created by a person—an artist, writer, scientist or engineer. The law protects this product from being used in an unauthorized fashion. Many of these products include creative artistic work such as writing, music, drawing, photography, and film. Laws protecting intellectual property are of four different categories. These include copyright, patent, trademark, and trade secrets.

Digital content is also subject to intellectual property laws. Products such are computer software and other content that is developed on a computer are considered the intellectual property of either the person or the organization that created it. In a digital world, access to digital artifacts such as music and movies is very easy. Consequently, distribution becomes vulnerable to unauthorized use. These activities are illegal and have consequences. Examples of such software are BitTorrent, Napster, etc.

Plagiarism is copying someone's work and passing off as one's own. There are serious consequences to plagiarism. Some of the ways to avoid plagiarism is to give credit to the source of the information. Even if it is only a summary or paraphrasing, it is ethical to give credit to the sources used to provide the information.

There are many ways to add a license to the work created. Creative Commons is a not-for-profit organization that have various forms of licenses that can be used to protect original work from being plagiarized.

All Creative Common licenses have this symbol and this button that can be added.

Below is a full list of all Creative Common licenses that are available.

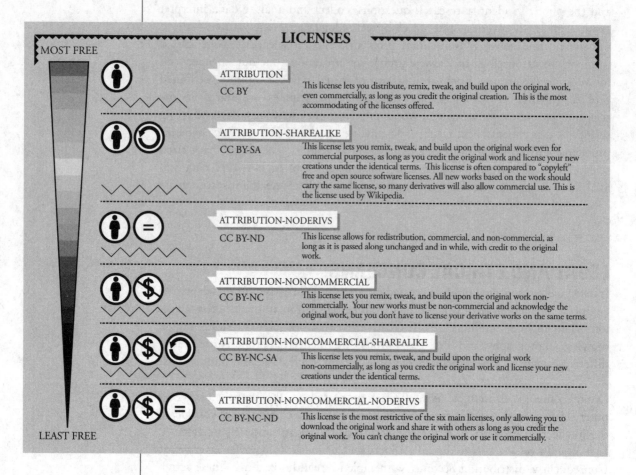

LICENSES

MOST FREE

ATTRIBUTION

CC BY

This license lets you distribute, remix, tweak, and build upon the original work, even commercially, as long as you credit the original creation. This is the most accommodating of the licenses offered.

ATTRIBUTION-SHAREALIKE

CC BY-SA

This license lets you remix, tweak, and build upon the original work even for commercial purposes, as long as you credit the original work and license your new creations under the identical terms. This license is often compared to "copyleft" free and open source software licenses. All new works based on the work should carry the same license, so many derivatives will also allow commercial use. This is the license used by Wikipedia.

ATTRIBUTION-NODERIVS

CC BY-ND

This license allows for redistribution, commercial, and non-commercial, as long as it is passed along unchanged and in while, with credit to the original work.

ATTRIBUTION-NONCOMMERCIAL

CC BY-NC

This license lets you remix, tweak, and build upon the original work non-commercially. Your new works must be non-commercial and acknowledge the original work, but you don't have to license your derivative works on the same terms.

ATTRIBUTION-NONCOMMERCIAL-SHAREALIKE

CC BY-NC-SA

This license lets you remix, tweak, and build upon the original work non-commercially, as long as you credit the original work and license your new creations under the identical terms.

ATTRIBUTION-NONCOMMERCIAL-NODERIVS

CC BY-NC-ND

This license is the most restrictive of the six main licenses, only allowing you to download the original work and share it with others as long as you credit the original work. You can't change the original work or use it commercially.

LEAST FREE

Many software products, especially crowdsourced ones, are open source. Open source is primarily with software products. Anyone can use, modify, and share it, since it is available on public domains. This contrasts with proprietary software, where the team that created the software are the only people who can modify it. To use the software, the consumer would need to get explicit permission and comply with the conditions placed by the software creators. With open source software, the authors make the source code available to others who would like to view that code, learn from it or share it. An excellent example of this is the GNU Image Manipulation Program.

The term open source originated in software development. However, the term "open source" in today's environment implies that the initiative embraces the ideas of collaboration, transparency, and community-oriented development.

Open access literature refers to digital artifacts. The Internet has made many articles available online and free of charge. Open access aims to make many academic publications free of most copyright and licensing restrictions. These research articles are available through open access archives and repositories as well as open access journals.

"Open access seeks to grant free and seeks to grant free and open online access to academic information, such as publications and data. A publication is defined 'open access' when there are no financial, legal or technical barriers to accessing it—that is to say when anyone can read, download, copy, distribute, print, search for and search within the information, or use it in education or in any other way within the legal agreements." (*Source: https://www.openaccess.nl/en/what-is-open-access*)

SAFE COMPUTING

Information about a person that can uniquely identify them, such as their educational, medical, financial, or employment information, is known as Personally Identifiable Information (PII). Individuals can be used to identify, contact, or locate an individual. Examples of data elements that can identify an individual include name, email address, fingerprint, etc. It is every individual's responsibility to safeguard their PII. Because of advances in technology such as the Internet, the PII has become a component of personal privacy. Websites, search engines, other social media sites store user information using cookies, history of mouse-clicks, and browsing history to target consumers with relevant ads. All this comes at the expense of user privacy.

There are several possible ways to misuse PII because of the data available online.

- Placement of PII online to enhance a user's online experiences
- Storage of PII online to simplify online purchases
- Exploitation of commercial and governmental curation of information by ignoring privacy and other protections, leading to the unintended use of information placed online that may have a harmful impact
- Use of PII for stalking or for identity theft or for other criminal acts
- The difficulty of deletion of information placed online
- Collection of your current location and time spent at previous locations
- Acquisition of information about a person from what is posted on social media and other sources'

Many of online accounts can be made a great deal safer from malicious attacks just by using better passwords. The best way to improve cybersecurity is by creating a strong password.

The weakest passwords are ones that use the following:

- names of family and friends
- birthday or those of family/friends
- places lived or have lived including cities or street names

Because the Internet is full of information about people's personal lives, it is most likely easily guessed if a password contains that person's information. Multifactor authentication is a security feature offered to improve account security. Many websites, applications, mobile devices now offer this service. MFA is a Two-Factor Authentication. Suppose an MFA is set up for a given account (website, application, or device) while logging in with the username and password. In that case, the account server asks for a second, independent form of authentication. It verifies it before granting access into the system. A comparison to this process is similar to real-life systems; to prove one's identity, systems ask for an Id and one more proof of identification (such as a passport).

Cybersecurity

Cybersecurity is also known as information security. It is the protection of a system against the unauthorized or criminal use of a system. It is the practice of ensuring integrity, confidentiality, and availability of information against unauthorized access. Cybersecurity's primary purpose is to protect networks, devices, programs, and data from external and internal threats.

The threat of cyberattacks requires vigilant security measures. These require implementation across information systems such as application security, identity management & data security, and network security. Because the technological landscape keeps evolving and the adoption of software is ever increasing, more and more information is becoming digital and accessible through networks and across the Internet. Cyberattackers use illegal approaches to gain unauthorized access to computers, devices, networks, applications, and databases.

Below is a list of cyberattacks that criminals and attackers use to exploit software:

Malware	Ransomware
Phishing	Distributed denial of service
Vulnerable software	Remote code execution
Brute force	SQL injection
Insider threat	Password attacks

The following are useful definitions on the various ways cyberattacks occur:

Phishing	Deceiving a user into providing personal information that can then be used to access sensitive online resources, such as bank accounts and emails
Computer Virus	Programs that can repeatedly duplicate themselves and gain authorized access to a computer often after attaching themselves to legitimate programs
Malware	Software that is capable of taking control over or harming a computing system
Keylogging	Recoding every keystroke made by a computer user hoping to gain fraudulent access to user names, passwords, and other sensitive and confidential information
Rogue access point	Data sent over public networks can be intercepted, analyzed, and modified. One way that this can happen is through a rogue access point: a wireless access point that can intercept, analyze, and modify data sent over public networks.

Encryption and Decryption

Data encryption is the process in which data is encoded into another form, then is converted to its original readable form with the help of a secret key (this is called a decryption key). Data, or plaintext, is encrypted with an encryption algorithm and an encryption key. Data encryption aims to protect digital data confidentiality as it is stored on computer systems and transmitted using the Internet or other computer networks. Encrypted data is commonly referred to as ciphertext, while unencrypted data is called plaintext. The conversion of encrypted data into its original form is called decryption. It is the reverse process of encryption. It decodes the encrypted information so that an authorized user can only decrypt the data because decryption requires a secret key or password.

A strong encryption-decryption system ensures privacy. As information travels over the Internet, it is necessary to scrutinize the access requests from various sources. Data that is encrypted before being sent through the Internet include text files, images, email, etc. At the receiving end, decryption software needs to enter a key to access the encrypted data. The decryption software extracts and converts the garbled data and transforms it into words and images easily understandable by a system. The decryption process is either manual or automatic.

There are two main types of encryption:

- asymmetric encryption (also known as public-key encryption)
- symmetric encryption.

These encryption algorithms help with authentication and ensure the integrity of systems. The process results in ciphertext, which only can be viewed in its original form if decrypted with the correct key.

Symmetric-key ciphers use the same secret key for encrypting and decrypting a message or file. While symmetric-key encryption is much faster than asymmetric encryption, the sender must exchange the encryption key with the recipient before the message can get decrypted. Asymmetric cryptography is also known as public-key cryptography. This form of cryptography uses two different keys, one public and one private. As it is named, the public key is one that everyone has access to, but the private key must be protected.

To summarize, cyberattacks occurring everywhere cybersecurity tools must all work in harmony cybercriminals. It is important to understand what is at stake, and society needs to take action to protect society's most vital information and digital data.

KEY TERMS
Computing Innovations
Legal and Ethical Concerns
Beneficial and Harmful Effects of Computing
Digital Divide
Artificial Intelligence
Machine Learning
Personally Identifiable Information (PII)
Encryption
Crowdsourcing
Citizen Science
Intellectual Property
Creative Commons
Plagiarism
Open source
Cybersecurity (Information Security)
Decryption

CHAPTER 7 REVIEW DRILL

1. Computing innovation is not always met with approval from the lawmakers in society. This is because

    (A) all computing innovations cause problems
    (B) computing innovations once deployed can sometimes cause unexpected problems
    (C) all computing innovations have predictable behavior
    (D) the impact a computing innovation has on society does not last forever

2. The digital divide in the time of Coronavirus became more evident because

    (A) the people who could afford the technology had better access to the vaccines
    (B) the people who could afford the technology had access to education and the news in society
    (C) the people who could afford the technology could pay for high-speed Internet
    (D) the people who could afford the technology knew how to hook up computers and other digital devices

3. In order to remove bias from software, which of the following steps must be taken?

    I. The data that is collected and provided to the AI algorithms should be gathered from diverse sources.
    II. There should be efforts taken to technically remove bias from the algorithms.
    III. The algorithms should be removed from use in society.

    (A) I, II, III
    (B) I and II
    (C) I and III
    (D) II and III

4. Citizen science is a form of crowdsourcing. Which of the following answer choices justify this statement?

    (A) Citizen science is scientific research conducted by distributed individuals who contribute relevant data to research using their own computing devices. This is a form of crowdsourcing.
    (B) Citizen science is distributed in how it is conducted. This is a form of crowdsourcing.
    (C) Citizen science is all about research. Crowdsourcing is very helpful in conducting research.
    (D) Citizen science helps collect data. Crowdsourcing is very useful in facilitating collection of large volumes of data.

5. One of the most important technologies needed for crowdsourcing is

    (A) knowing how to write computer programs
    (B) access to the Internet
    (C) the ability to attend online classes
    (D) having a webcam, microphone, and speaker

6. Intellectual property is defined as

   (A) something that a person owns (that is, they have paid to use the product)
   (B) something that while free cannot be distributed
   (C) something that, because it is created by a person, cannot be sold or distributed
   (D) something that a person has created like a song, story, movie and can be sold or distributed with permission

7. The best way to avoid plagiarism is

   (A) to get the permission of the author before using their work
   (B) to give credit by citing the sources
   (C) to pay for the work that is being used
   (D) to not use the resource and make all work original

8. Information about a person such as name, age, email identification is called

   (A) personalized data
   (B) metadata
   (C) cookie data
   (D) Personally Identifiable Information

9. Which of the following list can be described as a cyberattack?

   Select <u>two</u> answers.

   (A) Operating System failure
   (B) Hard disk crash
   (C) Distributed Denial of Service
   (D) Ransomware

10. The process of converting data into its original readable form is called

   (A) encryption
   (B) decryption
   (C) asymmetric key
   (D) packet transfer

Summary

○ While computing innovations are typically designed to achieve a specific purpose, they may have unintended consequences.

○ A single effect can be viewed as both beneficial and harmful by different people, or even by the same person.

○ Computing innovations can be used in ways that their creators had not originally intended:
  • The World Wide Web was originally intended only for rapid and easy exchange of information within the scientific community.
  • Targeted advertising is used to help businesses, but it can be misused at both individual and aggregate levels.
  • Machine learning and data mining have enabled innovation in medicine, business, and science, but information discovered in this way has also been used to discriminate against groups of individuals.

○ Some of the ways computing innovations can be used may have a harmful impact on society, the economy, or culture.

○ Responsible programmers try to consider the unintended ways their computing innovations can be used and the potential beneficial and harmful effects of these new uses, but it is not possible for a programmer to consider all the ways a computing innovation can be used.

○ The *digital divide* refers to differing access to computing devices and the Internet, based on socioeconomic, geographic, or demographic characteristics.
  • The digital divide can affect both groups and individuals.
  • The digital divide raises issues of equity, access, and influence, both globally and locally.
  • The digital divide is affected by the actions of individuals, organizations, and governments.

○ Computing innovations can reflect existing human biases because of biases written into the algorithms or biases in the data used by the innovation.

○ Programmers should take action to reduce bias in algorithms used for computing innovations as a way of combating existing human biases.

o Widespread access to information and public data facilitates the identification of problems, development of solutions, and dissemination of results.

o Citizen science is scientific research conducted in whole or part by distributed individuals, many of whom may not be scientists, who contribute relevant data to research using their own computing devices.

o *Crowdsourcing* is the practice of obtaining input or information from a large number of people via the Internet.

o Material created on a computer is the intellectual property of the creator or an organization. The use of material created by someone else without permission and presented as one's own is plagiarism and may have legal consequences.

o Some examples of legal ways to use materials created by someone else include:
  • Creative Commons—a public copyright license that enables the free distribution of an otherwise copyrighted work. This is used when the content creator wants to give others the right to share, use, and build upon the work they have created.
  • open source—programs that are made freely available and may be redistributed and modified
  • open access—online research output free of any and all restrictions on access and free of many restrictions on use, such as copyright or license restrictions

o The use of material created by someone other than you should always be cited.

o As with any technology or medium, using computing to harm individuals or groups of people raises legal and ethical concerns. Computing can play a role in social and political issues, which in turn often raises legal and ethical concerns. Some examples of these include:
  • the development of software that allows access to digital media downloads and streaming
  • the existence of computing devices that collect and analyze data by continuously monitoring activities

- Personally Identifiable Information (PII) is information about an individual that identifies, links, relates, or describes them. Examples of PII include:
  - Social Security number
  - age
  - race
  - phone number(s)
  - medical information
  - financial information
  - biometric data

- PII and other information placed online can be used to enhance a user's online experiences.

- PII stored online can be used to simplify making online purchases.

- Commercial and governmental curation of information may be exploited if privacy and other protections are ignored. Information placed online can be used in ways that were not intended and that may have a harmful impact. For example, an email message may be forwarded, tweets can be retweeted, and social media posts can be viewed by potential employers.

- PII can be used to stalk or steal the identity of a person or to aid in the planning of other criminal acts.

- Once information is placed online, it is difficult to delete.

- Authentication measures protect devices and information from unauthorized access. Examples of authentication measures include strong passwords and multifactor authentication.

- *Encryption* is the process of encoding data to prevent unauthorized access. *Decryption* is the process of decoding the data. Two common encryption approaches are:
  - Symmetric key encryption involves one key for both encryption and decryption.
  - Public key encryption pairs a public key for encryption and a private key for decryption.

- *Phishing* is a technique that attempts to trick a user into providing personal information. That personal information can then be used to access sensitive online resources, such as bank accounts and emails.

- *Keylogging* is the use of a program to record every keystroke made by a computer user in order to gain fraudulent access to passwords and other confidential information.

o   *Malware* is software intended to damage a computing system or to take partial control over its operation. This is often found on suspicious or free programs.

o   A *computer virus* is a malicious program that can copy itself and gain access to a computer in an unauthorized way. Computer viruses often attach themselves to legitimate programs and start running independently on a computer.

o   Data sent over public networks can be intercepted, analyzed, and modified. One way that this can happen is through a rogue access point.

o   A *rogue access point* is a wireless access point that gives unauthorized access to secure networks.

o   A malicious link can be disguised on a web page or in an email message.

Chapter 8
End of Chapter
Drill Answers and
Explanations

CHAPTER 4

1. **D** Metadata is a data about data, information that gives more details about the data itself. In this case, the time at which the song was recorded, while useful information is not information about the song itself.

2.

00110001_2	49_{10}
11100000_2	224_{10}
11000011_2	195_{10}
11110010_2	242_{10}
10010100_2	148_{10}
10101110_2	174_{10}
1101000_2	104_{10}
01011100_2	92_{10}
00001100_2	12_{10}
10111111_2	191_{10}

3.

123_{10}	01111011_2
210_{10}	11010010_2
75_{10}	01001011_2
103_{10}	01100111_2
25_{10}	00011001_2
77_{10}	01001101_2
235_{10}	11101011_2
102_{10}	01100110_2
200_{10}	11001000_2
45_{10}	00101101_2

4. **C** Choice (D), while true, is not really an advantage. Choice (C) is the advantage of lossy compression. Choices (A) and (B) are not valid responses.

5. **D** This is true because even a slightest loss of information may cause the program to not run. Images, video and music files can withstand some loss of data and retain the quality of data after transmission and decompression.

CHAPTER 5

1. **C** In most programming languages variables are assigned data using the assignment statement. Boolean is a special type of data type that holds only 2 values, true or false. The other data types are int, double, string, etc.

2. **A** A variable or a list is a data abstraction; when the programmer creates a variable, it is a collection of characters, numbers or strings. But the value of the variable is stored in the computer's memory as a bunch of bits. This is data abstraction or information hiding. Choice (D) is a process used to solve a problem. Choices (B) and (C) deals with procedures and not with variables, which is what the question is about.

3. **A** In most programming languages when dealing with the arrays, the first element in an array starts with a 0. However, in the Exam Reference Sheet, the index value starts with 1, and it is important to pay attention to this detail.

4. **A** An algorithm is a detailed step-by-step process used to solve a problem. While (B) and (C) may be true, they are not part of the definition of an algorithm. An algorithm can be written in English, pseudocode, or any other programming language.

5. **C** Strings are formed by a list (or an array) of characters. Most programming languages "add" strings together, which really means concatenation.

6. **B** The logical operators are OR and AND. In most programming languages, (A) is the symbol usually for assignment statements and (C) and (D) are symbols for arithmetic operators.

7. **A** Sequencing (where one actions leads to the next in a predetermined order), selection (also called decision statements, IF statements) and iteration (repetition) are considered building blocks of algorithms. Sequencing has to be a part of every algorithm. Selection and Repetition are very important, and most algorithms need these blocks to solve harder problems.

8. **C** Different algorithms for the same problem have different levels are efficiency, including ones that are so inefficient they become impractical to use, so eliminate (A). Although it may be possible to calculate the memory the algorithm will use for variable storage, memory used for executing the instructions can vary in different executions, so eliminate (B). Algorithms are informal descriptions of a program, so they don't have to follow a set format. Eliminate (D). Any problem can be solved in multiple ways, perhaps slight tweaks of another method or most drastic changes. The answer is (C).

9. **A** Procedural abstraction is, by definition, the use of a function to perform a particular repeated task so that the programmer only needs to be concerned with the end result of the function call. Thus, by using abstraction, the programmer can call a function anytime a particular task is required rather than recreating the individual steps of the task on every instance. The answer is (A).

10. **D** All of the answer choices are valid statements about simulations. Choice (B) is a formal definition of simulations. Choices (A) and (C) are advantages of simulations.

CHAPTER 6

1. **A** Bandwidth is measured as bits per second (bps).

2. **B** The path that the data takes when it is sent from one computer to another is called a route.

3. **A** Open Internet protocol standards allow anyone to set up a service online using the appropriate and established protocol; no permission is required from anyone else to make it available to everyone on the Internet. While (B), (C), and (D) may be true, that is not why they are called open standards.

4. **C** The fact that there is more than one way to send data between two points on the Internet increases the reliability of the Internet. This idea of there being more than one route is called redundancy. The Internet system was designed with built-in redundancy. While (A), (B) and (D) are significant features of the Internet, they are not the reason the Internet is reliable.

5. **D** The World Wide Web is the different from the Internet. The Internet, which is a network of computers, is scalable and reliable with a fault-tolerant design build into the system. The WWW is one system (most user-friendly and popular) to access the Internet.

CHAPTER 7

1. **B** Choices (A) and (C) are not true. Choice (D), while true, is not a good reason to not approve a computing innovation.

2. **B** Choice (A) is not related to the digital divide or technology. Choices (C) and (D) existed in non-pandemic times.

3. **B** Statement III will not remove bias from the algorithm. Statements I and II are steps taken to solve the problem.

4. **A** The three key features of citizen science are that it is distributed, conducted by people using their own devices, and is scientific research. The other answer choices do not cover all the three features.

5. **B** The other features will help with crowdsourcing, are not needed for the process to be successful.

6. **D** The most important aspect of intellectual property is that users have to seek explicit permission or need to understand how to clearly acknowledge the contribution of the creator of the movie/song etc. The other answer choices may or may not be true in all cases.

7. **B**   Choice (B) is the practical solution. Choices (A) and (D) not be always possible. Choice (C) may not be needed in all cases.

8. **D**   Personally Identifiable Information is data that can be used to uniquely identify and individual. Name, age, and email can potential be used for this purpose.

9. **C, D** Choices (A) and (B) are computer hardware failures. Choices (C) and (D) are cyberattacks.

10. **B**   Encryption is the conversion of data from a readable format to an unreadable one. This is reversible. The reverse process is called decryption. Choice (C) can be used for encryption but does not support the definition stated in the question. Choice (D) is not related to the encryption/decryption

Part VI
Practice Tests

Practice Test 2

AP® Computer Science Principles Exam

SECTION I: Multiple-Choice Questions

DO NOT OPEN THIS BOOKLET UNTIL YOU ARE TOLD TO DO SO.

At a Glance
Total Time
2 hours
Number of Questions
70
Percent of Total Score
70%
Writing Instrument
Pencil required

Instructions

Section I of this examination contains 70 multiple-choice questions. Fill in only the ovals for numbers 1 through 70 on your answer sheet.

Indicate all of your answers to the multiple-choice questions on the answer sheet. No credit will be given for anything written in this exam booklet, but you may use the booklet for notes or scratch work. After you have decided which of the suggested answers is best, completely fill in the corresponding oval on the answer sheet. Give only one answer to each question. If you change an answer, be sure that the previous mark is erased completely. Here is a sample question and answer.

Sample Question   Sample Answer

Chicago is a
(A) state
(B) city
(C) country
(D) continent

Use your time effectively, working as quickly as you can without losing accuracy. Do not spend too much time on any one question. Go on to other questions and come back to the ones you have not answered if you have time. It is not expected that everyone will know the answers to all the multiple-choice questions.

About Guessing

Many candidates wonder whether or not to guess the answers to questions about which they are not certain. Multiple-choice scores are based on the number of questions answered correctly. Points are not deducted for incorrect answers, and no points are awarded for unanswered questions. Because points are not deducted for incorrect answers, you are encouraged to answer all multiple-choice questions. On any questions you do not know the answer to, you should eliminate as many choices as you can, and then select the best answer among the remaining choices.

GO ON TO THE NEXT PAGE.

Quick Reference

Instruction	Explanation
Assignment, Display, and Input	

Text:
 	
`a ← expression`
 	
Block:
 	
`a ◄── expression`
	Evaluates `expression` and then assigns a copy of the result to the variable a.

Text:
 	
`DISPLAY(expression)`
 	
Block:
 	
`DISPLAY expression`
	Displays the value of `expression`, followed by a space.

Text:
 	
`INPUT()`
 	
Block:
 	
`INPUT`
	Accepts a value from the user and returns the input value.

Arithmetic Operators and Numeric Procedures	

Text and Block:
 	
`a + b`
`a - b`
`a * b`
`a / b`
	The arithmetic operators +, -, *, and / are used to perform arithmetic on a and b.
	
	For example, `17 / 5` evaluates to `3.4`.
	
	The order of operations used in mathematics applies when evaluating expressions.

Text and Block: `a MOD b`	Evaluates to the remainder when a is divided by b. Assume that a is an integer greater than or equal to 0 and b is an integer greater than 0. For example, `17 MOD 5` evaluates to 2. The MOD operator has the same precedence as the * and / operators.

Text:
 	
`RANDOM(a, b)`
 	
Block:
 	
`RANDOM a, b`
	Generates and returns a random integer from a to b, including a and b. Each result is equally likely to occur.
	
	For example, `RANDOM(1, 3)` could return 1, 2, or 3.

Instruction	Explanation
Relational and Boolean Operators	
Text and Block: a = b a ≠ b a > b a < b a ≥ b a ≤ b	The relational operators =, ≠, >, <, ≤, and ≥ are used to test the relationship between two variables, expressions, or values. A comparison using relational operators evaluates to a Boolean value. For example, a = b evaluates to true if a and b are equal; otherwise it evaluates to false.
Text: NOT condition Block: NOT (condition)	Evaluates to true if condition is false; otherwise evaluates to false.
Text: condition1 AND condition2 Block: (condition1) AND (condition2)	Evaluates to true if both condition1 and condition2 are true; otherwise evaluates to false.
Text: condition1 OR condition2 Block: (condition1) OR (condition2)	Evaluates to true if condition1 is true or if condition2 is true or if both condition1 and condition2 are true; otherwise evaluates to false.
Selection	

Text:
 	
IF(condition)
 	
{
 	
\<block of statements>
 	
}
 	
Block:
 	
IF (condition)
    (block of statements)
	The code in block of statements is executed if the Boolean expression condition evaluates to true; no action is taken if condition evaluates to false.

Instruction	Explanation
Selection—Continued	

Text:
 	
`IF(condition)`
 	
`{`
 	
`<first block of statements>`
 	
`}`
 	
`ELSE`
 	
`{`
 	
`<second block of statements>`
 	
`}`
 	
Block:
 	
`IF (condition)`
`    first block of statements`
`ELSE`
`    second block of statements`
	The code in `first block of statements` is executed if the Boolean expression `condition` evaluates to `true`; otherwise the code in `second block of statements` is executed.

Iteration	

Text:
 	
`REPEAT n TIMES`
 	
`{`
 	
`<block of statements>`
 	
`}`
 	
Block:
 	
`REPEAT n TIMES`
`    block of statements`
	The code in `block of statements` is executed n times.

Text:
 	
`REPEAT UNTIL(condition)`
 	
`{`
 	
`<block of statements>`
 	
`}`
 	
Block:
 	
`REPEAT UNTIL (condition)`
`    block of statements`
	The code in `block of statements` is repeated until the Boolean expression `condition` evaluates to `true`.

Instruction	Explanation
List Operations	
For all list operations, if a list index is less than 1 or greater than the length of the list, an error message is produced and the program terminates.	

Text:
 	
`aList ← [value1, value2, value3, ...]`
 	
Block:
 	
`aList ◄── value1, value2, value3`
	Creates a new list that contains the values `value1`, `value2`, `value3`, and ... at indices 1, 2, 3, and ... respectively and assigns it to `aList`.

Text:
 	
`aList ← []`
 	
Block:
 	
`aList ◄── []`
	Creates an empty list and assigns it to `aList`.

Text:
 	
`aList ← bList`
 	
Block:
 	
`aList ◄── bList`
	Assigns a copy of the list bList to the list `aList`.
	
	For example, if `bList` contains [20, 40, 60], then `aList` will also contain [20, 40, 60] after the assignment.

Text:
 	
`aList[i]`
 	
Block:
 	
`aList i`
	Accesses the element of `aList` at index `i`. The first element of `aList` is at index 1 and is accessed using the notation `aList[1]`.

Text:
 	
`x ← aList[i]`
 	
Block:
 	
`x ◄── aList i`
	Assigns the value of `aList[i]` to the variable x.

Text:
 	
`aList[i] ← x`
 	
Block:
 	
`aList i ◄── x`
	Assigns the value of x to `aList[i]`.

Text:
 	
`aList[i] ← aList[j]`
 	
Block:
 	
`aList i ◄── aList j`
	Assigns the value of `aList[j]` to `aList[i]`.

Text:
 	
`INSERT(aList, i, value)`
 	
Block:
 	
`INSERT aList, i, value`
	Any values in `aList` at indices greater than or equal to `i` are shifted one position to the right. The length of the list is increased by 1, and `value` is placed at index `i` in `aList`.

Instruction	Explanation
List Operations—Continued	

Instruction	Explanation

Text:
 	
`APPEND(aList, value)`
 	
Block:
 	
`APPEND aList, value`
	The length of `aList` is increased by 1, and `value` is placed at the end of `aList`.

Text:
 	
`REMOVE(aList, i)`
 	
Block:
 	
`REMOVE aList, i`
	Removes the item at index `i` in `aList` and shifts to the left any values at indices greater than `i`. The length of `aList` is decreased by 1.

Text:
 	
`LENGTH(aList)`
 	
Block:
 	
`LENGTH aList`
	Evaluates to the number of elements in `aList`.

Text:
 	
`FOR EACH item IN aList`
`{`
`<block of statements>`
`}`
 	
Block:
 	
`FOR EACH item IN aList`
`block of statements`
	The variable `item` is assigned the value of each element of `aList` sequentially, in order, from the first element to the last element. The code in `block of statements` is executed once for each assignment of `item`.

Procedures and Procedure Calls	

Text:
 	
`PROCEDURE procName(parameter1,`
`                parameter2, ...)`
`{`
`<block of statements>`
`}`
 	
Block:
 	
`PROCEDURE procName parameter1,`
`                   parameter2, ...`
`block of statements`
	Defines `procName` as a procedure that takes zero or more arguments. The procedure contains `block of statements`.
	
	The procedure `procName` can be called using the following notation, where `arg1` is assigned to `parameter1`, `arg2` is assigned to `parameter2`, etc.:
	`procName(arg1, arg2, ...)`

Instruction	Explanation
Procedures and Procedure Calls—Continued	

Text:
 	
`PROCEDURE procName(parameter1,`
`                parameter2, ...)`
 	
`{`
`<block of statements>`
`RETURN(expression)`
`}`
 	
Block:
 	
```PROCEDURE procName parameter1,``` `parameter2, ...`
```block of statements```
```RETURN expression```
	Defines `procName` as a procedure that takes zero or more arguments. The procedure contains `block of statements` and returns the value of `expression`. The `RETURN` statement may appear at any point inside the procedure and causes an immediate return from the procedure back to the calling statement.
	
	The value returned by the procedure `procName` can be assigned to the variable `result` using the following notation:
	`result ← procName(arg1, arg2, ...)`

Text:
 	
`RETURN(expression)`
 	
Block:
```RETURN expression```
	Returns the flow of control to the point where the procedure was called and returns the value of `expression`.

Robot	
If the robot attempts to move to a square that is not open or is beyond the edge of the grid, the robot will stay in its current location and the program will terminate.	

Text:
 	
`MOVE_FORWARD()`
 	
Block:
```MOVE_FORWARD```
	The robot moves one square forward in the direction it is facing.

Text:
 	
`ROTATE_LEFT()`
 	
Block:
```ROTATE_LEFT```
	The robot rotates in place 90 degrees counterclockwise (i.e., makes an in-place left turn).

Text:
 	
`ROTATE_RIGHT()`
 	
Block:
```ROTATE_RIGHT```
	The robot rotates in place 90 degrees clockwise (i.e., makes an in-place right turn).

Text:
 	
`CAN_MOVE(direction)`
 	
Block:
```CAN_MOVE direction```
	Evaluates to `true` if there is an open square one square in the direction relative to where the robot is facing; otherwise evaluates to `false`. The value of `direction` can be `left`, `right`, `forward`, or `backward`.

This page intentionally left blank.

GO ON TO THE NEXT PAGE.

COMPUTER SCIENCE PRINCIPLES
SECTION I
Time—2 hours
Number of Questions—70
Percent of total exam grade—70%

Directions: Choose one best answer for each question. Some questions at the end of the test will have more than one correct answer; for these, you will be instructed to choose two answer choices.

1. The metadata from an image you took was released. Which of the following information could not be determined from the metadata?

    (A) The names of the people in the picture
    (B) Where you took the picture
    (C) When you took the picture
    (D) Size of the image

2. A student is designing a new classroom library record system. She has based it on 9 bits. How many possible books can she store in the library?

    (A) 18
    (B) 81
    (C) 511
    (D) 512

3. Which of the following would be an example of multifactor authentication?

    (A) Requiring a password to log in to the main website and an additional password to enter a chatroom feature of the website
    (B) Requiring an email to verify joining a website
    (C) Requiring both a text message code and password to log in to a website
    (D) Allowing users to setup a password or use their fingerprint to log in to an application

4. Elon Musk, CEO of SpaceX, is currently planning a launch of thousands of Starlink satellites which will create constellations that can offer high-speed Internet anywhere on the planet. The plan is to ultimately create an interconnected network of about 12,000 small satellites in low orbit around Earth. Which of the following descriptions best describes his actions?

    (A) Through the launching of these satellites, Elon Musk is increasing the chance of crowdsourcing.
    (B) Elon Musk and SpaceX's actions will most likely help reduce the digital divide.
    (C) Elon Musk and his Starlink satellites are an example of citizen science.
    (D) Starlink satellites will most likely become a rogue access point.

GO ON TO THE NEXT PAGE.

5. The following grid contains a robot represented as a triangle. The robot is initially facing right. Which of the following code lines can replace the missing code to move the robot to the grey square?

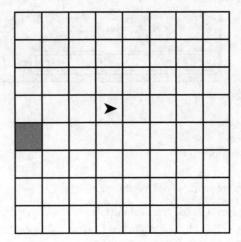

```
REPEAT 3 TIMES
{
    <missing code>
}
MOVE_FORWARD()
REPEAT 2 TIMES
{
    ROTATE_LEFT()
    MOVE_FORWARD()
}
ROTATE_RIGHT()
MOVE_FORWARD()
MOVE_FORWARD()


(A)  MOVE_FORWARD()
     ROTATE_RIGHT()
(B)  ROTATE_RIGHT()
     MOVE_FORWARD()
(C)  MOVE_FORWARD()
     ROTATE_LEFT()
(D)  ROTATE_LEFT()
     MOVE_FORWARD()
```

GO ON TO THE NEXT PAGE.

6. A teacher is dividing her students in groups of 3 for an in-class project. She has created a computer program that will tell her whether or not she is able to equally distribute her students into groups of 3. Which of the following can replace the missing code to evaluate whether her classes can be divided into groups of 3 students evenly?

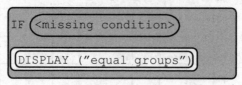

```
IF (<missing condition>)
    DISPLAY ("equal groups")
```

(A) numStudents MOD 2 + 1 = 3
(B) numStudents MOD 3 = 0
(C) numStudents / 3 = 0
(D) numStudents / 3 - 3 = 0

7. Which of the following best describes an example of crowdsourcing?

(A) In 2020, similar to the past 12 years, Google released the Google Doodle challenge, which asked students to design a doodle that expressed kindness. This challenge allowed Google to deepen their engagement with users.
(B) Code.org presents Hour of Code each year for students to engage in different types of coding to promote the idea that anyone can code.
(C) FoxSports.com streams the Super Bowl to allow anyone with Internet access to watch the game free. This increased the availability of the Super Bowl to many people.
(D) In July 2020, Loon, a part of Google's parent company Alphabet, launched high-altitude balloons in Kenya to deliver the Internet to rural and remote areas. These balloons would allow more people access to the Internet.

8. Which of the following provides an example of identity theft in relation to Personally Identifiable Information?

(A) You receive an email from your bank stating that your savings and checking accounts have been locked because of suspicious withdrawals. The email instructs you to click on the link in order to reset your passwords and receive more details about the suspicious activity.
(B) A friend sends you an email with an attachment. You expect that it's something important and download it. Your computer then starts acting strange and is slow responding.
(C) Your credit report shows a fraudulent identity, where your social security number has been combined with fake details. This identity was used to file a tax return and open several credit card accounts.
(D) A friend posts on social media from your account, pretending to be you.

9. A picture has been compressed and each pixel value was averaged and converted to greyscale. Which of the following statements, best describes the compression?

(A) The original image cannot be restored since the above compression was lossy compression.
(B) The original image cannot be restored since the above compression was lossless compression.
(C) The original image can be restored since the above compression was lossy compression.
(D) The original image can be restored since the above compression was lossless compression.

GO ON TO THE NEXT PAGE.

10. The following data table below shows how long each of the processes take depending on the number of binary bits.

Task	8 bits	80 bits	800 bits
Backing up an audio file	0.5 seconds	2.0 seconds	8 seconds
Creating a copy of an audio file	1 second	2 second	3 second
Searching an audio file	0.5 seconds	5 seconds	50 seconds
Deleting an audio file	0.25 seconds	0.75 seconds	2.25 seconds

Using this information, which of the following would take the shortest amount of time for 1000 bytes?

(A) Deleting an audio file
(B) Backing up an audio file
(C) Searching an audio file
(D) Creating a copy of an audio file

11. Which of the following descriptions shows computing bias for the facial recognition system?

(A) Sylvia uses facial recognition in order to open the doors of her apartment when she is carrying heavy bags, but it doesn't allow the delivery driver access.
(B) The facial recognition system is being used in the subway to reduce crime but not for fare collection and subway access.
(C) In China, interlocking facial recognition cameras track where people are, what they are up to, and who they associate with—and are ultimately used to help assign people a single score based on whether the government considers them trustworthy.
(D) Rekognition, Amazon's face-ID system, once identified Oprah Winfrey as male and is why many companies are abandoning facial recognition research.

12. Currently, the list of processes below are being completed sequentially. Since there are 2 processors available, what 2 processes could be done in parallel to best improve execution time?

Task	Processing Time
X	110 sec
Y	85 sec
Z	20 sec

(A) Y and Z would be done sequentially and X would be run parallel.
(B) X and Y would be done sequentially and Z would be run parallel.
(C) Z and Y would be done sequentially and X would be run parallel.
(D) Execution time would not be improved by running a parallel process.

GO ON TO THE NEXT PAGE.

13. What type of data is returned by the following procedure, equalNums?

```
PROCEDURE equalNums(num)
{
    counter ← 1
    done ← true
    REPEAT UNTIL(counter ≥ num)
    {
        counter ← counter + 1
    }
    IF (counter > num)
    {
        done ← false
    }
    DISPLAY(counter)
    RETURN (done)
}
```

(A) Boolean
(B) String
(C) Number
(D) Expression

14. Space-X has provided a set of criteria to determine whether an applicant is eligible for the next Mars mission. The person must be between the ages of 25 through 35, inclusive, and must be able to lift 50 lbs. The algorithm has a variable called age which represents the applicant's age and a variable called capable which stores the amount of weight an applicant can lift. Which of the following Boolean expressions will correctly evaluate whether an applicant is allowed to go on the next Mars mission?

(A) age ≥ 25 OR (age ≤ 35 AND capable ≥ 50)
(B) age ≥ 25 OR age ≤ 35 AND capable ≥ 50
(C) (age ≥ 25 AND age ≤ 35) AND capable ≥ 50
(D) age > 25 OR age < 35 OR capable ≥ 50

15. For which of the following situations below would it be best to use a heuristic in order to find a solution that runs in a reasonable amount of time?

   I. How many moves it will take for a computer to beat a human player
  II. Finding the route to multiple desired destinations
 III. Calculating student GPA

(A) II only
(B) I and II only
(C) III only
(D) I, II, and III

GO ON TO THE NEXT PAGE.

16. Comparing the 2 algorithms below, which statement best compares time and identifies the algorithm that runs faster, given that calling the procedure `countX()` takes approximately 1 minute to run each time it is called?

Algorithm A

```
x ← 0
y ← 0
REPEAT n TIMES {
    x = countX();
}
REPEAT n TIMES {
    y = countX();
}
```

Algorithm B

```
x ← 0
y ← 0
REPEAT n TIMES {

    REPEAT n TIMES {
        countX();
    }
}
```

(A) Both algorithms take the same amount of time.

(B) Algorithm B is faster as it takes 2 * n minutes to run, while Algorithm A takes 4 * n minutes to run.

(C) Algorithm A is faster as it takes 4 * n minutes to run, while Algorithm B takes 8 * n minutes to run.

(D) Algorithm A is faster as it 2 * n minutes to run, while Algorithm B takes 1 * n^2 minutes to run

GO ON TO THE NEXT PAGE.

17. Given the following network configurations, which shows fault tolerance due to redundancy between terminals A and C?

   I.   Network A

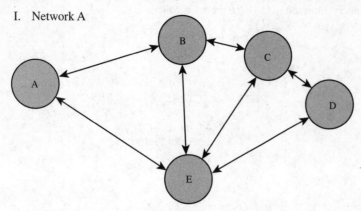

   II. Network B

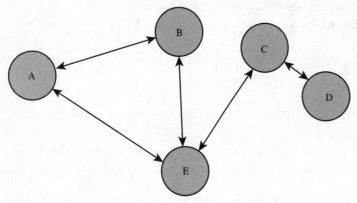

   III. Network C

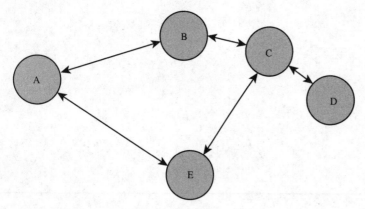

   (A) I, II, and III
   (B) I only
   (C) I and III only
   (D) I and II only

GO ON TO THE NEXT PAGE.

18. Which of the following situations shows the use of Creative Commons?

    (A) Sally needs images of dogs for her presentation at school, she googles pictures of dogs and, even though they are copyrighted, she doesn't have to credit the photographer.

    (B) Preston is working on creating a new song to raise money by putting together sounds others have created; he uses audio clips which he found that had an attribution license.

    (C) Mrs. Alexander photocopies pages out of her book to share with students in her class who haven't purchased the book.

    (D) Steven quotes and cites an author who he interviewed for his book report.

19. Which of the following shows is NOT an example of phishing?

    (A) A user installs new software that they downloaded and then notices their computer is running slower and unexpected pop-up windows appear while browsing the Internet.

    (B) The user receives a link to a spoofed version of a popular website, designed to look like the real one, that asks them to confirm or update their account credentials.

    (C) Using an email address of the CEO of the company, the email asks the user to install a new app on their computer.

    (D) An email alerts users that there is an issue with their order and to confirm their payment information by opening the attachment and responding via email.

20. Given the following code, which expression is equivalent to the output displayed after this code segment is run?

```
x ← 8
y ← 5

REPEAT UNTIL(x < y)
{
    y ← y - 2
    x ← x - 5
}
DISPLAY (x*y)
```

    (A) 4 + 3 * -2 / 7
    (B) 4 + 3 * -2 / 1
    (C) 2 - 14 * -6 / 1
    (D) -2 + 14 * -2 / 4

21.

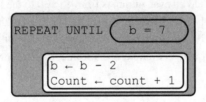

```
REPEAT UNTIL ( b = 7 )

    b ← b - 2
    Count ← count + 1
```

Currently the programmer wants this loop to take a value of b and decrease it until the value of b is 7 and count how many times it takes to change the value of b to 7. Unfortunately, it only works part of the time. What code could be changed to ensure that it works regardless of the value of b initially?

    (A) Change condition for b to be equal to or greater than 7
    (B) Change so that it sets b to 7 in loop
    (C) Change so loop will repeat n times
    (D) Change so that b is decreased by 1 each time

GO ON TO THE NEXT PAGE.

22. Steve has created 2 variables which hold integer values named num1 and num2. He needs to switch the values held in these variables so that the data in num1 is now contained in num2 and the data in num2 will now be contained in num1. Which of the following codes below will switch the data correctly?

(A) num2 ← num1
    num ← num2
    num1 ← num2

(B) temp ← num2
    num1 ← num2
    num2 ← temp

(C) temp ← num1
    num1 ← num2
    num2 ← temp

(D) num1 ← num2
    num2 ← num1

23. A programmer wants to write code which will evaluate each number from 1 to 30 and determine whether it is an odd number. Odd numbers will be added to the list oddNum and displayed. Evaluate the 2 code segments below to determine whether they will output the correct list.

Code Segment #1

```
oddNum ← []
number ← 1
REPEAT 30 TIMES
{
    IF(number MOD 2 = 1)
    {
    oddNum[number] ← number
    }
    number ← number + 1
}
DISPLAY(oddNum)
```

Code Segment #2

```
oddNum ← []
number ← 1
REPEAT 30 TIMES
{
    IF(number MOD 2 = 0)
    {
        APPEND(oddNum, number + 1)
    }
    number ← number + 1
}
DISPLAY(oddNum)
```

(A) Both code segments will correctly add all even numbers from 1 to 30 to the list.
(B) Only Code segment #1 will correctly add all even numbers from 1 to 30 to the list.
(C) Only Code segment #2 will correctly add all even numbers from 1 to 30 to the list.
(D) Neither code segment will correctly add all even numbers from 1 to 30 to the list.

GO ON TO THE NEXT PAGE.

24. The following code segment should allow a person to know how much the wind is blowing: If wind is less than 2 miles per hour, it should output "no wind at all"; if between 2 and 5 mph, it should output "a light breeze"; if greater than 15 mph but less than 30, it should say "getting gusty"; and if greater than 30 mph, it should say "make sure to hold on." The following conditional statement does not function properly for all cases.

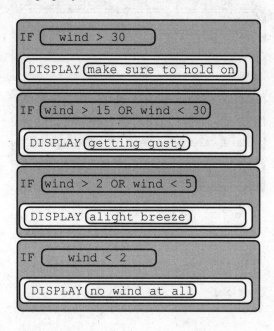

Which of the following corrections would allow the code to work for all cases?

(A) Make IF statements nested

(B) Reverse the order of the IF statements

(C) Change the OR to AND in both complex IF statements

(D) Make all comparisons for Boolean conditions greater than or less than and equal to

25. The `createNew` procedure takes 2 string parameters and concatenates the first 2 letters of the first string parameter in reverse order with the last 2 letters of the second string parameter and return a string. The precondition of the procedure is that all strings will have a length greater than 3. Which of the following inputs will correctly create a variable name word containing "acid"?

(A) `word ← createNew(acute, rapid)`

(B) `word ← createNew(castle, avoid)`

(C) `word ← createNew(car, paid)`

(D) `word ← createNew(caper, disk)`

GO ON TO THE NEXT PAGE.

26.

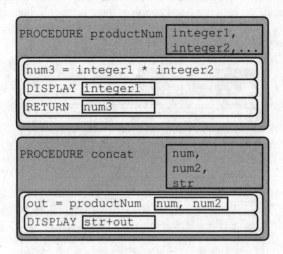

What is displayed as a result of the procedure call concat(3,5, " answer ")?

(A) 3 answer 5

(B) 15 answer 15

(C) 5 answer 3

(D) 3 answer 15

27. Procedure doSomething takes in 2 parameters, a list and integer, and follows the following algorithm.

1. Let min be the value at the first index of the list and max be the value at the last index of the list.
2. If max < min, then stop: target is not present in array. Return –1.
3. Compute mid as the average of max and min, rounded down (so that it is an integer).
4. If array[guess] equals target, then stop. Return guess.
5. If the guess was too low, that is, array[guess] < target, then set min = guess + 1.
6. Otherwise, the guess was too high. Set max = guess – 1.
7. Go back to step 2, repeat until procedure returns –1 or guess.

Which of the following are true statements about the procedure?

 I. It implements a binary search.
 II. It implements a sort of list from greatest to least.
III. It only works as intended when the list is sorted.

(A) I only

(B) II only

(C) I and III only

(D) II and III only

GO ON TO THE NEXT PAGE.

28. A flowchart is a way to visually represent an algorithm. The flowchart below is used to display a message under certain Boolean conditions. The flowchart uses the integer variable max.

Block	Explanation
Oval	The start or end of the algorithm
Diamond	A conditional or decision step, where execution proceeds to the side labeled true if the condition is true and to the side labeled false otherwise
Rectangle	One or more processing steps, such as a statement that assigns a value to a variable

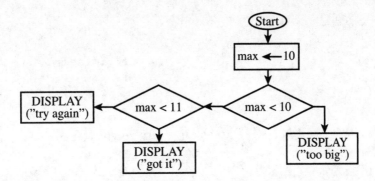

What is displayed as a result of executing the algorithm in the flowchart?

(A) Got it

(B) Too big

(C) Try again

(D) Not enough information is provided to determine the output.

29.

```
IF(closed)
{
        DISPLAY("Check back")
}
ELSE
{
        IF(code < 10)
        {
            DISPLAY("Open in next hour")
        }
        ELSE
        {
            DISPLAY("Open Now")
        }
}
```

If the variable closed has the value false and code has the value of 10, what is displayed as a result of running the code segment above?

(A) Check back

(B) Open in next hour

(C) Check back Open in next hour

(D) Open Now

GO ON TO THE NEXT PAGE.

30. The division of motor vehicles uses the following system to determine whether a driver needs to take a driving test, which is stored in a Boolean variable called `test`. The program for the system contains 2 variables: `age`, which holds a numeric value for the applicant's age, and class, which is a Boolean variable, whether or not they have taken a class. Which of the following code segments correctly sets the value of `test` variable?

Fifteen-year-old drivers need to have taken a course but do not require a driving test. Those drivers 16 years and older must take a course but are still required to take a driving test.

(A)
```
test ← false
IF (class)
{
    test ← true
}
IF (age = 15)
{
    test ← false
}
```

(B)
```
test ← false
IF (class)
{
    test ← true
}
IF (age ≥ 16)
{
    test ← false
}
```

(C)
```
test ← false
IF (age ≠ 16)
{
    test ← false
}
IF (class)
{
    test ← true
}
```

(D)
```
test ← true
IF (age < 16)
{
    test ← false
}
IF (class)
{
    test ← true
}
```

GO ON TO THE NEXT PAGE.

31. Which of the following code segments will allow the robot to get to the grey square from its current position?

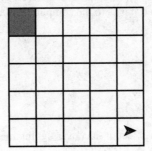

```
PROCEDURE TARGET(steps)
over ← steps/2
     REPEAT over TIMES
     {
         ROTATE LEFT()
         REPEAT steps TIMES
         {
              FORWARD()
         }
     }
```

(A) TARGET(2)

(B) TARGET(4)

(C) TARGET(1)

(D) TARGET(5)

32.

```
list ← [5, 3, 12, 8, 9, 10]
a ← 1
b ← LENGTH(list)

REPEAT UNTIL (b < a)
{
    temp ← list[a]
    list[a] ← list[b]
    list[b] ← temp
    a++
    b--
}
```

Which of the following describes what is contained in the variable list after the code above runs?

(A) 5, 3, 12, 8, 9, 10

(B) 10, 9, 8, 12, 3, 5

(C) 10, 9, 8, 5, 3, 12

(D) 10, 9, 8, 12, 5, 3

GO ON TO THE NEXT PAGE.

33. The police contacted Claire because they believed her identity had been stolen. New credit card accounts were opened with her personal information and certain existing accounts had been accessed by someone other than her. The police determined that software on her computer was recording all inputs to the computer and transmitting that data to another user. This best describes what type of cyberthreat?

    (A) Malware
    (B) Phishing
    (C) Virus
    (D) Keylogger

34. Which of the following are true about the movement of data over the Internet?

    (A) If a packet is not received or is "dropped," all packets, not just the dropped packet, need to be resent.
    (B) Packets of data must be delivered in the same order they were sent otherwise the data will be corrupted.
    (C) Packets may choose longer paths as they process the information and addressing data.
    (D) A packet is divided into three parts; the header, payload and trailer, either containing data or address information so that the packet will be able to put together at the desired destination.

35. What is the benefit of having fault-tolerant Internet routing?

    (A) Fault tolerance increases downtime, which may cause substantial data loss.
    (B) Fault tolerance allows the reduction of redundancy allowing for best cost efficiency of the system.
    (C) Fault tolerance allows packets to follow the same paths, which allows for more traceability of data.
    (D) Fault tolerance increases the complexity of the Internet and has worked so well that so far no one has managed to break the entire Internet.

36. Which of the following demonstrates the largest privacy concern?

    (A) Katherine's bank sends her an email asking her to call her local branch about a potential security breach.
    (B) A website uses cookies to track what users do when they visit it.
    (C) When Anna searches using Google, the company is able to share data from its search engine across a wide variety of services, including 3rd party companies.
    (D) Steve logs on to the personal Wi-Fi at his home.

37. Which of the following would NOT be an unethical use of computer technology?

    (A) Looking up code for to an assignment that you are struggling with as you prepare for the Create Task
    (B) Weird Al Yankovic using the instrumental composition of the song "Smells Like Teen Spirit" as a base for his own lyrics, which poke fun at the band Nirvana
    (C) Downloading the newest Star Wars movie since you aren't able to go see it in the theater
    (D) A student putting images in his presentation from the Internet without checking the sources to determine copyright

38. Which of the following cannot be represented by a single binary digit?

    (A) Result in MOD
    (B) Grade in school
    (C) Black and white pixels in an image
    (D) Position of a light switch

GO ON TO THE NEXT PAGE.

39. Which of the following best describes lossless compression?

(A) A sound file is compressed and now has reduced size of data but has reduced sound quality.

(B) A sound file is compressed and emailed and when it reaches final recipient it is restored to its original details, quality, and size.

(C) An image file has been compressed by averaging each color of pixel.

(D) A sound file is compressed by removing all redundant sounds in the file.

40. In Florida, sharks are tagged to provide information on the health of the different species and also migration patterns. Tags that researchers place on sharks collect the following information.

- Location of shark
- Speed of shark
- Internal temperature of shark
- Depth of shark movements

Additionally, when the shark is tagged, data is collected on the species and gender of it.

What cannot be determined by this data alone?

(A) Whether sharks travel in groups

(B) Average body temperature of great white sharks

(C) How fast sharks can swim while in 30' deep water

(D) How location of shark causes a change in body temperature and speed

41. The bookstore assigns a binary number to each reading level in the children's book section. Reading level 0 are picture books and those in the young adult section are assigned 1011101, which is equal to what decimal number?

(A) 93

(B) 101

(C) 109

(D) 189

42. Which best describes the terms Internet and World Wide Web?

(A) Both are the same and are interchangeable terms.

(B) The World Wide Web is what the Internet was called before it expanded to be world wide.

(C) The Internet is a link of computers and servers, while the World Wide Web is a protocol which specifies how people can use the Internet.

(D) World Wide Web is a system of linked pages, programs, and files and it uses the Internet.

43. During a storm, Bob's computer is having difficulty loading websites, and when they do load, they seem to take a much longer time than normal. Which best describes what could being occurring?

(A) The storm is causing issues and the network is fault-tolerant, which is causing a slow connection.

(B) Because of lower available bandwidth, Bob's computer is having issues loading the websites.

(C) Redundancy is causing Bob's computer to be slow when loading web pages.

(D) Packets may have not arrived at the correct router, which is causing Bob's computer to be unable to load the web page.

GO ON TO THE NEXT PAGE.

44. Johnny snaps his friend via SnapChat and tells him about a party in which there was illegal activity that he went to. He then realizes that this wasn't smart and deletes it. The following week, his school principal calls him into the office to discuss the party. Which best describes how this occurred?

    (A) Johnny's friend had to tell the principal because since Johnny deleted the message it is not possible for the data to be available.

    (B) The principal is able to see snap messages that Johnny sent as it is public information.

    (C) The principal is talking to all students in the high school about the party and doesn't know if Johnny was there or not.

    (D) It is possible Johnny's snap was reshared or used for an unintended purpose even if he deleted it because once information is placed online it is very difficult completely delete.

45. Which of the following statements are most true about program documentation?

    (A) Program documentation is not required as it is mostly a tool for unskilled programmers and those just learning who do not know to make descriptive variable names.

    (B) Program documentation only needs to be done when the program is complete; otherwise it is redundant.

    (C) Programming documentation should be done throughout program development so that what code segments do and how they were developed is documented.

    (D) Documentation is only required if you use code from other sources.

46. When making a program, a student encounters code that, although it has no syntax issues and runs, it still does not work correctly. What type of error is most likely occurring?

    (A) Syntax error
    (B) Run-time error
    (C) A user error
    (D) A logic error

GO ON TO THE NEXT PAGE.

47. What explanation best fits the data about Monthly Revenue over different periods of time in the graphs shown below?

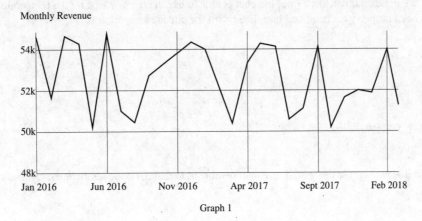

Graph 1

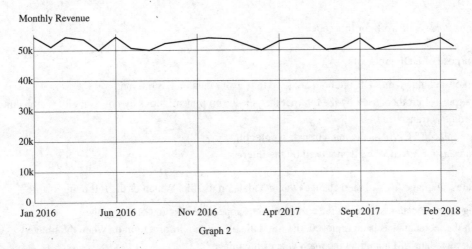

Graph 2

(A) Monthly revenue for these years was almost identical as shown by Graph 2. Graph 1 must show outlier data.

(B) Although the data looks fairly stable, when the axis is adjusted to better fit the data range, the visualization in Graph 1 shows there was variation across these years.

(C) The 2 graphs must be 2 different data sets as they show different information and trends.

(D) In order to best understand what is occurring with monthly revenue over these years, more data must be analyzed.

GO ON TO THE NEXT PAGE.

48. A chef is unable to use the ovens in the kitchen when their temperature is at or below 120° C. The following code segment is intended to print a message indicating whether or not the chef is able to use the ovens based on the temperature. Assume that the variable degrees has been properly declared and initialized with the outside temperature.

```
IF (degrees ≥ 120)
{
    DISPLAY("Ovens can be used")
}
ELSE
{
    DISPLAY("Ovens cannot be operated")
}
```

Which of the following initializations for degrees, if any, will demonstrate that the code segment may not work as intended?

(A) degrees = 120
(B) degrees = 119
(C) degrees = 130
(D) All initializations will work for this code.

49. What is the purpose of UDP protocol?

(A) UDP is more reliable than TCP, but both are used to transfer data on the Internet.
(B) UDP is a transfer protocol used by the Internet that speeds up transmissions by not formally establishing a connection before data is transferred.
(C) UDP has replaced TCP/IP as the main transfer protocol.
(D) UDP is a transport protocol but is not used by the Internet.

50. A student creates an image file and then changes the metadata on the file. Which of the following is true?

(A) Changing the metadata may impact the colors or other appearance factors of the image.
(B) Although the metadata has been removed, the file will still contain information on when the image was created.
(C) Changing metadata will not affect the main data of the image.
(D) When metadata is deleted, it will not impact the image file size.

51. Which of the following is not an effective tool for extracting information from a large dataset?

(A) Search tools
(B) Data filtering systems
(C) Visualization of data through graphs and charts
(D) Compressing data

GO ON TO THE NEXT PAGE.

52. Which of the following lines in the code segment show a data abstraction?

```
Line 1:    DISPLAY ("Welcome to the Random Number Picker")
Line 2:    DISPLAY ("Do you want to get a random number")
Line 3:    user ← INPUT()
Line 4:    numbers ← [5,12,7,3,0,9]
Line 5:    REPEAT UNTIL(user == "no")
Line 6:    {
Line 7:         choice ← RANDOM(1,LENGTH(numbers)-1)
Line 8:         DISPLAY(numbers[choice])
Line 9:         DISPLAY ("Do you want to get a random number")
Line 10:        user ← INPUT()
Line 11:   }
```

(A) Line 5

(B) Line 3

(C) Line 4

(D) Line 7

53. A new grading system is being used at High Valley High School. The grade average will be calculated traditionally, but the lowest and highest grades will be eliminated. The following procedures have been created:

1. `NumberGrades()` calculates how many grades are inputted by the user.
2. `MaxGrade()` finds the maximum grade inputted.
3. `MinGrade()` finds the minimum grade inputted.
4. `SumGrades()` finds the sum of all grades inputted.

Which of the following sequences will correctly calculate the grade average according to the new system?

(A) First `MaxGrade()` and `MinGrade()` are subtracted from `SumGrades()` and then divided by `NumberGrades()`

(B) `SumGrades()` divided by `NumberGrades()` minus 2

(C) `SumGrades()` divided by `NumGrades()` minus `MaxGrade()` minus `MinGrade()`

(D) First `MaxGrade()` and `MinGrade()` are subtracted from `SumGrades()` and then divided by `NumberGrades()` minus 2

54. Consider the following code segment.

```
oldValues = [true, false, true, true]
Values2 = []
for EACH item IN oldValues
{
    IF (item)
    {
        APPEND(Values2, item)
    }
}
```

What, if anything, will be the contents of `Values2` as a result of executing the code segment?

(A) [true, false, true, true]

(B) [true, true, true]

(C) []

(D) [false]

GO ON TO THE NEXT PAGE.

55. A medical device R&D team has a new drug delivery system to test and plans to use a simulation. Which of the following is NOT an advantage of using simulation?

(A) A simulation will allow researchers to help find unexpected behavior of the drug delivery system.

(B) Running a simulation will lessen the cost of developing the new drug delivery system.

(C) A simulation of a drug delivery system can allow researchers to examine possible long-term effects of system itself.

(D) A simulation will allow a greater population to understand all possible effects of the new drug delivery system without having complete knowledge of the system.

56. Computing innovations can be used in ways their original inventors did not intend or imagine. Which of the following is an unintended consequence of 3D printing?

(A) Production of small tools and parts for robotics has become easily accessible and has no health, monetary, or proprietary down-sides.

(B) Toy makers may lose millions and have had to deal with increased piracy issues.

(C) Model making for architects and designers is becoming an increasingly specialized field.

(D) 3D printing is less of a health risk than most manufacturing processes, which has led to a healthier workforce.

57. How does the computer system verify that a website is secure?

(A) The server hosting the website will present a digital certificate and your browser determines whether it is trusted.

(B) The trust model allows you to trust any website which claims it is secure without verification.

(C) Secure websites automatically encrypt all data using symmetric encryption.

(D) Computer systems use standard protocols to determine ownership by examining the IP address of the website.

Questions 58–62 refer to the information below:

A company is developing an upgrade to its VR system. The current system uses a full room of equipment to create an experience so that a person is able to look around the artificial world, move around in it, and interact with virtual features or items. The new upgraded system will use a headset for a similar experience. Both systems incorporate sensory and force feedback that collect data on position, movement, and response, using haptic technology to ensure an immersive experience. The old system was a stationary system and used a single static IP at the company's location. A user would enter their height and gender in order to start a simulation each time they used the system. Data was collected on simulations and haptic sensor data.

The new headset has a built-in screen processor and battery, as well as several viewfinders that provide stable spatial orientation and position recognition relative to the coordinates of peripheral devices. A single processor is self-contained in the headset, in comparison to the older model which used to render better, higher quality images. The new system is able to be used with any stable Internet connection and will enable users to create an account. The account setup will require an email address, name, height, and gender to access the VR system. The new system will log data on length of play, scores, simulations used and log haptic data. The company is hoping, that by creating a system that can be used in any environment where the Internet is available, more users will be able to use their system.

GO ON TO THE NEXT PAGE.

58. Which of the following is the MOST plausible data privacy concern of the upgraded system?

   (A) The company could analyze which simulations are most popular and use this information to create new simulations of that type.
   (B) Medical professionals could analyze the data to determine the effects of use of the system on response time of users.
   (C) The storage of the upgraded system data will be much larger and could possibly require the company to utilize cloud storage.
   (D) The new system will contain your information including email address, simulations used, and time spent in simulations. Since there is no disclosure by the company of how this data will be used, it may be possible for the company to sell your information to third party vendors for targeted advertising.

59. Which of the following is a potential effect of the VR application, rather than a purpose of the application?

   (A) The immersive nature of virtual and augmented reality can induce stress or anxiety after wearing a full occlusion headset for more than a few minutes.
   (B) Medical colleges are able train doctors and nurses in complex medical procedures easier.
   (C) Students are able to interactively experience historical events while remaining in the classroom.
   (D) A scientist is able to manipulate atoms and molecules without the use of an electron microscope, using VR simulation instead to analyze reactions.

60. Which of the following statements is most likely to be true about the trade-offs of using the new VR system?

   (A) Processing time and graphic quality may be decreased on the new stand-alone headset system.
   (B) More people will be able to experience VR, but the company will have more control over personal data and the applications being used on their systems.
   (C) Due to the less efficient processor in the stand-alone system, the stand-alone system will be less expensive but also run fewer detailed simulations.
   (D) Although graphic quality may decrease, the processing time and types of simulations will increase on the new stand-alone headset.

61. Which of the following data is necessary for the new VR system to process in order to enable a user to run it?

   (A) IP address, email address, name, height, and gender
   (B) E-mail address, height, gender, and name
   (C) None: it can be run the same as the old system
   (D) E-mail address, name, and age

62. Which of the following data is not provided directly from the user but is necessary for the upgraded system to operate as described?

   (A) Height of user
   (B) Head movement and position data
   (C) Age of user
   (D) Choice of simulation

GO ON TO THE NEXT PAGE.

63. What are the advantages of procedural abstraction?

Select <u>two</u> answers.

(A) An advantage of using procedural abstractions is that coding time is reduced.

(B) Procedural abstraction reduces debugging time since, when the same code is used in multiple places, changes to the code or fixing errors in the code only need to occur in a single spot.

(C) Procedural abstraction eliminates the need for global variables, which will cause the program to be much less complex.

(D) Procedural abstraction allows the solving of complex issues by focusing on the intricacies and not hiding any details.

64. Which of the following are examples of distributed computing?

Select <u>two</u> answers.

(A) A one player game where puzzles are complex

(B) Verizon cellular communication system

(C) Program which calculates GPA of an individual student

(D) Air traffic control systems

65. Which of the following statements are always true about data compression?

Select <u>two</u> answers.

(A) When data compression is completed, fewer bits means less information.

(B) When data compression is completed, quality is not always impacted, but you cannot revert to the original file.

(C) Data compression is dependent on 2 factors: the amount of redundancy and the type of compression used.

(D) Data compression reduces the number of bits of data but does not always impact the amount of information stored.

66. Which of the following are challenges that are found with processing data, regardless of data size?

Select <u>two</u> answers.

(A) Data processing may require parallel systems since data may not be able to processed with a single computer.

(B) Data may contain invalid or incomplete data.

(C) Data may need to processed in order to make it uniform without changing the meaning of the data.

(D) Data processing may affect the amount of information that is able to be extracted from it.

67. Which of the following are examples of analog data?

Select <u>two</u> answers.

(A) Position of a runner on a cross country course

(B) Measure of weight on bathroom scale

(C) Blood pressure reading on blood pressure cuff

(D) Volume of music playing on cell phone

68. Which of the following describes asymmetric encryption?

Select <u>two</u> answers.

(A) Alice sends an encrypted message to Bob and tells him the key she used to encrypt the message so he can read it.

(B) Alice sends Bob an encrypted message which she used a private key to encrypt and then Bob uses a public key that Alice published online to decrypt the message.

(C) Alice stores her tax information on her computer and uses a password to protect it. Without the password, Alice will be unable to open the documents.

(D) A server at Bob's work generates both a public and private key so that different users can access the data.

GO ON TO THE NEXT PAGE.

69. Ron and Brenda are designing a computer program together. They have produced a beta version for testing and want users to test the functionality of the program. What are some advantages of this collaboration?

Select <u>two</u> answers.

(A) Users are able to test the limitations of the program and report bugs, which will help both Ron and Brenda.

(B) Users are able to add code to the program and increase functionality that Ron and Brenda did not originally include in it.

(C) Having a diverse group of testers will allow for varied responses, enabling Ron and Brenda to anticipate the needs of varied users.

(D) Using collaboration for developing the program may increase because of the wide variety of possible users.

70. If this code executes what value could be displayed?

Select <u>two</u> answers.

```
x ← 2
b ← RANDOM(1, 5)
REPEAT UNTIL (b < 1)
{
    IF(b MOD 2 = 1)
    {
            x ← x * 2
    }
    ELSE
    {
            x ← x + 2
    }
    b ← b - 1
}
DISPLAY(x)
```

(A) 1

(B) 4

(C) 28

(D) 160

STOP

END OF EXAM

Practice Test 2:
Answers and
Explanations

PRACTICE TEST 2 ANSWER KEY

1.	A	36.	C
2.	D	37.	B
3.	C	38.	B
4.	B	39.	B
5.	A	40.	A
6.	B	41.	A
7.	A	42.	D
8.	C	43.	B
9.	A	44.	D
10.	D	45.	C
11.	D	46.	D
12.	A	47.	B
13.	A	48.	A
14.	C	49.	B
15.	B	50.	C
16.	D	51.	D
17.	C	52.	C
18.	B	53.	D
19.	A	54.	B
20.	B	55.	D
21.	D	56.	B
22.	C	57.	A
23.	C	58.	D
24.	C	59.	A
25.	B	60.	C
26.	D	61.	B
27.	C	62.	B
28.	A	63.	A, B
29.	D	64.	B, D
30.	A	65.	C, D
31.	B	66.	B, C
32.	B	67.	A, C
33.	D	68.	B, D
34.	D	69.	A, C
35.	D	70.	B, C

PRACTICE TEST 2 EXPLANATIONS

1. **A** Metadata summarizes basic information about data. The metadata is descriptive information about the image file. Most cameras store location, time, and file data, but metadata does not include descriptive information. The answer is (A).

2. **D** Binary is a base 2 system. In general, N bits (binary digits) are required to represent 2^N unique values. Using the same logic, 2^9 where 9 represents the number of bits, 512 unique values are able to be represented. The answer is (D).

3. **C** Multifactor authentication is a type of access control where at least 2 types of evidence are met by the user. The types of evidence are knowledge, possession, and inherence. Knowledge requires a user to answer a question about information they know. Possession requires a check in with an alternative device and inherence is normally completed via biometric authentication. Choice (A), although it gives 2 requests for evidence, they are both of the knowledge type. Choices (B) and (D) only require 1 request for evidence. Choice (C) requires both a knowledge type of evidence shown by the password request and then a possession evidence required from the text message code. The answer is (C).

4. **B** A simple explanation of the digital divide is that people's access to computing and the Internet differs based on socioeconomic or geographic characteristics. Therefore, Elon Musk's Starlink satellites will help some groups access technology and content that they previously could not access. Therefore, the answer is (B).

5. **A** In the initial robot picture, the robot is facing towards the right of the page since the point of the arrow always displays which direction the robot is pointed. Following the code for (A), the robot will be in the space below its initial position but facing upward after repeating this code 3 times. After moving forward, it will be facing upward, and after repeating the loop two times, the robot will be two squares to the right of the gray square but facing down. Finally, the last 3 statements move the robot to the ending gray square, pointing to the left. The answer is (A).

6. **B** The MOD function analyzes whether there is remainder. If the remainder of the number of students when divided by 3 is zero, then the students can evenly distribute into groups of 3. In a MOD statement, the first number is the dividend and the second number is the divisor. Therefore, (B) states if `numStudent` is divided by 3, then there will be equal groups of three students each. The answer is (B).

7. **A** Crowdsourcing is simply the idea that many online users are combining their work or efforts to help fund projects, generate ideas, or create services. Google uses crowdsourcing to allow students to have input into the brand and therefore effectively engage people with their company. The answer is (A).

8. **C** Personally Identifiable Information is any data that can be used to identify a specific individual. Social Security numbers, mailing or email address, and phone numbers have most commonly been considered PII, but technology has expanded the scope of PII considerably. It can include an IP

address, login IDs, social media posts, or digital images. Geolocation, biometric, and behavioral data can also be classified as PII. Choice (C) is the correct answer because it shows the use of PII in order to create a new identity and commit crimes.

9. **A** Lossy compression algorithms are techniques that reduce file size by discarding the less important information. Since pixel values are averaged, the original pixel value cannot be restored; therefore, this is lossy compression. The answer is (A).

10. **D** The table shows processing times for 8 bits, 80 bits, and 800 bits. 1000 bytes is 8000 bits since each byte is 8 bits. Therefore, examining the pattern between the columns, you can see that increasing the number of bits by a multiple of 10 adds an additional second for creating a copy of an audio file; the processing time for 8000 bits would be 4 seconds. The processing time for backing up an audio file is 32 seconds, searching an audio file is 500 seconds, and deleting an audio file is 6.75 seconds. The answer is (D).

11. **D** Computing bias is defined as errors in a computing system that create unfair and incorrect outcomes. In this example, Oprah Winfrey is incorrectly identified as a male. Computing bias is often seen in facial recognition systems since facial recognition algorithms vary in their performance across different face types. They have a tendency to performance worse on darker skin tones and the female population. The answer is (D).

12. **A** Execution time is optimized when the workload of the two processors is as close to equal as possible, so that one processor does not finish too early and has to wait for the other processor to finish. In order to accomplish this, Y and Z would need to run sequentially, which would take 105 seconds, close to 110 seconds that task X takes. The answer is (A).

13. **A** The variable which is returned contains either the value `true` or `false`, which is best described as a Boolean variable. The answer is (A).

14. **C** The first part of the Boolean expression determines if their age is between 25 and 35, inclusively, and the second part determines whether they are able to lift 50 lbs. The answer is (C).

15. **B** A heuristic solution is an algorithm that finds an approximate solution. Calculating student GPA requires a very exact solution. I and II both require brute force to try every possible solution; however, the computer can approximate the result to determine a possible solution. The answer is (B).

16. **D** Each time Algorithm A runs the first or second loop it takes 1 minute. The number of times it runs is dependent on n. Each time Algorithm B runs it takes 1 minute, but since it is a nested loop, it multiplied by n^2. The answer is (D).

17. **C** In Network A, there are many paths, including A-B-C, A-E-B-C, and A-E-C, which make it fault-tolerant due to redundancy. Also, in Network C, there are 2 different paths, A-B-C and A-E-C. But in Network B, in order to access C from A, you must go through node E. Therefore, only Networks A and C are fault tolerant, which means that the answer is (C).

18. **B** Creative Commons licensing allows copyright owners to specify the ways in which their works can be used or distributed. Creative Commons licenses do not replace copyright law. Therefore, (A) would still be a violation of copyright. Also, (D) shows proper credit being given according to the copyright laws. Choice (C) is a violation of copyright. Choice (B) is the answer because Preston uses materials that have a Creative Commons license, which allows their use as long as attribution is given.

19. **A** A phishing attack is an attempt to trick individuals into providing personal information, often by getting them to fill out a form on a malicious website. All of the above show examples of phishing except for (A), which is an example of a virus. Choice (A) is the correct answer.

20. **B** The loop runs 2 times first when x is 8 and y is 5. Since x is not less than y, y becomes 5 – 2 = 3 and x becomes 8 – 5 = 3. Since x is still not less than y, it runs again: y becomes 3 – 2 = 1 and x becomes 3 – 5 = –2. The loop does not run again since –2 is less than 1. So the code displays –2 times 1, which is –2. Looking at the answers, due to order of operations, the expressions should be multiplied first, then divided, and then added or subtracted. For (B), if you do this you get 4 + –6 / 1 and then 4 + –6, which equals –2. Choice (A) does not equal –2; instead it equals 3.14. Choice (C) equals 86 and (D) equals –9. Choice (B) is correct.

21. **D** Currently if b is an even number and you decrease by 2 in the loop each time, it will never equal to 7. If you, instead, decrease by 1 each time, then when b is an even or odd number, it will work as intended. The correct choice is (D).

22. **C** In order for the data to not be overwritten, it needs to be stored in a temporary value. Choice (C) stores num1 in a temporary variable, then num2 value is put in num1 and, after that, num2 is assigned the value of num1, which was stored as a temporary variable. Choice (C) is the correct answer.

23. **C** Code Segment #1 correctly evaluates whether the number is odd but it does not correctly add it to the list since oddNum is a blank list and therefore cannot be indexed at each number. Code Segment #2 correctly evaluates whether the number is odd and then appends it to the list. Since only Code Segment #2 works, (C) is the correct answer.

24. **C** When the wind speed is greater than 30 then the current code will output "make sure to hold on", "getting gusty", and "a light breeze". The OR statements provide that, if either part of the conditional statement is true, it will display the output. It should require both parts of the statement to be true; for example, the wind needs to be greater than 15 AND less than 30 for getting gusty to be correct. The correct answer is therefore (C).

25. **B** In order to make the word "acid", you need the first 2 letters of the first parameter to be "ca" since the procedure extracts these letters and reverses their order. For the second parameter, you need the string to end with the letters "id". These two parameters are then concatenated, linked together. Choices (C) and (B) both appear to work, but the question states that there is a precondition for the procedure that requires the string parameters to have a length greater than 3; the parameter "car" is not, so therefore the answer is (B).

26. **D** The procedure `productNum` takes in 2 integers, displays the first parameter number and then returns the product of the 2 numbers. The procedure `concat` adds the string parameter to the output from the `productNum` procedure and displays the output. The answer is (D).

27. **C** The procedure `doSomething` implements a binary search, which works by repeatedly dividing in half the portion of the list that could contain the item, until you've narrowed down the possible locations to just one, and if the item is not found, it returns –1. Therefore, statement I is correct. Eliminate (B) and (D), which do not include statement I. A binary search though requires the list to be sorted, so statement III is also true. Eliminate (A), which does not include statement III. The correct answer is (C).

28. **A** After start max is set to 10, which is not less than 10, the flowchart evaluates whether max is less than 11, which is true. So it displays "got it". The answer is (A).

29. **D** For this conditional statement, if the variable `closed` is true, then it will display "Check back", otherwise it will go to the ELSE statement. Then, if `code` is less than 10, it will display "Open in next hour", otherwise it will display "Open Now". Since `closed` is false and the code has a value of 10, this will display "Open Now"; the answer is (D).

30. **A** Choice (A) sets `test` to `false`, and if they have taken a class, then it is set to `true`. Only does it set to `false` if age is 15. The correct answer is (A).

31. **B** Each time the procedure runs, the robot rotates to the left and then moves forward however many times indicated by the argument. In order to move to this spot, the robot would need to turn left and move forward 4 spots; if it does this twice, which is equal to steps divided by 2, then the robot will reach the destination. The answer is (B).

32. **B** The code creates a list and 2 variables, which initializes a with the value of 1 and b to the length of the list. The loop repeats until b is less than a. It then swaps the items at the end of the list with those at the beginning. Once the loop is complete, all items of the list will be reversed. The answer is (B).

33. **D** Keylogger is a program that records user input, allowing a third party to gain fraudulent access to passwords and other confidential information. The answer is (D).

34. **D** Data is broken into a number of packets that are sent independently over whatever route is most efficient and reassembled at the destination. Each packet contains address information that identifies the sending computer and intended recipient. Using these addresses, network switches and routers determine the most efficient way to transfer the packet to its destination. Because it is possible for packets to follow very different routes, the receiving end needs to know the order in which the packets are to be assembled, and to request any be resent, if they are received corrupted or incomplete. Due to this, the answer is (D).

35. **D** A fault-tolerant system is one that can experience failure (or multiple failures) in its components, but still continue operating properly. Although there have been some catastrophic failures around the world, due to the fault tolerance of the Internet, not one of these has managed to disable the entire Internet system. The answer is (D).

36. **C** Computer privacy issues deal with storing, reusing, sharing data with third parties, and sharing information about oneself on the Internet. For (A), replying to such an email may be risky, but calling a local branch does not carry the same risks. For (B), although it seems it would be a possible privacy issue, cookies traditionally cannot be used to obtain personal information from your computer. For (D), though public Wi-Fi can be an easy access point for cybercriminals to eavesdrop and gain private information, private Wi-Fi in your home is more secure. Google has been frequently in the news for their privacy issues and sharing of data. Even the CEO has stated that if you don't want someone knowing what you doing then you probably shouldn't be doing it. The answer is (C).

37. **B** Weird Al Yankovic is covered by fair use since it is a parody. All others contain ethical issues, including plagiarism and piracy. The answer is (B).

38. **B** A binary digit can be used to express anything with 2 possible values. Choice (A) can be expressed as a binary digit if the divisor is 2, since the result of an integer MOD 2 is either 1 or 0. Choice (C) can be expressed as a binary digit since there are only two possible colors. Choice (D) can be as well since the light switch can be either in position "on" or "off." The only that cannot be is the grade binary is a grade in school, which is either 0 to 100 or A, B, C, D or F. The answer is (B).

39. **B** Lossless compression restores and rebuilds data to its original form after decompression, while lossy compression eliminates the data which is not noticeable and cannot be restored to its original form. Therefore, (B) is the correct answer.

40. **A** The individual tag on a shark does not contain data about the location of sharks nearby, and while it is possible to correlate this data with other shark tags, whether sharks travel in groups cannot be determined by this data alone. The answer is (A).

41. **A** Binary numbers are 8 bits where each bit is either a 0 or a 1. To convert to a decimal number, add the power of 2 represented by each bit, if the bit in that place is 1. Here there is a 1 in 2^0 column, 2^2 column, 2^3 column, 2^4 column, and 2^6 column. Adding these values together $(1 + 4 + 8 + 16 + 64)$ yields 93. The correct answer is (A).

42. **D** As the correct answer, (D) states the World Wide Web is simply a system of linked pages, programs, and files, while the Internet is a computer network consisting of interconnected networks. The World Wide Web does use the Internet.

43. **B** Bandwidth of a computer network is the maximum amount of data that can be sent in a fixed amount of time. During a storm, people are more likely to be home using Internet-connected devices, limiting the amount of broadband available per customer. Thus, web pages will either not load or load slowly. The correct answer is (B).

44. **D** Materials posted online are very difficult to delete and can be used in ways not intended by the original creator. For example, tweets can be retweeted or screenshots can be taken of snaps or text messages. The correct answer is (D).

45. **C** Program documentation is a written description of the function of code segments, events, procedures or programs, and how they were developed. Documentation should be completed throughout development and is a helpful tool whether working individually or especially when working collaboratively. Choice (C) is the correct answer.

46. **D** A logic error is a mistake in the program that causes it to act incorrectly, while a syntax error occurs when the programming rules are not followed. A run-time error occurs when a mistake occurs in the program when it operates. The correct answer is (D).

47. **B** The data is identical in these two graphs. The first graph has a y-axis that goes from 48,000 to 56,000, while the second graph shows a y-axis range from 0 to 60k. When the x-axis is adjusted, the trends are able to be better visualized. Choice (B) is the correct answer.

48. **A** When degrees is 120, the expression `degrees ≥ 120` evaluates to true, so "Ovens can be used" is printed. This shows that the code does not work as intended because it was supposed to display "Ovens cannot be operated" when the temperature is at or below 120°C. The answer is (A).

49. **B** HTTP, UDP, TCP and IP are all open protocols used by the Internet. UDP is a standardized method for transferring data between two computers in a network. Compared to other protocols, UDP accomplishes this process in a simple fashion: it sends packets (units of data) directly to a target computer without establishing a connection first. The correct answer is (B).

50. **C** Metadata is defined as data about data. It may contain information such as date of creation, file size, camera used, etc. Deleting this data will not impact the overall primary data. Choice (C) is correct.

51. **D** Data compression can reduce the number of bits used to store data, but it does not help extract information for analysis. The correct answer is (D).

52. **C** Data abstraction is assigning a collection of data a single name as a reference to help manage complexity of code. Here the data abstraction, numbers, is created using a list. The answer is (C).

53. **D** In order to calculate the grade average in the new system, the maximum grade and the minimum grade are subtracted. Since 2 grades are removed, the total number of grades will be what is returned from the procedure `NumberGrades()` minus two. The answer is (D).

54. **B** When the IF statement is true and when the item in the list contains the value `true`, then `true` will be added to the `newVals` list. Since there are 3 true values in the initial list, `oldValues`, then the new list, `Values2`, will contain 3 true values. The answer is (B).

55. **D** To create a simulation, a thorough understanding is needed of the system and an awareness of all the factors involved with it. Without this understanding, it is difficult to interpret the results. Additionally, it is not possible to test all possible effects. The answer is (D).

56. **B** Computing innovations, such as the 3D printer, often have both beneficial and harmful effects, which are often unintended. Since 3D printing models and CAD software are so readily available and easy to learn, the toy market is struggling with copyright and piracy issues. The correct answer is (B).

57. **A** Certificate based authentication, which is the basis of the trust model, allows users to securely access a server by exchanging a digital certificate. Since the certificate is signed, it is only possible to connect to the real server and is therefore secure. The correct answer is (A).

58. **D** Both (A) and (B) do not connect the user's identity to the data. Choice (C) provides only a storage concern. Data privacy concerns often revolve around whether and how data is shared with third parties. Choice (D) states that user data may be shared with other companies and used for targeting advertising without the user's consent or knowledge. The answer is (D).

59. **A** The purpose of the VR innovation is the why: Why does it exist? What problem does it address? What is the goal/objective? An effect is something that can occur from using the VR application. Choices (B), (C), and (D) all discuss potential purposes of the VR application, but (A) is a possible negative effect of VR.

60. **C** A trade-off is a decision that involves diminishing or losing one quality or property of a system in return for gains in other aspects. In the new VR system, the system went from requiring a whole room setup to now being a stand-alone headset, but due to this trade-off, the new system uses a less powerful processor and cannot render images and graphics of the same quality. Choice (C) is the correct answer.

61. **B** The new system requires email address and name in addition to the previously required height and gender. The answer is (B).

62. **B** The user must provide height and choose which simulation to use, but sensors analyze head movement and position data in order for the VR environment to function. Choice (B) is correct.

63. **A, B** If you only have to write a code segment one time and code statements that call it, you save the time of coding the same routine multiple times; this reduces programming and debugging time. The correct answers are (A) and (B).

64. **B, D** Distributed computing is defined as a computational model in which multiple devices are used to run a single program. Air traffic control systems rely heavily on information about the location of hundreds or thousands of airplanes and sensors at each airfield working together. Cellular networks require multiple cell phone towers and coverage areas to communicate and work together to allow users to travel without losing service. The correct answers are (B) and (D).

65. **C, D** Data compression is the process of reducing the amount of data or bits needed for storage or transfer of particular information. Lossless data compression reduces the number of bits but stores all the same information so the original files can be restored. The amount of data compression that can be achieved is dependent on whether lossy or lossless compression is done and the amount of redundant data. The answers are (C) and (D).

66. **B, C** Data processing has 4 main challenges that are not dependent on the size of the data set. These include the need to clean data, the need to combine data sources, elimination of incomplete data, and invalid data. The answers are (B) and (C).

67. **A, C** Analog data has values that change smoothly over time. Digital data represents discrete measurements. Both (A) and (C) are examples of analog data and are the correct answers.

68. **B, D** Asymmetric encryption requires 2 different keys which are linked to encrypt and decrypt the data. Choices (B) and (D) are the answers since they describe the use of 2 different keys for encryption.

69. **A, C** Having a variety of users will increase perspective, and allowing more users to test the code will allow a great chance of all errors being located. Users are not able to add code and collaboration decreases bias. The answers are (A) and (C).

70. **B, C** When b is given the lowest value of 1, then the loop only iterates 1 time, since b modulus 1 equals 1, it takes x which has a value of 2 and multiplies it by 2 yielding 4. This value is displayed by the program. When b is given the maximum value of 5, then the loop iterates 5 times. The first iteration b is 5 and x is 2, and since b modulus 2 is 1, then x becomes 4. The second iteration b is 4 and x is 4, and since b modulus 2 is not 1, then x becomes 6. The third iteration b is 3 and x is 6, and since b modulus 2 is 1, then x becomes 12. The fourth iteration b is 2 and x is 12, and since b modulus 2 is not 1, then x becomes 14. The fifth iteration b is 1 and x is 14, and since b modulus 2 is 1, then x becomes 28. The answers are (B) and (C).

HOW TO SCORE PRACTICE TEST 2

Section I: Multiple Choice

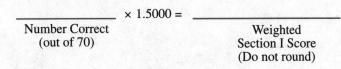

_____ × 1.5000 = _____
Number Correct   Weighted
(out of 70)   Section I Score
                                (Do not round)

Section II: Create Performance Task

(This is completed and submitted outside of test time. See if you can find a teacher or classmate to score your Create Performance Task using the guidelines in Chapter 2.)

Task Score: _____ × 7.5000 = _____
            (out of 6)   (Task Score
                                        Do not round)

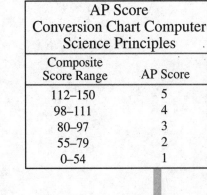

AP Score Conversion Chart Computer Science Principles	
Composite Score Range	AP Score
112–150	5
98–111	4
80–97	3
55–79	2
0–54	1

Composite Score

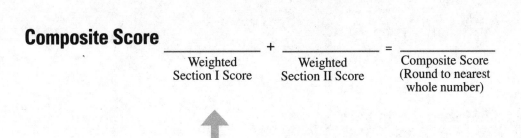

_____ + _____ = _____
Weighted   Weighted   Composite Score
Section I Score   Section II Score   (Round to nearest
                                    whole number)

Practice Test 3

AP® Computer Science Principles Exam

DO NOT OPEN THIS BOOKLET UNTIL YOU ARE TOLD TO DO SO.

At a Glance

Total Time
2 hours
Number of Questions
70
Percent of Total Score
70%
Writing Instrument
Pencil required

Instructions

Section I of this examination contains 70 multiple-choice questions. Fill in only the ovals for numbers 1 through 70 on your answer sheet.

Indicate all of your answers to the multiple-choice questions on the answer sheet. No credit will be given for anything written in this exam booklet, but you may use the booklet for notes or scratch work. After you have decided which of the suggested answers is best, completely fill in the corresponding oval on the answer sheet. Give only one answer to each question. If you change an answer, be sure that the previous mark is erased completely. Here is a sample question and answer.

Sample Question   Sample Answer

Chicago is a
(A) state
(B) city
(C) country
(D) continent

Use your time effectively, working as quickly as you can without losing accuracy. Do not spend too much time on any one question. Go on to other questions and come back to the ones you have not answered if you have time. It is not expected that everyone will know the answers to all the multiple-choice questions.

About Guessing

Many candidates wonder whether or not to guess the answers to questions about which they are not certain. Multiple-choice scores are based on the number of questions answered correctly. Points are not deducted for incorrect answers, and no points are awarded for unanswered questions. Because points are not deducted for incorrect answers, you are encouraged to answer all multiple-choice questions. On any questions you do not know the answer to, you should eliminate as many choices as you can, and then select the best answer among the remaining choices.

GO ON TO THE NEXT PAGE.

Quick Reference

Instruction	Explanation
Assignment, Display, and Input	
Text: a ← expression Block: a ◄— expression	Evaluates expression and then assigns a copy of the result to the variable a.
Text: DISPLAY (expression) Block: DISPLAY expression	Displays the value of expression, followed by a space.
Text: INPUT () Block: INPUT	Accepts a value from the user and returns the input value.
Arithmetic Operators and Numeric Procedures	
Text and Block: a + b a - b a * b a / b	The arithmetic operators +, -, *, and / are used to perform arithmetic on a and b. For example, 17 / 5 evaluates to 3.4. The order of operations used in mathematics applies when evaluating expressions.
Text and Block: a MOD b	Evaluates to the remainder when a is divided by b. Assume that a is an integer greater than or equal to 0 and b is an integer greater than 0. For example, 17 MOD 5 evaluates to 2. The MOD operator has the same precedence as the * and / operators.
Text: RANDOM (a, b) Block: RANDOM a, b	Generates and returns a random integer from a to b, including a and b. Each result is equally likely to occur. For example, RANDOM(1, 3) could return 1, 2, or 3.

Instruction	Explanation
Relational and Boolean Operators	
Text and Block: a = b a ≠ b a > b a < b a ≥ b a ≤ b	The relational operators =, ≠, >, <, ≤, and ≥ are used to test the relationship between two variables, expressions, or values. A comparison using relational operators evaluates to a Boolean value. For example, a = b evaluates to `true` if a and b are equal; otherwise it evaluates to `false`.
Text: NOT condition Block: NOT [condition]	Evaluates to `true` if condition is `false`; otherwise evaluates to `false`.
Text: condition1 AND condition2 Block: [condition1] AND [condition2]	Evaluates to `true` if both condition1 and condition2 are `true`; otherwise evaluates to `false`.
Text: condition1 OR condition2 Block: [condition1] OR [condition2]	Evaluates to `true` if condition1 is `true` or if condition2 is `true` or if both condition1 and condition2 are `true`; otherwise evaluates to `false`.
Selection	

Text:
 	
IF(condition)
 	
{
 	
<block of statements>
 	
}
 	
Block:
 	
IF [condition]
　　[block of statements]
	The code in `block of statements` is executed if the Boolean expression `condition` evaluates to `true`; no action is taken if `condition` evaluates to `false`.

Instruction	Explanation
Selection—Continued	

Text:
 	
IF(condition)
 	
{
 	
\<first block of statements>
 	
}
 	
ELSE
 	
{
 	
\<second block of statements>
 	
}
 	
Block:
 	
IF (condition)
　　first block of statements
ELSE
　　second block of statements
	The code in first block of statements is executed if the Boolean expression condition evaluates to true; otherwise the code in second block of statements is executed.

Iteration	

Text:
 	
REPEAT n TIMES
 	
{
 	
\<block of statements>
 	
}
 	
Block:
 	
REPEAT n TIMES
　　block of statements
	The code in block of statements is executed n times.

Text:
 	
REPEAT UNTIL(condition)
 	
{
 	
\<block of statements>
 	
}
 	
Block:
 	
REPEAT UNTIL (condition)
　　block of statements
	The code in block of statements is repeated until the Boolean expression condition evaluates to true.

Instruction	Explanation
List Operations	
For all list operations, if a list index is less than 1 or greater than the length of the list, an error message is produced and the program terminates.	
Text: aList ← [value1, value2, value3, ...] Block: `aList ◀── value1, value2, value3`	Creates a new list that contains the values value1, value2, value3, and ... at indices 1, 2, 3, and ... respectively and assigns it to aList.
Text: aList ← [] Block: `aList ◀── []`	Creates an empty list and assigns it to aList.
Text: aList ← bList Block: `aList ◀── bList`	Assigns a copy of the list bList to the list aList. For example, if bList contains [20, 40, 60], then aList will also contain [20, 40, 60] after the assignment.
Text: aList[i] Block: aList `i`	Accesses the element of aList at index i. The first element of aList is at index 1 and is accessed using the notation aList[1].
Text: x ← aList[i] Block: `x ◀── aList i`	Assigns the value of aList[i] to the variable x.
Text: aList[i] ← x Block: `aList i ◀── x`	Assigns the value of x to aList[i].
Text: aList[i] ← aList[j] Block: `aList i ◀── aList j`	Assigns the value of aList[j] to aList[i].
Text: INSERT(aList, i, value) Block: `INSERT aList, i, value`	Any values in aList at indices greater than or equal to i are shifted one position to the right. The length of the list is increased by 1, and value is placed at index i in aList.

Instruction	Explanation
List Operations—Continued	
Text: APPEND(aList, value) Block: APPEND `aList, value`	The length of aList is increased by 1, and value is placed at the end of aList.
Text: REMOVE(aList, i) Block: REMOVE `aList, i`	Removes the item at index i in aList and shifts to the left any values at indices greater than i. The length of aList is decreased by 1.
Text: LENGTH(aList) Block: LENGTH `aList`	Evaluates to the number of elements in aList.

Text:
 	
FOR EACH item IN aList
 	
{
 	
<block of statements>
 	
}
 	
Block:
 	
FOR EACH item IN aList
    `block of statements`
	The variable item is assigned the value of each element of aList sequentially, in order, from the first element to the last element. The code in block of statements is executed once for each assignment of item.

Procedures and Procedure Calls	

Text:
 	
PROCEDURE procName(parameter1,
                  parameter2, ...)
 	
{
 	
<block of statements>
 	
}
 	
Block:
 	
PROCEDURE procName `parameter1,`
`parameter2, ...`
    `block of statements`
	Defines procName as a procedure that takes zero or more arguments. The procedure contains block of statements.
	
	The procedure procName can be called using the following notation, where arg1 is assigned to parameter1, arg2 is assigned to parameter2, etc.:
	procName(arg1, arg2, ...)

Instruction	Explanation
Procedures and Procedure Calls—Continued	
| Text:<br><br>`PROCEDURE procName(parameter1,`<br>`                parameter2, ...)`<br><br>`{`<br><br>`<block of statements>`<br><br>`RETURN(expression)`<br><br>`}`<br><br>Block:<br><br>```
PROCEDURE procName  parameter1,
                    parameter2, ...

    block of statements
    RETURN expression
``` | Defines `procName` as a procedure that takes zero or more arguments. The procedure contains `block of statements` and returns the value of `expression`. The RETURN statement may appear at any point inside the procedure and causes an immediate return from the procedure back to the calling statement.<br><br>The value returned by the procedure `procName` can be assigned to the variable `result` using the following notation:<br>`result ← procName(arg1, arg2, ...)` |
Text:
 	
`RETURN(expression)`
 	
Block:
 	
`RETURN expression`
	Returns the flow of control to the point where the procedure was called and returns the value of `expression`.

Robot	
If the robot attempts to move to a square that is not open or is beyond the edge of the grid, the robot will stay in its current location and the program will terminate.	

Text:
 	
`MOVE_FORWARD()`
 	
Block:
 	
`MOVE_FORWARD`
	The robot moves one square forward in the direction it is facing.

Text:
 	
`ROTATE_LEFT()`
 	
Block:
 	
`ROTATE_LEFT`
	The robot rotates in place 90 degrees counterclockwise (i.e., makes an in-place left turn).

Text:
 	
`ROTATE_RIGHT()`
 	
Block:
 	
`ROTATE_RIGHT`
	The robot rotates in place 90 degrees clockwise (i.e., makes an in-place right turn).

Text:
 	
`CAN_MOVE(direction)`
 	
Block:
 	
`CAN_MOVE direction`
	Evaluates to `true` if there is an open square one square in the direction relative to where the robot is facing; otherwise evaluates to `false`. The value of `direction` can be `left`, `right`, `forward`, or `backward`.

```

This page intentionally left blank.

GO ON TO THE NEXT PAGE.

COMPUTER SCIENCE PRINCIPLES
SECTION I
Time—2 hours
Number of Questions—70
Percent of total exam grade—70%

Directions: Choose one best answer for each question. Some questions at the end of the test will have more than one correct answer; for these, you will be instructed to choose two answer choices.

1. Which of the following represents the minimum number of bytes that are required to represent the number 2719 in binary?

   (A) 1 byte
   (B) 2 bytes
   (C) 3 bytes
   (D) 4 bytes

2. Dania has a rectangular garden of $(11011110100)_2$-foot length and $(10101111000)_2$-foot width; she wants to fence her garden where the fence costs $5 per foot. Which of the following represents the total cost of fencing Dania's garden?

   (A) $15,300
   (B) $20,100
   (C) $25,100
   (D) $31,800

GO ON TO THE NEXT PAGE.

3. Which of the following represents the correct descending order (from greatest to least) of the numbers given below?

$$(1101101)_2, (176)_{10}, (10001111)_2$$

(A) $(1101101)_2 > (176)_{10} > (10001111)_2$
(B) $(10001111)_2 > (1101101)_2 > (176)_{10}$
(C) $(1101101)_2 > (10001111)_2 > (176)_{10}$
(D) $(176)_{10} > (10001111)_2 > (1101101)_2$

4. Consider the Guess procedure below which is intended to receive a binary number constructed of zeros and ones:

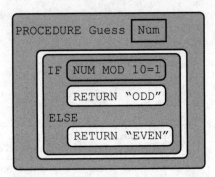

Which of the following procedure calls results in displaying "EVEN" as an output?

(A) DISPLAY (Guess(100101010010))
(B) DISPLAY (Guess(101101011011))
(C) DISPLAY (Guess(111011010011))
(D) DISPLAY (Guess(111111000111))

GO ON TO THE NEXT PAGE.

5. The procedure Guess below is intended to receive an integer and return its binary representation in a string.

```
PROCEDURE Guess(NUM)
{
    REPRESENTATION ← ""
    REPEAT UNTIL (NUM=0)
    {
    REPRESENTATION ← REPRESENTATION + NUM MOD 2
    NUM ← <missing expression>
    }
    RETURN REPRESENTATION
}
```

The algorithm of the method is illustrated in the flowchart below:

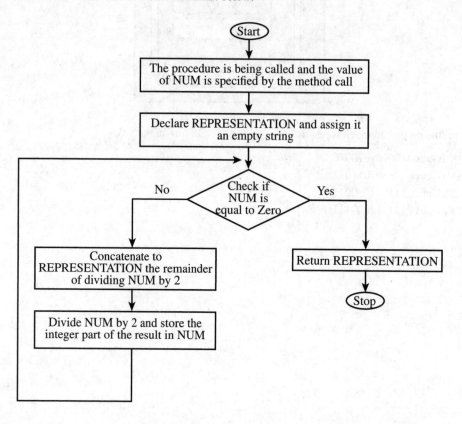

Of the following, which option should replace <missing expression> in order to make the procedure work properly as intended?

(A) NUM / 2

(B) (NUM MOD 2) / 2

(C) NUM / 2 - (NUM MOD 2) / 2

(D) (NUM MOD 2) * 2 - (NUM MOD 2) / 2

GO ON TO THE NEXT PAGE.

6. Which of the following is the LEAST accurate about analog data and digital data?

   (A) Values represented in analog data change smoothly and continuously, whereas digital data have discrete values.
   (B) When representing an analog image digitally, the greater the resolution of the digital image, the closer it represents the analog image.
   (C) When representing an analog picture digitally, the number of bits used per a regular interval doesn't affect the accuracy of the resulting image.
   (D) When representing an analog image digitally, the physical dimensions of the digital image have no correlation to the accuracy of the resulting image.

Questions 7–8 refer to the information below.

American Standard Code for Information Interchange (ASCII) is an encoding scheme that assigns numeric codes for keyboard characters, numbers, and symbols.

The table below represents part of the ASCII table and shows some English letters along with their decimal ASCII codes. Each symbol is represented using 7 binary digits in ASCII.

Character	Decimal Code
S	83
L	76
A	65
V	86
D	68
U	85
G	71
T	84

7. What is the maximum number of symbols can be represented using the ASCII system according to the specifications given above?

   (A) 64
   (B) 128
   (C) 256
   (D) 512

GO ON TO THE NEXT PAGE.

8. Using some of the ASCII characters given in the table, Joe created a digital signal with a bitrate of 1 bit/ second to represent the letters he used. What are the characters that Joe used as shown in the digital signal below?

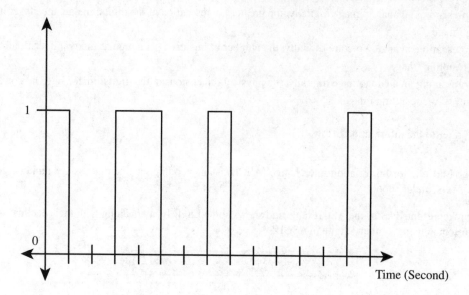

Time (Second)

(A) DS

(B) UG

(C) ST

(D) LA

9. Which of the following is/are correct about lossy and lossless compression techniques?

   I.   In lossy compression techniques, the exact original data can't be restored.

   II. Lossy compression techniques work better than lossless techniques in terms of reducing files sizes.

   III. If the quality of the file after the compression is done matters, then it is better to use lossy compression techniques.

(A) I only

(B) I and II only

(C) I and III only

(D) I, II, and III

GO ON TO THE NEXT PAGE.

10. Suzy is texting her mother; she wants to save her time and send the message as soon as she can, so she wrote this message:

    "I am wrtng to infrm y tht my mbl is ot of chrg and gng to trn off..dn't wry"

    the original intended message was:

    "I am writing to inform you that my mobile is out of charge and going to turn off…...don't worry"

    Which of the following best describes what Suzy did to compress her text message?

    I. Suzy used a lossy compression technique to reduce the size of the message so it can be sent as soon as possible.
    II. Lossless compression was used by Suzy as the recipient will receive the compressed message along with a dictionary of symbols to substitute for where symbols were used to reconstruct the original message.
    III. The technique that Suzy used is not suitable for text compression as it relies on the recipient's ability to fill in the gaps to understand the message.

    (A) I only
    (B) I and II only
    (C) I and III only
    (D) I, II, and III

Questions 11–12 refer to the information below.

The table below summarizes data collected from people of different ages about the number of cups of water they consume per day.

Number of people	Age (years)	Number of cups
113	3	1
65	5	2
99	8	4
78	11	6
60	14	8
86	17	10
75	21	10
93	25	10

11. Which hypothesis is true based on the data given above?

    I. Little kids need to consume water much more that adults.
    II. Teenagers consume the least number of water cups.
    III. People tend to consume more water as they are getting older.

    (A) I only
    (B) III only
    (C) II and III only
    (D) I, II, and III

GO ON TO THE NEXT PAGE.

12. The graph below was created to visualize a portion of the data given in the dataset above.

Number of water cups a day for each age group

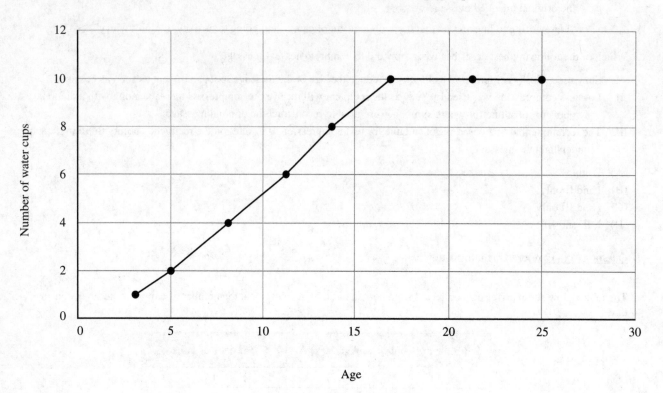

Age

Which of the following is correct about the given graph and data?

I. The graph shows a positive correlation among the two variables age and number of water cups from the age of 3 until the age of 17.

II. It is impossible to identify a correlation among variables based on the available data.

III. There is a linear relationship among the age and number of water cups variables from the age of 3 until the age of 17.

(A) I only
(B) III only
(C) II and III only
(D) I and III only

13. Which of the following is the final value assigned to the variable a after executing the code segment below?

```
a ← 10
b ← 6
c ← 5
b ← a - c
c ← b*2
a ← b MOD c
```

(A) 0
(B) 2
(C) 5
(D) 10

GO ON TO THE NEXT PAGE.

14. Which of the following is correct about the metadata of a dataset of images?

   I. It can include the date of creation, the size of the dataset, and its content.

  II. It can increase the effective use of the dataset by providing additional information about it.

 III. It helps in pre-curating the dataset such as exporting, saving, and structuring it.

   (A) I only

   (B) II only

   (C) III only

   (D) I, II, and III

15. In order for an employee of a particular company to access a workstation, the employee must first provide a user name and password. Once this is done, the employee is prompted to input a code received on their mobile phones via SMS message. Only when this code is inputted, can the user access the workstation. This process is an example of which of the following?

   (A) Digital divide

   (B) Lossless compression

   (C) Public key encryption

   (D) Multifactor authentication

16. Which of the following represents the final output of the code segment below?

```
x ← 1
y ← 2
z ← 3
temp ← "x"+"y"+"z"
DISPLAY(temp)
```

   (A) 3

   (B) 4

   (C) 6

   (D) xyz

17. Messy datasets lead to inaccurate results when they are used in applications. Of the following, which is incorrect about cleaning and filtering datasets?

   (A) Filtering data helps in finding information and recognizing patterns in data.

   (B) Filtering allows you to keep the full dataset unchanged but shows the portion that needs work.

   (C) Manually applying cleaning and filtering processes on big datasets is much faster and more accurate than using computer programs.

   (D) Cleaning data makes the data uniform without changing its meaning by fixing problems related to incomplete data, invalid data, and duplicated data.

GO ON TO THE NEXT PAGE.

Questions 18–19 refer to the information below.

A researcher is going to publish on the Internet some research that he conducted on his own. He wants to make some of his research available for users' distribution and modification under certain conditions.

18. Which of the following represents the material created by this researcher?

   (A) Crowdsourcing
   (B) Intellectual property
   (C) Citizen science
   (D) Documentaries

19. Which of the following is correct if the researcher decided to use the Creative Commons license?

   (A) The researcher will make his research open source.
   (B) The researcher wants to sell his research.
   (C) The researcher has the capacity to decide how his works can be legitimately utilized and conveyed.
   (D) The research is going to make his research open access.

20. Which of the following represents the final value assigned to the variable flag?

```
x ← 1
y ← 2
z ← 3
flag ← NOT(x ≥ y OR z ≠ y)
```

   (A) true
   (B) false
   (C) 5
   (D) 4

21. A string is an ordered sequence of characters where each character is given an index number starting from 1. For example, in the string "ABCDXYZ", the character A has the index 1, B has the index 2, and so on.

The procedure substring has two versions **substring(String, start, end)** and **substring(String, start)**. Both substring versions return string value.

The table below shows both versions of substring along with examples showing how can they be called and the returned string after calling each one of them:

Substring method	Example of how to call the procedure	Returned value
substring(String, start, end)	Substring("Hello CSP", 4, 6)	lo
substring(String, start)	Substring("Hello CSP", 2)	Hello CSP

What is the final value assigned to the variable temp after executing the program below?

```
str ← "Computer Science"
temp ← substring(str, 4, 7)+" "+substring(str, 10)
```

   (A) put Science
   (B) Science Com
   (C) Com Computer
   (D) Science Scie

GO ON TO THE NEXT PAGE.

22. Which of the following represents the final contents of aList after executing the code segment below?

```
aList ← [4, 5, 3, 4, 2, 5, 1]
mark1 ← aList[1]
mark2 ← aList[2]
mark3 ← aList[3]
APPEND(aList, (mark1+mark2+mark3)/3)
```

(A) [4, 5, 3, 4, 2, 5, 1]
(B) [4, 5, 3, 4, 2, 5, 1, 4]
(C) [4, 5, 3, 4, 2, 5, 1, 1]
(D) [4, 5, 3, 4, 2, 5, 1, 5, 4]

23. Refer to the code segment below:

```
List1 ← [12, 13, 22, 4, 7]
List2 ← [-4, -5, -21, -8]
INSERT(List1, 2, list2[3])
REMOVE(List2, LENGTH(List1) - 2)
APPEND(List1, LENGTH(List2)+ 5)
```

Which of the following represents the final values assigned to List1 and List2?

(A) List1: [12, -21, 13, 22, 5]
List2: [-4, -5, -21, -5]
(B) List1: [12, -21, 13, 22, 4]
List2: [-4, -5]
(C) List1: [12, -21, 13, 22, 4, 9]
List2: [-4, -5, -21, -1]
(D) List1: [12, -21, 13, 22, 4, 7, 8]
List2: [-4, -5, -21]

24. Refer to the procedure below. The procedure is intended to find and return the biggest number in the list arr that is received as an argument:

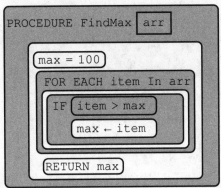

The procedure above is not working properly as intended with all test cases. Which of the following test cases should be passed to FindMax and results in returning an incorrect value?

(A) [0, 205]
(B) [-1, 0, 101]
(C) [1, 6, 9, 13]
(D) [105, 105, 93]

GO ON TO THE NEXT PAGE.

25. The following grid contains a robot represented as a triangle. The robot is initially facing right.

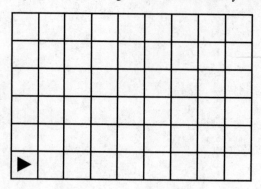

The procedure RollingDice() does not receive any arguments. The procedure controlRobot controls the robot to move it as instructed, the procedure receives two arguments: round and direction.

```
PROCEDURE RollingDice()
{
 temp ← RANDOM(1, 6)
  RETURN temp
}


PROCEDURE controlRobot(rounds, direction)
{
 REPEAT rounds TIMES
 {
    IF(direction)
        {
        ROTATE_RIGHT()
        }
    ELSE
        {
     ROTATE_LEFT()
      }
    steps←RollingDice()
    REPEAT steps TIMES
    {
            MOVE_FORWARD()
    }
 direction←NOT(direction)
 }
}
```

GO ON TO THE NEXT PAGE.

Which of the following is a possible placement for the robot after executing the procedure call below?

```
controlRobot(2, false)
```

(A)

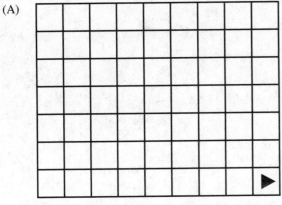

(C)

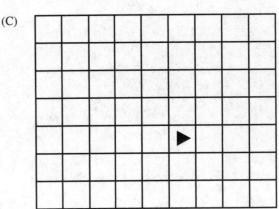

(B)

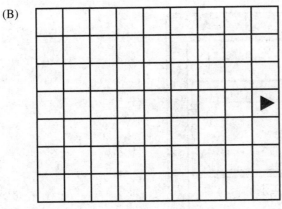

(D)

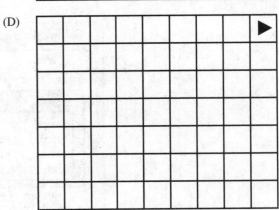

26. Refer to the program below:

```
temp←31
str←"Programming is interesting"
REPEAT UNTIL(temp MOD 15=0)
{
str←substring(str, 5 )
temp←temp - 4
}
DISPLAY(str)
```

The procedure substring(str, value) returns portion of the string str starting from the character at index value till the end of str.

Which of the following represents the final output after executing the code segment above?

(A) ing
(B) esting
(C) is interesting
(D) ing is interesting

GO ON TO THE NEXT PAGE.

27. Which of the following represents the final value assigned to the variable temp after executing the code segment below?

```
P←false
Q←true
temp←88
REPEAT UNTIL((P OR Q) AND P)
{
temp←temp-10
Q← NOT((P OR Q) AND P)
}
```

(A) 58

(B) 38

(C) 18

(D) Cannot specify because an infinite loop

28. Refer to the program below:

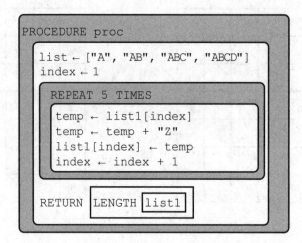

```
PROCEDURE proc
    list ← ["A", "AB", "ABC", "ABCD"]
    index ← 1
    REPEAT 5 TIMES
        temp ← list1[index]
        temp ← temp + "Z"
        list1[index] ← temp
        index ← index + 1

    RETURN LENGTH list1
```

Which of the following represents the return of the above procedure?

(A) 3

(B) 4

(C) 5

(D) An error message will be produced and the program will be terminated.

29. A computer program for teenagers indicates that it should be used only if the player's age is 12 or more and the player has agreed to the program's use terms and conditions.

The variable age holds the age of the player, and the variable terms holds a Boolean value of true if the player agreed on the terms and conditions or false otherwise.

Which of the following expressions evaluates to true if and only if a player meets the criteria?

(A) (age ≥ 12) AND NOT(terms)

(B) (age > 12 OR age = 12) AND terms

(C) (age > 12 AND age = 12) OR terms

(D) (age ≥ 12) OR NOT(terms)

GO ON TO THE NEXT PAGE.

30. The program below uses a conditional to help a student to decide which major he can study in the university.

```
IF (preferredSubject = "sciences" AND absenteeism< 5)
{
    Major ← "Chemistry"
}
ELSE
{
    IF (preferredSubject = "sciences" AND absenteeism<10)
    {
            major ← "Computer Science"
    }
}
```

In which of the following situations will major be "Computer Science"?

(A) `preferredSubject` is sciences and the `absenteeism` is 7
(B) `preferredSubject` is sciences and the `absenteeism` is 1
(C) `preferredSubject` is sciences and the `absenteeism` is 3
(D) `preferredSubject` is sciences and the `absenteeism` is 10

31. The program below specifies as either an equilateral triangle, an isosceles triangle, or a scalene triangle, the type of a triangle which has the sides A, B, and C as described below:

- An equilateral triangle has three equal sides
- A scalene triangle has three different sides
- Isosceles triangle which has two equal sides

```
IF (A = B AND B = C)
{
    type ← "equilateral triangle"
}
ELSE
{
    IF (A ≠ B AND B ≠ C)
    {
      type ← "scalene triangle"
    }
    ELSE
    {
      IF (A = B OR B = C OR A = C)
      {
          type ← "isosceles triangle"
      }
    }
}
```

The program is not working properly with all test cases.

Which of the following yields an incorrect result after executing the program?

(A) When A = 5, B = 5, and C = 5
(B) When A = 5, B = 5, and C = 8
(C) When A = 5, B = 8, and C = 5
(D) When A = 8, B = 5, and C = 5

GO ON TO THE NEXT PAGE.

32. Refer to the program below:

```
X ← 5
Y ← 10
Z ← -3
temp ← 100

IF ( X > 4 AND Y MOD 2 = 1)
{
    temp ← temp + 15
}
ELSE
{
    IF (Y MOD 3 = 1 AND temp / 10 = 5)
    {
      temp ← temp - 20
    }
    ELSE
    {
      IF (Z ← 0 OR (X + Y) MOD 4 = 0)
      {
          temp ← 10
      }
    }
}
```

Which of the following represents the final value assigned to the variable `temp`?

(A) 115
(B) 100
(C) 80
(D) 10

GO ON TO THE NEXT PAGE.

Questions 33–34 refer to the procedure below.

Consider that each of arr1 and arr2 have the same number of values.

```
PROCEDURE Mystery(arr1, arr2)
{
    index ← 1
    status ← false
    REPEAT UNTIL(index > LENGTH(arr1))
    {
        value ← arr1[index]
        FOR EACH item IN arr2
        {
            IF(value = item)
            {
                status ← true
            }
        }
        IF(status = false)
        {
            APPEND(arr2, value)
        }
        index ← index+1
        status ← false
    }
    RETURN (arr2)
}
```

33. Which of the following correctly describes the main function of the procedure Mystery?

    (A) Making two lists identical
    (B) Duplicating the common values among two lists
    (C) The values that are not in one list are to be copied from another list
    (D) The common values among two lists are to be removed from one of them

34. Which of the following represents the content of arr3 after executing the code segment below?

    ```
    arr1 ← [5, 7, 9, 2]
    arr2 ← [3, 7, 8, 5]
    arr3 ← Mystery (arr2, arr1)
    ```

    (A) [5, 7, 9, 2, 3, 8]
    (B) [3, 7, 8, 5, 9, 2]
    (C) [5, 7, 9, 2]
    (D) [3, 7, 8, 5]

GO ON TO THE NEXT PAGE.

35. The following grid contains a robot represented as a triangle. The robot is initially facing right.

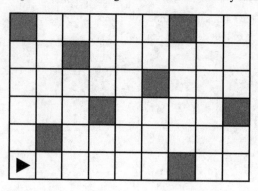

The robot can move into the white square only.

Which of the following programs will place the robot as illustrated below?

The procedure below controls the robot to move it as instructed, the procedure receives two arguments: round and direction.

```
I.  REPEAT 4 TIMES
    {
        MOVE_FORWARD()
    }
    ROTATE_LEFT()
    REPEAT 4 TIMES
    {
        MOVE_FORWARD()
    }
    ROTATE_RIGHT()
    REPEAT 4 TIMES
    {
        MOVE_FORWARD()
    }
```

```
II.  PROCEDURE goAhead(steps)
     {
         REPEAT steps TIMES
         {
             MOVE_FORWARD()
         }
     }
     goAhead(4)
     ROTATE_LEFT()
     goAhead(4)
     ROTATE_RIGHT()
     goAhead(4)
```

(A) I only

(B) II only

(C) I and II only

(D) Neither I nor II

GO ON TO THE NEXT PAGE.

Questions 36–37 refer to the procedure below.

```
PROCEDURE CheckIt(arr)
{
      size ← LENGTH(arr)
      index1 ← 1
      REPEAT UNTIL (index1 > size)
    {
            index2 ← 1
            REPEAT UNTIL (index2 > size)
            {
                  IF(index1 = index2)
                {
                  index2 ← index2 + 1
                }
                  IF(arr[index1] = arr[index2])
                  {
                        RETURN false
                  }
                  index2 ← index2 + 1
            }
        index1 ← index1 + 1
    }
      RETURN true
}
```

The procedure above was called as shown below but an error message was generated:

```
aList ← [5, 7, 9, 2]
CheckIt(aList)
```

36. Which of the following best describes the error in the program?

(A) At the last iteration, the index will exceed the length of the argument list. Index2 in the comparison
    (arr[index1] = arr[index2]) will be out of the list bounds.

(B) The index used to access the argument list will be negative in the last iteration, which results in terminating the program and
    producing an error message.

(C) Having two return statements in the program will cause a problem that terminates the program.

(D) Having nested iterations will cause an error of accessing values that are not existing in the list.

GO ON TO THE NEXT PAGE.

37. The procedure `CheckIt` is fixed as shown below:

```
PROCEDURE CheckIt(arr)
{
      size ← LENGTH(arr)
      index1 ← 1
      REPEAT UNTIL index1 > size
   {
         index2 ← 1
         REPEAT UNTIL index2 > size
         {
               IF(index1 = index2)
            {
                 index2 ← index2 + 1
            }
               IF(index2 ≤ size)
               {
                     IF(arr[index1] = arr[index2])
                     {
                     RETURN false
                     }
                     index2 ← index2 + 1
               }
         }
            index1 ← index1 + 1
   }
      RETURN true
}
```

Which of the following represents the returned value after the procedure call below?

```
aList ← [5, 7, 9, 2]
CheckIt(aList)
```

(A) false

(B) true

(C) true false

(D) false true

GO ON TO THE NEXT PAGE.

38. Refer to the search algorithm below that should be applied on a list of integers of n values indexed from 1 to n.

    Step 1: Create the variable number and set it to the value you are looking for.
    Step 2: Create the variable index and set it to 1.
    Step 3: Check if the value at index is equal to number, if so, then return index and stop. Otherwise, add 1 to index.
    Step 4: Repeat step 3 until index is greater than n.
    Step 5: Return −1 and stop.

    Of the following, which is the search algorithm that is described above?

    I.   Linear Search
    II. Binary Search
    III. Sequential Search

    (A) I only
    (B) II only
    (C) I and II only
    (D) I and III only

39. Which of the following is true about the binary search algorithm?

    I.   Data must be in sorted order to use the binary search algorithm.
    II. The maximum number of comparisons when applying binary search on a list of 800 elements is less than 15.
    III. Most of the time, applying binary search algorithm on a sorted list is less efficient than applying sequential search algorithm.

    (A) I only
    (B) II only
    (C) I and II only
    (D) I and III only

40. Natural Language processing HCI is a subfield of artificial intelligence that helps machines to understand human spoken or written words. Sam is a computer programmer, who is specialized in creating smart applications. Sam creates a language recognition application to be used on smart phones. The application accepts the user input and analyzes the meaning of it to perform the task or reply accordingly. For example, when a user asks to open a specific program or wants to save a text on the phone notes, the user instructs the application verbally and the algorithm tries to make sense of the user inputs. Word associations, analysis of context, and previous queries can be used to help the algorithm give satisfying results as well as speed up the process, but in all cases the solution can't be guaranteed to be optimal.

    Which of the following best describes Sam's application and algorithm?

    (A) It is impossible for an application to perform this task or it may not be able to perform it in a reasonable amount of time.
    (B) The application uses a heuristic algorithm as no optimal solution is guaranteed.
    (C) The problem is undecidable as the algorithm's given solution can't solve all instances of it.
    (D) The algorithm has a polynomial efficiency and can't run in a reasonable amount of time.

GO ON TO THE NEXT PAGE.

41. The two algorithms below are intended to display the result of the following series where n is a positive number:

$$n^2 + (n-1)^2 + (n-2)^2 + \ldots + 25 + 16 + 9 + 4 + 1$$

For example, if n is 6, then the method should display 91 as illustrated below:

$$36 + 25 + 16 + 9 + 4 + 1 = 91$$

Algorithm 1:

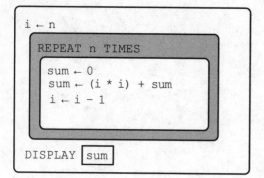

Algorithm 2:

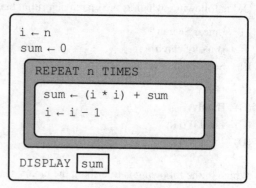

Which of the following correctly describes the result of using both of algorithm 1 and algorithm 2?

(A) Algorithm 1 correctly displays the series result but algorithm 2 does not.
(B) Algorithm 2 correctly displays the series result but algorithm 1 does not.
(C) Both of algorithm 1 and algorithm 2 display the correct result.
(D) Neither of the algorithms work correctly as intended.

42. Which of the following is correct about computer networks and routing?

I. Computer networks are interconnected computers and computing devices that have the ability to send and receive data within the network.

II. To send data from a computer to another in a network, the routing process finds a path from the sender to the receiver.

III. The Internet is the network of the interconnected networks that use standardized protocols to manage sending and receiving data through it.

(A) I only
(B) II only
(C) I and II only
(D) I, II, and III

GO ON TO THE NEXT PAGE.

43. Refer to the figure below that represents a network that connects 5 computing devices:

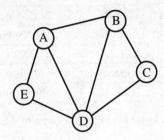

Of the following, which is incorrect about the network above?

(A) The network is fault-tolerant as it is able to support failures that happen.

(B) There is redundancy of rounding between all the computing devices in the network.

(C) If the line that connects station E with station A is disconnected, the whole network will stop working.

(D) If station C is out of response due to a technical issue, the network will keep working by avoiding it and using different routes.

44. Transmission Control Protocol (TCP) is an Internet protocol that facilitates exchanging messages on the Internet. Which of the following is NOT correct about the TCP protocol?

   I. TCP has its own addressing system, and unlike other protocols, it doesn't use the IP protocol.

   II. When sending messages, the TCP layer on the sender's side divides the messages into smaller packets to be forwarded by routers in the network.

   III. The TCP layer on the sender's side numbers the packets to help the TCP layer on the receiver side put them in the correct order.

(A) I only

(B) II only

(C) III only

(D) I and III only

45. Which of the following is the Internet protocol that is described as an application level, client-server protocol, used to transmit hypermedia documents from servers to clients' computing devices and allows users to communicate data on the World Wide Web?

(A) UDP

(B) TCP

(C) DNS

(D) HTTP

GO ON TO THE NEXT PAGE.

46. The following Internet service providers (ISPs) offer Internet service for individuals as per the table below:

ISP	Bandwidth
Hi-Fi	15000Kbps
Tele	25Mbs
Speedy	9Mbps
Data-Com	9000Kbps

Of the following, which is the ISP that can transfer the highest amount of data per second?

(A) Hi-Fi

(B) Tele

(C) Speedy

(D) Data-Com

47. An IA solutions company has 850 employees, and each employee needs a computer and a mobile phone to be connected to the Internet at the same time during the whole workday.

Suppose that all employees are at work, what is the minimum number of bits needed in a binary number to provide addresses for all these devices so every single device in the company is assigned a unique address for connection to the Internet?

(A) 9

(B) 10

(C) 11

(D) 12

48. Refer to the steps below that describe how to send a message from computer A to computer B via the Internet using TCP/IP after establishing the connection between them:

- IP generates the IP addresses of the sender and the receiver and TCP breaks the message into packets and adds metadata to packets.

- Every packet will be sent through the connections and can take a different route between the source and the destination, depending on whether the original route becomes congested or unavailable.

- Packets may arrive out of order or even they may not arrive at all.

- Packets reception is acknowledged by TCP at the destination and they are reassembled.

Which of the following is guaranteed when using TCP?

I. Speed

II. Accuracy

III. Reliability

(A) I only

(B) II only

(C) I and II only

(D) II and III only

49. Which of the following represents an instance where UDP is better to be used than TCP?

(A) Emails

(B) Online video games

(C) Online payments

(D) Loading websites

GO ON TO THE NEXT PAGE.

Questions 50–51 refer to the information below.

A computational task consists of 6 processes where each process should be executed on one processor only. The amount of time needed for each process is shown in the table below:

Process	Time needed to be executed on a processor
A	35 seconds
B	10 seconds
C	50 seconds
D	60 seconds
E	40 seconds
F	25 seconds

To execute and perform the task, two computers will be used. Computer 1 has one processor and computer 2 has two processors that can work in parallel. All processors in both computers are identical and can execute one process at a time.

The processes of the task are to be executed as follows, assuming that all processes and independent:

Process	Time needed to be executed on a processor	Computer to execute the process
A	35 seconds	Computer 2
B	10 seconds	Computer 2
C	50 seconds	Computer 1
D	60 seconds	Computer 2
E	40 seconds	Computer 2
F	25 seconds	Computer 1

50. Which of the following is a computational model that is followed when the executing the task?

    I. Parallel computing

   II. Sequential computing

  III. Distributed computing

(A) I only

(B) I and II only

(C) I and III only

(D) I, II, and III

51. Which of the following represents the approximate least possible time needed to execute the six process by the two computers when all processors in computer 1 and computer 2 work simultaneously?

(A) 55

(B) 75

(C) 85

(D) 95

GO ON TO THE NEXT PAGE.

52. Refer to the circuit shown below that is composed of two AND operators, one OR operator and one NOT operator. The AND and OR operators take two inputs and each one of the generate one output while the NOT operator takes one input that is unknown in the given circuit and generates one output.

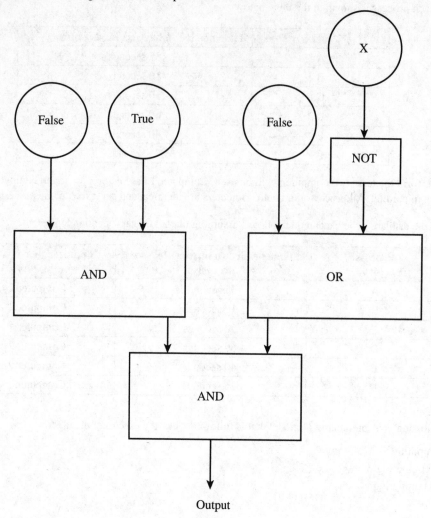

Which of the following correctly describes the final output of the circuit?

(A) The output of the circuit is true if X is true.

(B) The output of the circuit is true if X is false.

(C) The output of the circuit is always true regardless of what is the value of X.

(D) The output of the circuit is always false regardless of what is the value of X.

GO ON TO THE NEXT PAGE.

53. Which of the following best describes Keylogging?

(A) The use of a program to record every keystroke made by a computer user in order to gain fraudulent access to passwords and other confidential information

(B) A technique that attempts to trick a user into providing personal information

(C) A malicious program that can copy itself and gain access to a computer in an unauthorized way

(D) A software intended to damage a computing system or to take partial control over its operation

54. Consider the following program:

```
i ← n
REPEAT 5 TIMES {
    i ← i + i
}

REPEAT 3 TIMES {
    i ← i * i
}
DISPLAY(i)
```

Which of the following expressions represents the result of the program?

(A) $(5 * n)^8$

(B) $(8 * n)^4$

(C) $(16 * n)^4$

(D) $(32 * n)^8$

55. A nutrition specialist maintains a dataset of different products of cereals with the following information about each item in the dataset:

- Product name
- Manufacturer
- Calories
- Carbohydrates
- Vitamins
- Ratings by people

Of the following, which can't be determined using this dataset?

(A) The product name with the highest number of ratings for each manufacturer

(B) The number of products that are produced by the same manufacturer

(C) The product that has the highest number of sales

(D) The products that should be avoided by people who are on a diet

56. Which of the following situations reveals digital divide?

(A) COVID-19 pandemic forced schools to close and students all over the world—in cities and rural areas—had to follow online studying models, despite not all of them having stable access to the Internet or adequate computing devices

(B) A teacher conducts classes in the computer lab of a school where every student has a computer on which to perform his tasks

(C) A group of students are conducting a research using their computers of the same model that are connected to the Internet at their homes

(D) A school changed the teaching model to online and offered every student and teacher a laptop and a tablet to be used to conduct lessons and perform tasks

GO ON TO THE NEXT PAGE.

57. A programming team is developing an ordering procedure for products sold on a company's website.

The model website began with a simple version of the ordering procedure. Based on feedback received from its testers, the programming team developed new features and improved existing features based on testers comments. The process kept repeating until the final version of the program was produced.

Which of the following is the development model that was followed by the programming team?

I. Iterative development model
II. Incremental development model

(A) I only
(B) II only
(C) Both I and II
(D) Neither I nor II

Questions 58–62 refer to the information below.

A small bank has decided to develop a mobile app for its users, which the bank will create. All data at will be stored the local branch. The bank has resisted making this change because its users live in a small town where everyone knows each other. The bank realizes that by creating an online system, customers will have concerns that will require additional features.

The mobile app is requiring its customers to come to the bank and sign a form agreeing to the risks of the system and choose a pin number. When current customers come to the bank, they only need to provide their names to the bank teller to access their account information. When users accesses the new system, however, they will be required to provide their email addresses and chosen pin numbers. The app will then instruct the user to do only the following:

• Access account #
• Read account balance
• Retrieve bank statement and transaction history from the last 60 days
• Process current checks/payments being processed
• Close bank account

58. Which of the following is the most plausible data storage concern of the new mobile banking system?

(A) The new mobile banking app will require a large amount of storage for the computer system and may cause the cost of banking for customers to rise.
(B) Since the bank is storing all data at their local branch, storage capacity may be a concern. It may require additional server updates or additional computer hardware.
(C) Storage of the data will require almost the identical amount of storage of the traditional bank and therefore no data storage concerns will occur with the new system.
(D) Storage of customer data may require cloud storage, which will leave bank customers with more privacy and security concerns due to possible hacking.

59. Which of the following statements is most likely to be true about the trade-offs of customers enrolling in the mobile bank app?

(A) The mobile banking app will allow customers to have more ease of access but will limit functionality.
(B) Customers can travel more and have more protection of their money due to the security of the mobile banking app.
(C) The mobile banking app will improve the digital divide for customers of the bank but will limit customer-banker interactions.
(D) The bank tellers are able to more easily access information for customers because of their training, but using the app may take more time to access information due to customer inexperience.

GO ON TO THE NEXT PAGE.

60. Which of the following is most likely to be a benefit of having a mobile banking app?

    (A) The mobile banking app will allow its customers who are traveling to deposit checks and see information on their account.
    (B) The mobile banking app will allow customers easier access to their accounts as less information is required to access them.
    (C) Customers will be able to deposit checks, transfer money, and access account information from their own homes.
    (D) Customers will be able to access bank information and close bank accounts outside of normal banking hours.

61. Which of the following input data is needed by the mobile banking app that was NOT needed by the original system?

    (A) Email address, account number, and pin number
    (B) Pin number, signed agreement, and email address
    (C) Email address and account number
    (D) No additional information is needed.

62. Which of the following data is necessary for the mobile bank app to allow customer access to bank statement data from 3 months ago?

    (A) The customer is required to sign a form agreeing to risks of the new system and choose a pin number.
    (B) No additional data is necessary to access bank statement data; using the mobile app will be identical to going to the physical bank location.
    (C) Although use of the new system requires you to sign a form agreeing to risks of the mobile banking app and choose a pin number, the app will be unable to access bank statement data older than 60 days.
    (D) To access bank statement data, the user will be required to input email address and pin number.

63. Consider the following program:

```
i ← RANDOM(5, 8)
n ← 3
REPEAT UNTIL n > 5
{
    i ← 2 * i + 1
    n ← n + 1
}
    DISPLAY(i)
```

Of the following, which is a possible output of the program?

Select <u>two</u> answers.

    (A) 42
    (B) 55
    (C) 62
    (D) 71

GO ON TO THE NEXT PAGE.

64. The head pharmacist for a group of pharmacies plans to create a program that contains all 80,000 medicine products, their expiration dates, and warns when any product is going to expire in one month.

Of the following, which must be used within his program?

Select two answers.

(A) Selection
(B) Iteration
(C) Procedures
(D) Sorting

65. Which of the following is correct about computing innovations?

Select two answers.

(A) The creators of the computing innovations can't consider all the possible ways their innovations are going to be used, but they should consider the potential beneficial and harmful effects of new uses.
(B) Computing innovations only relate to computer science and are not related to other fields such as medicine, art, engineering, and agriculture.
(C) Computing innovations have regularly had unintended advantageous impacts by driving progress in other areas.
(D) Unintended consequences of computing innovations are generally problematic.

66. In an event-driven program, an event associated with an action supplies input data for a program. Which of the following generates an event to execute program statements?

Select two answers.

(A) Calling a procedure
(B) Clicking a mouse
(C) Pressing a keyboard key
(D) Opening an application

67. A list of integers has n values indexed from 1 to n. The algorithm shown below is intended to add 5 to each number in the list and display the average of the list after the modification.

Step 1: Create the variable index and set it to 1.
Step 2: Create the variable total and set it to 0.
Step 3: Add the value at index to total, then Add 5 to the value at index.
Step 4: Increase index by 1.
Step 5: Repeat steps 2, 3 and 4 until index is greater than n.
Step 6: Create average variable and set it to total / n.
Step 7: Display the value of average.

The algorithm above is not doing the task properly. Which of the following modifications must be applied to the algorithm to fix it?

Select two answers.

(A) Swap steps 5 and 6.
(B) Swap steps 2 and 3.
(C) Change Step 3 into: Add 5 to the value at index, the add the value at index total.
(D) Change step 5 into: Repeat steps 3 and 4 until index is greater than n.

GO ON TO THE NEXT PAGE.

68. Jone is designing a cooking program that is intended to explain how to cook a recipe.

The segment below is a portion of his big program and is supposed to do the following:

- The user will enter the recipe name.
- The user will enter the number of items needed for the recipe.
- Using a loop, the user will enter the ingredients one by one to a list that was previously declared as an empty list.
- A loop to iterate through the list is used to display all the content of the list that holds the ingredients to display them.

```
aList ← []
recipe ← INPUT()
NumberOfItems ← INPUT()
REPEAT NumberOfItems TIMES
{
 Ingredient ← INPUT()
 APPEND(aList, Ingredient)
}
DISPLAY("These are the ingredients of "+ recipe+": ")
index ←  /*MISSING VALUE */
REPEAT UNTIL(index<1)
{
 DISPLAY( aList[index])
 index ← index - 1
}
```

Which of the following values should be assigned to index variable so that the code will work properly as intended and all ingredients in the list are displayed with no errors?

Select two answers.

(A) NumberOfItems
(B) LENGTH (aList)
(C) LENGTH (aList) + 1
(D) NumberOfItems * 2

69. A machine learning model was created to classify students into either eligible to sit for the AP Computer Science Principles Exam or not eligible. The model was trained using a dataset composed of entries representing the student gender and a programming diagnostic test score. The dataset contains a total of 4323 records with the following details:

500 female records and 3823 male records
600 Java records and 2823 Python records

Which of the following best describes a possible result of using this model in all schools to decide the students' eligibility to sit for the AP Computer Science Principles Exam?

Select two answers.

(A) Because the dataset contains biased data that checks Java and Python programming languages, the learning model may not be fair to students with other programming language skills.
(B) The model will help in making proper decisions about the students' eligibility to sit for the AP Computer Science Principles Exam.
(C) The model may give poor results for female students compared to male students because of bias in the dataset.
(D) The model will be able to specify the eligibility of the student if he/she sat for AP Statistics Exam with a score of 3 or higher.

GO ON TO THE NEXT PAGE.

Refer to the table below for information that was taken from a bigger dataset:

Year	% of Internet Usage
2016	42%
2017	46%
2018	54%
2019	56%
2020	60%

70. Of the following, which option best describes the given information in the table?

Select <u>two</u> answers.

(A) It represents metadata of the dataset, which describes the dataset and provides additional information about its content.

(B) It is considered part of the dataset content.

(C) Changes or deletions to it will cause an update to the primary content of the dataset.

(D) It helps in making the data structured and clean and can be used for finding, organizing, and managing information.

STOP

END OF EXAM

Practice Test 3:
Answers and
Explanations

PRACTICE TEST 3 ANSWER KEY

1.	B	36.	A
2.	D	37.	B
3.	D	38.	D
4.	A	39.	C
5.	C	40.	B
6.	C	41.	B
7.	B	42.	D
8.	D	43.	C
9.	B	44.	A
10.	C	45.	D
11.	B	46.	B
12.	D	47.	C
13.	A	48.	D
14.	D	49.	B
15.	D	50.	D
16.	D	51.	B
17.	C	52.	D
18.	B	53.	A
19.	C	54.	D
20.	B	55.	C
21.	A	56.	A
22.	B	57.	A
23.	D	58.	B
24.	C	59.	A
25.	C	60.	D
26.	B	61.	B
27.	D	62.	C
28.	D	63.	B, D
29.	B	64.	A, B
30.	A	65.	A, C
31.	C	66.	B, C
32.	D	67.	C, D
33.	C	68.	A, B
34.	B	69.	A, C
35.	C	70.	A, D

PRACTICE TEST 3 EXPLANATIONS

1. **B**   To convert a decimal number to binary, keep dividing the number by 2. When dividing by 2, take the integer part of the result and repeat the process until you reach a result of 0. The resulting remainders will be the binary equivalent in reverse order. The table below shows how to convert 2,719 to binary.

	Result	Remainder
2719/2	1359	1
1359/2	679	1
679/2	339	1
339/2	169	1
169/2	84	1
84/2	42	0
42/2	21	0
21/2	10	1
10/2	5	0
5/2	2	1
2/2	1	0
1/2	0	1
STOP		

Take the remainders from the bottom up to get the binary number 101010011111. As each 8 bits are 1 byte, this means that 2,719 needs at least 2 bytes to be represented in binary especially since no partial bytes can be used. The answer is (B).

2. **D**   To make it easy, start by converting the binary numbers to decimal numbers, then perform the mathematical calculations to answer the question. To convert a binary number to a decimal number, use the power of two table.

Power of 2	2^{10}	2^9	2^8	2^7	2^6	2^5	2^4	2^3	2^2	2^1	2^0
Value	1,024	512	256	128	64	32	16	8	4	2	1
Binary number	1	1	0	1	1	1	1	0	1	0	0

Now, the last step is to add all the power of 2 values under which the binary number cell is filled with 1. In this case, they are 1,024 + 512 + 128 + 64 + 32 + 16 + 4 = 1,780.

Convert, the second number the same way.

Power of 2	2^{10}	2^9	2^8	2^7	2^6	2^5	2^4	2^3	2^2	2^1	2^0
Value	1,024	512	256	128	64	32	16	8	4	2	1
Binary number	1	0	1	0	1	1	1	1	0	0	0

The result is $1,024 + 256 + 64 + 32 + 16 + 8 = 1,400$.

The garden is rectangular, so she needs to calculate the perimeter then multiply it by the cost: $(1,780 \times 2 + 1,400 \times 2) \times \$5 = \$31,800$. The answer is (D).

3. **D** To convert from binary to decimal, we will add all of powers of 2 represented by the bits that hold 1. Start with $(1101101)_2$.

Power of 2	2^6	2^5	2^4	2^3	2^2	2^1	2^0
Value	64	32	16	8	4	2	1
Binary number	1	1	0	1	1	0	1

Therefore, $(1101101)_2 = 64 + 32 + 8 + 4 + 1 = 109$. Now, do the same for $(10001111)_2$.

Power of 2	2^7	2^6	2^5	2^4	2^3	2^2	2^1	2^0
Value	128	64	32	16	8	4	2	1
Binary number	1	0	0	0	1	1	1	1

Therefore, $(10001111)_2 = 128 + 8 + 4 + 2 + 1 = (143)_{10}$. The correct descending order is $(176)_{10} > (10001111)_2 > (1101101)_2$. The answer is (D).

4. **A** A binary number is even when the right most digit is 0. The code NUM MOD 10 always produces the right most digit of the number. If it is 1, ODD is returned; EVEN will be returned otherwise. All of the given numbers in the options are odd according to the explanation except (A), which includes an even binary number. The answer is (A).

5. **C** In the procedure Guess, the line with <missing expression> is the second line in a REPEAT loop, and therefore, must correspond with the second step of the loop in the algorithm diagram. This step stores the integer part of the result when NUM is divided by 2. Try a value for NUM. Let NUM = 9. If NUM = 9, then NUM / 2 = 4.5, so the integer part is 4. Eliminate any choice that doesn't result in 4. Choice (A) is 9 / 2 = 4.5, so eliminate (A). Choice (B) = (1 MOD 2) / 2 = 1 / 2 – 0.5, so eliminate (B). Choice (C) is 9 / 2 – (9 MOD 2) / 2 = 4.5 – 1 / 2 = 4.5 – 0.5 = 4, so keep (C). Choice (D) is (9 MOD 2) * 2 – (9 MOD 2) / 2 = 1 * 2 – 1 / 2 = 1 – 0.5 = 0.5, so eliminate (D). The answer is (C).

6. **C** Choice (C) is the least accurate option. If you are representing an analog image digitally, you should try to produce the best digital image that represents the analog one. In order to catch all the details and give the impression of analog data, you need to add more pixels/bits to represent every square inch (this means that the higher the resolution of the image, the better). In order to represent more pixels per square inch, you need more bits, which contradicts (C).

7. **B** As there are 7 bits used to represent any symbol in ASCII, there are $2^7 = 128$ symbols that can be represented using this system. The answer is (B).

8. **D** First, start by converting the digital signal to binary number: 10011001000001. Now, as you have 14 bits, this gives two groups of bits with each group representing a letter. The first group is 1001100; convert it to the decimal number 76, which is 'L'. The second group of bits is 1000001; convert it the decimal number 65, which 'A'. The answer is (D).

9. **B** Both statements I and II are correct as lossy techniques work on deleting some parts of the original file in order to reduce the size, which leads to the loss of the deleted data. At the same time, it works better in reducing files sizes. Statement III is incorrect because if the priority after the compression is the quality of the file, then it is better to use lossless techniques as no data will be deleted and all the data of the files can be restored. The answer is (B).

10. **C** All choices include statement I, so there is no need to consider it. (Note that statement I is correct because it is consistent with the method used and the reason for it.) Statement II is incorrect as there are no lossless compression techniques used by Suzy, and no dictionary of symbols was used by her to reach the conclusion that a lossless technique compressed the text message. Eliminate (B) and (D), which include statement II. Statement III is correct as Suzy worked on removing some letters from the message and keeping the ones that are important for the recipient to understand the message. In this case, she is relying on the recipient's ability to fill in the gaps to understand the message, which makes it an improper way to compress text messages. Eliminate (A), which does not include III. The answer is (C).

11. **B** Statement I is not correct since the table only describes the number of cups people drink rather than the number they *need to consume*. Eliminate (A) and (D), which include statement I. Statement II is not correct as the data shows that younger children consume less water than do teenagers. Eliminate (C), which includes statement II. Only one choice remains, so there is no need to continue. However, note that statement III is correct as the data in the table shows consistent growth in water consumption as people get older. The answer is (B).

12. **D** Since the graph illustrates a linear, increasing relationship from the ages 3 to 17, statements I and III are correct. Statement II contradicts statements I and III, so statement II is incorrect. The answer is (D).

13. **A** The variables are assigned the initial values of a = 10, b = 6, and c = 5. Next, b is assigned a - c = 10 - 5 = 5. Then c is assigned b * 2 = 5 * 2 = 10. Finally, a is assigned b MOD c = 10 MOD 5 = 0. The answer is (A).

14 **D** Metadata is data about data. This can include creation date or size of the dataset, so statement I is correct. The information in metadata can help with more effective use of the data, so statement II is also correct. Metadata can also be used to help structure or organize the data, which can help in pre-curating the data, so statement III is also correct. The answer is (D).

15. **D** Digital divide is the gap between the different levels of technological access that is available to different users. There is nothing about that here, so eliminate (A). Similarly, there is no mention of any sort of compression or encryption, so eliminate (B) and (C) as well. Multifactor authentication is a method of computer access control in which a user is only granted access after successfully presenting several separate pieces of evidence to an authentication mechanism. This typically includes at least two of the following categories: information (something they know), ownership (something they have), and inherence (something they are). The answer is (D).

16. **D** In the assignment of temp, "x", "y", and "z" refer to the strings "x", "y", and "z" and are unrelated to the variables x, y, and z. The answer is (D).

17. **C** Choice (C) is not true because cleaning and filtering processes done manually are much slower than done on a computer. The answer is (C).

18. **B** Crowdsourcing makes questions or assignments available to a large group of people to get input for the purpose of innovation or development. Although the researcher made his research public, there's no indication that he's looking for input, so eliminate (A). Similarly, there is no indication that the researcher is looking for input from non-scientists, so eliminate (C). Also, nothing indicates that the researcher is creating documentaries, so eliminate (D). Although the researcher is choosing to make the research public, it is still his creation and, therefore, his intellectual property. The answer is (B).

19. **C** When material is open source, the source code itself is free to me modified by other users. In the case described, only the research itself is allowed to be modified rather than the source code, so eliminate (A). Creative Commons does not involve selling research, so eliminate (B). Creative Commons does allow the author to put restrictions on use, so it is not open access. Eliminate (D). Creative Commons allows the owner of the intellectual property to control how his or her work is used. The answer is (C).

20. **B** Eliminate (C) and (D), since the NOT operator will yield a Boolean rather than a number. Now determine the Boolean value of flag. The statement x ≥ y is false if x = 1 and y = 2, but z ≠ y is true if z = 3 and y = 2. Since one of those statements is true, the statement (x ≥ y OR z ≠ y) is true. Therefore, the statement NOT (x ≥ y OR z ≠ y) is false. Since this is the value assigned to flag, the answer is (B).

21. **A** The variable temp will be assigned the result of concatenating substring(str, 4, 7)+ " " + substring(str, 10). The result of substring(str, 4, 7) is the substring of str from index 4 to index 6, which is "put". Then it will concatenate " ", which is a space. Finally, it will concatenate substring(str, 10), which is the substring of str from index 10 till the end of str, which is "Science". Therefore, the answer is (A).

22. **B** The list, aList, will be appended by (mark1 + mark2 + mark3) / 3. Since mark1 is assigned 4, mark2 is assigned 5, and mark3 is assigned 3, the value that is appended is (4 + 5 + 3) / 3 = 4. Therefore, the appended list is [4, 5, 3, 4, 2, 5, 1, 4]. The answer is (B).

23. **D** The command INSERT(List1, 2, List2[3]) will insert the value at index 3 in List2 to index 2 in List1, making List1 = [12, –21, 13, 22, 4, 7]. Since List1 – 2 = 6 – 1 = 4, the command REMOVE(List2, LENGTH(List1) - 2) deletes the 4th element of List2, making List2 = [–4, –5, –21]. Finally, since LENGTH(List2) + 5 = 3 + 5 = 8, the value 8 is appended to the end of List1 to make List1 = [12, –21, 13, 22, 4, 7, 8]. The answer is (D).

24. **C** The variable max is initially 100. Therefore, if all the contents of the list are less than 100, then the condition IF(item > max) will never be met and the value of max will not change. This causes returning 100 as the biggest number, which is incorrect result. Since [1, 6, 9, 13] only contains values less than 100, FindMax will return the wrong value if this array is passed. The answer is (C).

25. **C** As the number of rounds are 2 and the initial direction is left (false), then the robot will start by rotating to its left, causing it to point upwards. Then the number of steps the robot will move will be specified by calling RollingDice procedure, which returns an integer from 1 to 6. Therefore, in the first round the robot will be somewhere above its current row. This means that (A) is incorrect because the robot is placed in the same row. After the robot moves to the correct row in the first round, its direction will be reversed. The final statement of the first round, flips the direction to true. In the 2nd round, the robot will be directed to its right. The number of steps it moves will be specified by calling RollingDice, which have a maximum return of 6. This means that the furthest to the right the robot can be is in the 7th column, so (B) and (D) are both incorrect. The answer is (C).

26. **B** The variable temp is initially set to 31, and the string str is initially set to "Programming is interesting". Since 31 MOD 15 ≠ 0, execute the repeat. Set str to substring(str, 5), which is the substring of str starting with the character at index 6 and going to the end of the string, leaving "amming is interesting". The variable temp is set to temp – 4 = 31 – 4 = 27. Since 27 MOD 15 ≠ 0, execute the repeat again. Set str to substring(str, 5), which is "g is interesting". The variable temp is set to temp – 4 = 27 – 4 = 23. Since 23 MOD 15 ≠ 0, execute the repeat again. Set str to substring(str, 5), which is "interesting". The variable temp is set to temp – 4 = 23 – 4 = 19. Since 19 MOD 15 ≠ 0, execute the repeat again. Set str to substring(str, 5), which is "esting". The variable temp is set to temp – 4 = 19 – 4 = 15. Since 15 MOD 15 = 0, end the loop. Display str, which is "esting". The answer is (B).

27. **D** The loop will keep repeating as long as the condition (P OR Q) AND P is false. For an AND statement to be true, both statements must be true. Since P is initially false, the condition (P OR Q) AND P is false, regardless of whether (P OR Q) is true. The rest of the code changes the Q value with no change to the P value, which makes P always false. Therefore, the condition will always be false which causes an infinite loop. The answer is (D).

28. **D** For all list operations, if a list index is less than 1 or greater than the length of the list, an error message is produced, and the program terminates. The list List1 has 4 values, and the loop repeats 5 times, increasing index by 1 each time. Therefore, in the 5th interval, index is 5, which exceeds the bounds of the array, causing an error message and terminating the program. The answer is (D).

29. **B** This Boolean expression has two parts as per the following description: (1) player's age is 12 or more and (2) player agreed to the program's use terms and conditions. Since both conditions must be true, an AND operator is needed between the age condition and the terms condition. Eliminate (C) and (D), which uses OR. Between (A) and (B), the first conditions are equivalent, so look at the second. The variable terms must be true to fit the requirements, so eliminate (A). The answer is (B).

30 **A** All of the choices say that preferredSubject is "sciences", so ignore that part. To assign "Computer Science" to major, first the program must reach the ELSE, so absenteeism must be greater than or equal to 5. Eliminate (B) and (C). Now, the IF condition inside the ELSE statement must be true, so absenteeism must be less than 10. Eliminate (D). The answer is (A).

31. **C** Nested conditional statements are used in this program, so that the sequence matters here. Choice (A) will satisfy the initial IF condition, since (A = B AND B = C), and type will be correctly assigned "equilateral triangle". For (B), neither the condition (A = B AND B = C) nor the condition (A ≠ B AND B ≠ C) are met but (A = B OR B = C OR A = C) is met, which causes the type to be correctly assigned "isosceles triangle". For (C), the condition (A = B AND B = C) is not met but (A ≠ B AND B ≠ C) is met, so type will be assigned "scalene triangle". However, two sides, A and C, are equal, so this triangle is actually isosceles. Therefore, this test case shows that the program does not always work properly. Check (D) to be sure. In (D), neither the condition (A = B AND B = C) nor the condition (A ≠ B AND B ≠ C) are met but (A = B OR B = C OR A = C) is met, which causes the type to hold "isosceles triangle", which is the correct assignment. Only (C) yields an incorrect result. The answer is (C).

32. **D** The condition of the first IF statement, which is (X > 4 AND Y MOD 2 = 1), will be false since Y MOD 2 = 10 MOD 2 = 0. Since the first condition is false, you need to go to the ELSE and evaluate the second IF statement, which has condition (Y MOD 3 = 1 AND temp / 10 = 5). Since temp / 10 = 100 / 10 = 10, this is false, so go to the second ELSE and evaluate the third IF, which has the condition (Z < 0 OR (X + Y) MOD 4 = 0). Since Z = –3 < 0, this is true, so execute the statement IF statement and assign 10 to temp. The correct answer is (D).

33. **C** The procedure receives two lists, arr1 and arr2, and starts by instructing the index to start with 1 and status to be initially false. The procedure then takes the content of arr1, element by element, using a loop to check whether that value exists somewhere in arr2. If it does, then status will be turned into true, and therefore, the value will not be appended to arr2. This means that the procedure is intended to copy the contents of arr1 into arr2 without duplicating values: if a value in arr1 is already existing in arr2, it will not be appended to arr2. The answer is (C).

34. **B**   In this segment, `arr1` and `arr2` were created and filled with values `arr1 ← [5, 7, 9, 2]` and `arr2 ← [3, 7, 8, 5]`. However, when called by the procedure, they were passed in reverse order: `Mystery (arr2, arr1)`. This means that `arr1` held a copy of the list that was called in `arr2` outside the procedure and vice versa. Therefore, `arr1 = [3, 7, 8, 5]` and `arr2 = [5, 7, 9, 2]`. Follow the steps of the procedure: start by specifying `index` to start as 1 and `status` to be initially `false`. The procedure takes the content of `arr1`, element by element, and uses a loop to check `arr2`. If it has the current value from `arr1`, then `status` will be turned into `true`, and therefore, the value will not be appended to `arr2`. The procedure is intended to copy the content of `arr1` into `arr2` without duplicating values: if a value in `arr1` is already existing in `arr2`, it will not be appended to `arr2`. Therefore, `arr1` will be appended to the noncommon elements from `arr2`, which are 9 and 2. Therefore, the procedure will return [3, 7, 8, 5, 9, 2]. The answer is (B).

35. **C**   Both program I and program II perform the same exact task as described below. The robot moves forward 4 steps. The robot rotates to the left. The robot moves forward 4 steps. The robot rotates to the right. The robot moves forward 4 steps. Program I is written without using procedures; that's why it contains duplicated lines that perform the same task, which is move forward 4 steps, while program II implemented the same task using a procedure to encapsulate the code that is needed frequently, then it is called when needed.

36. **A**   Both indexes are given initial values of 1 and are never decreased. Therefore, their values cannot be negative. Eliminate (B). Two return statements will not cause an error as the procedure will terminate once the first one is reached. Eliminate (C). Neither iteration creates values that are used outside the iteration, so eliminate (D). In the final iteration, `index1` will be equal to `size`, and `index2` will be equal to `size + 1`, leading to an out of bounds error. Therefore, the correct answer is (A).

37. **B**   Even though there are multiple return statements, the procedure will terminate upon reaching the first, so there cannot be two returns. Eliminate (C) and (D). The procedure receives a list, it takes the items of the list one by one and it compares them to the other items in the array. If it finds to similar items, it returns `false` or otherwise, if there are no similar items, it will return `true`.

38. **D**   Linear search and sequential search refer to the same algorithm, which checks each element of a list in their order until a desired value is found, or all the list elements are checked. The algorithm performs this task where the loop is iterated through the list's content, looking for the value of the variable number: once found, then the index where it was found will be returned. If all list items were checked and none of them matches number, then −1 is returned. A binary search, however, must begin in the middle of an ordered list. The list in this algorithm is not assumed to be ordered nor does the search begin in the middle. The answer is (D).

39. **C**   The binary search algorithm starts at the middle of a sorted data set of numbers and eliminates half of the data; this process repeats until the desired value is found or all elements have been eliminated. Since the list must be sorted to use a binary search, statement I must be included. Eliminate (B). The maximum number of comparisons in a binary search is $\log_2(n)$, where n is the number of

items in the list. Though $\log_2(800)$ is hard to calculate, you can calculate powers of 2 to realize that $800 < 2^{10}$, so $\log_2(800) < 10 < 15$. Therefore, statement II is also true. Eliminate (A) and (D). Only one answer remains, so there is no need to continue. However, note that, since a sequential search algorithm must go through each item in the list individually until it finds the desired element, it is typically less efficient than a binary search. Therefore, statement III is not correct. The answer is (C).

40. **B** Choices (A) and (C) are not correct as nothing indicates that the problem of the application is undecidable or can't be solved in a reasonable amount of time. Choice (D) is also not correct as nothing in the given description indicates that the algorithm has a polynomial efficiency nor that the algorithm is given to calculate the efficiency to decide on its type. By definition, a heuristic is an approach to a problem that produces a solution that is not guaranteed to be optimal. The answer is (B).

41. **B** Algorithm 1 doesn't do the task properly. The problem of this algorithm is that sum is created inside the loop body, where sum is assigned 0 at the beginning of every single iteration. This prevents sum from holding the accumulative total of the squares of the numbers from n to 1. Eliminate (A) and (C), which state that Algorithm 1 works correctly. Algorithm 2 does the task correctly. It starts with n, and iterates through the numbers from n to 1 and finds the total of the squares of those numbers. The sum here is properly created outside the loop body, which enables it to hold the accumulative total of the squares of the numbers from n to 1. Eliminate (D), which says that Algorithm 2 does not work correctly. The answer is (B).

42. **D** All of the given options are correct. A computer network is a group of interconnected computing devices capable of sending or receiving data. Routing is the process of finding a path from sender to receiver. The Internet is a computer network consisting of interconnected networks that use standardized, communication protocols.

43. **C** The network above is fault-tolerant, as the stations are connected in a way that supports any failure: if one station stops working for any reason, the data will follow another path to be delivered to the destination. This is because there are redundant paths connecting the devices. For example, if you want to send data from station A to station D, you can follow more than one path to do so: you can use the direct link if it is available, send the data through station E, or send the data through B, and so on. Choice (C) contains incorrect information about the network; the network has redundant paths between all the stations, and the failure of one path or one station will not stop the network. The answer is (C).

44. **A** Statement I is not correct about the TCP. TCP is one of the Internet protocols the uses the IP protocol. The question asks for which statements are incorrect, so statement I must be included in the correct answers. Eliminate (B) and (C). Both statements II and III correctly describe how TCP exchanges messages between devices, starting by dividing the message into smaller chunks called packets and numbering them so the TCP layer on the receiver's side will be able to put them in the correct order to reconstruct the original message. Therefore, II and III should not be included. Eliminate (D). The answer is (A).

45. **D** HTTP stands for Hypertext Transfer Protocol that allows users to communicate data and hypermedia documents on the World Wide Web. It is considered the foundation of the World Wide Web and is used to load web pages using hyperlinks. The answer is (D).

46. **B** The Hi-Fi ISP transfers a maximum of 15000 Kbps data, which is equal to 15 Mbps as 1000 Kb = 1 Mb. Tele transfers a maximum of 25 Mbps data and Speedy has a maximum of 9 Mbps. Data-Com transfers a maximum of 9000 Kbps data, which is equivalent to 9 Mbps. This means that Tele can transfer the maximum amount of data per second. The answer is (B).

47. **C** Since there is a binary number assigned to each device, and each of the 850 employees needs two devices, there is a need for 2 × 850 = 1,700 binary numbers. Look for power of two that is 1700 or more. Since 2^{10} = 1,024, ten bits address is not enough to assign a unique address for every single device at the company. Since 2^{11} = 2,048, the minimum number of bits in the address should be 11. The answer is (C).

48. **D** TCP breaks the message into packets and assigns every single packet an order number. The packets are then sent through the Internet via routers that direct them to the proper paths, depending on whether the original route becomes congested or unavailable. Packets of the same message are not necessarily following the same path, which makes it possible to deliver the packets out of order. The order number that was added by the TCP layer of the sender will be used by the TCP layer at the receiver side to put the packets in the correct order and to acknowledge their reception. If any packet is not acknowledged, TCP at the sender side will resend it until it is acknowledged. TCP will make sure that all the packets are received. The process of acknowledging and resending unacknowledged packets may make the transmission take more time, but it ensures the accuracy and reliability of the reception. However, the various alternative routes could slow the message down, so speed is not guaranteed. The answer is (D).

49. **B** UDP is used in the instances in which speed has the highest priority. TCP is used in the instances in which reliability and accuracy are the priorities. In (A), (C), and (D), accuracy is the most important. In (B), speed is more important. The answer is (B).

50. **D** Two devices are going to be used, so distributed computing is used. Therefore, statement III is correct. Eliminate (A) and (B), which don't include III. Since computer 1 is used to execute process C and process F, one at a time, the sequential computing model is also used. Therefore, statement II is correct. Eliminate (C), which doesn't include II. Only one choice remains, so there is no need to continue. However, note that statement I is true because computer 2 has two parallel processors that are executing code simultaneously, so the parallel computing model is also used. The answer is (D).

51. **B** Computer 1 will perform its tasks in a total of 50 + 25 = 75 seconds. Computer 2 will perform its tasks for processor 1 in 60 + 10 = 70 seconds and for processor 2 in 40 + 35 = 75 seconds. Therefore, the whole task will be completed in 75 seconds.

52. **D** The circuit is represented as (False AND True) AND (False OR NOT X). The branch on the left side, (False AND True) evaluates to false. The circuit then becomes False AND (False OR NOT X). When one of the operands of an AND statement is false, the result is false regardless of the value of the other operand. Therefore, the answer is (D).

53. **A** Choice (A) is a correct description of the definition of keylogging. Choice (B) refers to phishing, (C) refers to a virus, and (D) refers to malware. The answer is (A).

54. **D** The problem begins by assigning i the value of a separate variable n. Then, it begins a loop that will repeat 5 times. In each iteration, the value i is assigned i + i. In the first iteration, i is assigned n + n = 2n. In the second iteration, i is assigned 2n + 2n = 4n. In the third iteration, i is assigned 4n + 4n = 8n. In the fourth iteration, i is assigned 8n + 8n = 16i. In the fifth iteration, i is assigned 16i + 16i = 32i. Then, the problem enters the second loop, which is repeated 3 times. In each iteration, the value i is assigned i * i. After the first iteration, i is assigned $32n * 32n = (32n)^2$. After the second iteration, i is assigned $(32n)^2 * (32n)^2 = (32n)^4$. Finally, after the third iteration, i is assigned $(32n)^4 * (32n^4) = 32n^8$. This value is displayed. The answer is (D).

55. **C** The database has information that ties ratings to manufacturers, so the highest number of rating per manufacturer can be determined. Eliminate (A). Similarly, individual products are tied to manufacturers, so the number of products that a manufacturer produces can be determined. Eliminate (B). There is no indication of sales information, so keep (C). An algorithm based on vitamins, carbohydrates, and calories can be used to determine which products should be avoided by people on a diet, so eliminate (D). The answer is (C).

56. **A** The digital divide is the gap in different people's ability to access computing technology. The COVID-19 pandemic highlighted the digital divide. Not all students all over the world have the same access to the Internet and computer devices, making remote learning much more difficult for some students than for others. In all other choices, the students have equal access to the computing technology available. The answer is (A).

57. **A** The iterative model starts with a simplified version that is improved based on feedback throughout the process, requiring programmers to revisit their earlier work to incorporate these comments. Therefore, this process exemplifies the iterative model. Eliminate (B) and (D), which do not include statement I. An incremental development process divides a large task into smaller subtasks to be implemented and perfected before combining the elements together into the larger program. There is no indication that this happened in this case. Eliminate (C), which included statement II. The answer is (A).

58. **B** The description above states that the bank has decided that all data for the mobile banking app will be stored at the local branch. Local storage of data may require updating or expanding the current computer system to ensure customers are able use the new mobile banking app. The answer is (B).

59. **A** The new mobile banking app will not allow customers to do everything that they can do in the local branch but will allow customers to complete these limited tasks with their bank accounts outside of traditional banking hours and without going to the branch, which increases their access. The answer is (A).

60. **D** Although the customers will now be able to access their bank information from outside the bank at any hour, the app will only be able to have a limited number of functions, including accessing account #, account balance, bank statement and transaction history from the last 60 days, processing current checks/payments, and closing bank accounts. The correct answer is (D).

61. **B** In order to use the mobile banking app, customers are required to come to the bank and sign a form agreeing to risks of the new system and choose a pin number. Then to access the mobile bank app, they will need this pin and their email address. The answer is (B).

62. **C** As the description of the new mobile banking system states, to use the new system, customers will first be required to sign a form agreeing to new risks of the mobile banking app and choose a pin number. Then, to log in to the system, the mobile banking app requires an email address and pin number, but the app will only be able to access bank statement and transaction history from the last 60 days. Since the listed functionality is the only functionality, the answer is (C).

63. **B, D** The value of i is a random number; it can be 5, 6, 7 or 8. The variable n is initially 3 and the loop will keep repeating as long as n is less than 6. Within the body of the loop, n is incremented by one, meaning the loop will be repeating 3 times. To know the possible outputs, execute the program 4 times, each time with one of the possible values of i. Consider i = 5. After the first iteration, i = 2 * 5 + 1 = 11. After the second iteration, i = 2 * 11 + 1 = 23. After the third iteration, i = 2 * 23 + 1 = 47. This is not a choice. Now consider i = 6. After the first iteration, i = 2 * 6 + 1 = 13. After the second iteration, i = 2 * 13 + 1 = 27. After the third iteration, i = 2 * 27 + 1 = 55. This is a choice, so select (B) and look for the second correct answer. Consider i = 7. After the first iteration, i = 2 * 7 + 1 = 15. After the second iteration, i = 2 * 15 + 1 = 31. After the third iteration, i = 2 * 31 + 1 = 63. This is not a choice. Finally, consider i = 8. After the first iteration, i = 2 * 8 + 1 = 17. After the second iteration, i = 2 * 17 + 1 = 35. After the third iteration, i = 2 * 35 + 1 = 71. This is a choice, so select (D) as well. The answers are (B) and (D).

64. **A, B** The program is going to check the expiration date for 80,000 products, which means that using loops and iteration in the program is a must. The program checks the expiration date for every single product and, if it is expiring in a month, it warns the pharmacist. This means that selection must be used here as well. Procedures can be implemented, but the algorithm does not require it. Also, although searching is used, sorting is not necessary. The answers are (A) and (B).

65. **A, C** Choice (A) is correct. Although programmers will never be able to anticipate all possible uses of their innovations, they should consider the potential beneficial and harmful effects as best as they can. Choice (B) is incorrect. Advances in computing have led to increased creativity in other fields,

including medicine, engineering, communications, and the arts. Choice (C) is correct because computing innovations can have greatly enhanced other fields. Similarly, (D) is incorrect as many unintended consequences and are not problematic.

66. **B, C** Event-driven programs determine flow based on input from users, sensors, or external messages. Clicking a mouse and pressing a keyboard key are examples of user input, so the answers are (B) and (C).

67. **C, D** The purpose of the algorithm is to add 5 to each number of the list and get the average of the list after this modification. In step 3, the algorithm should add 5 to the value at index before adding the value to the total. Otherwise, the total will contain the original total rather than the modified total. One correct answer is (C). Step 5, which repeats step 2, will recreate the total variable and assign it 0 in every single iteration. This causes a problem in which total will not hold the correct total of the numbers in the list. Therefore, (D) is also correct. The answers are (C) and (D).

68. **A, B** As an index variable will be used to access the list items, it should take the range [1, length of the list]. According to the program, the loop header specifies that `REPEAT UNTIL(index < 1)`. This means that you will start at the last item in the list and will finish after you access the first item in the list. To start at the last item, you can simply use the length value as an index, so (B) is correct. Moreover, when `aList` was initially created, the user was asked to input the number of ingredients, which was stored to the `NumberOfItems`. Therefore, this variable also contains the size of the list, so (A) is correct as well. The answers are (A) and (B).

69. **A, C** This model is trained on Java and Python records and gives biased results against people who are skilled with other programming languages. Moreover, as female records in the training data are far fewer than male records, there will be bias as well against females. This means that both (A) and (C) are correct.

70. **A, D** The information underneath the table is considered metadata, which is data about data. It describes the file that contains the data and gives general information about the content of the data, such as the size of the file and the date of creation, as in (A). Metadata also helps in making the data structured and clean and can be used for finding, organizing, and managing information, so (D) is correct. Updating the metadata will not affect the primary content of the dataset. Thus, the answers are (A) and (D).

HOW TO SCORE PRACTICE TEST 3

Section I: Multiple Choice

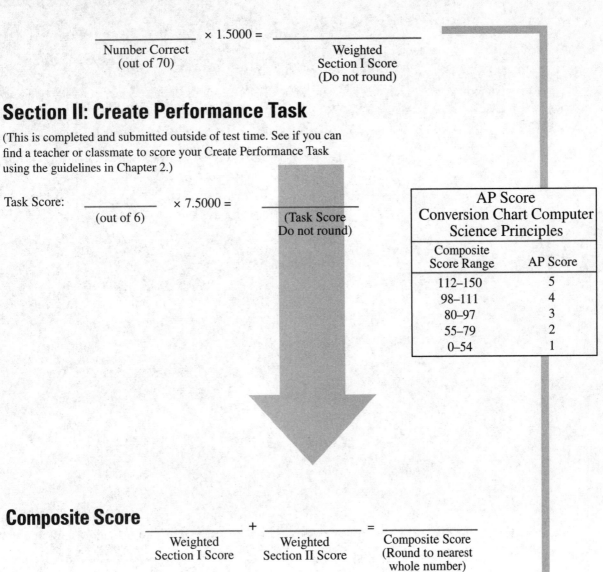

_____ × 1.5000 = _____
Number Correct   Weighted
(out of 70)   Section I Score
                                  (Do not round)

Section II: Create Performance Task

(This is completed and submitted outside of test time. See if you can find a teacher or classmate to score your Create Performance Task using the guidelines in Chapter 2.)

Task Score: _____ × 7.5000 = _____
             (out of 6)   (Task Score
                                           Do not round)

AP Score Conversion Chart Computer Science Principles

Composite Score Range	AP Score
112–150	5
98–111	4
80–97	3
55–79	2
0–54	1

Composite Score

_____ + _____ = _____
Weighted   Weighted   Composite Score
Section I Score   Section II Score   (Round to nearest
                                      whole number)

Appendix

Glossary

GLOSSARY

A

Abstraction: A way of hiding information

Algorithm: A clear, step-by-step, detailed computable set of instructions that returns a result in a finite amount of time

Algorithm Efficiency: How an algorithm performs with regards to both time and space

Application Program Interface (API):   Specifications for using a library's procedures and understanding how they behave

Artificial Intelligence: The development of computing systems capable of performing tasks that would otherwise rely on human intelligence

Assignment: The storing of a value to a variable

B

Bandwidth: The maximum amount of data that can be sent over a particular computer network in a fixed amount of time

Base Conversion: Taking a number written in one base (e.g., decimal) and rewriting it in another (e.g., binary)

Bias: The intentional or unintentional skewing of data to favor a particular result

Binary: Numbers represented with base 2 digits

Binary Search: A method of seeking an item in an ordered list through an iterated process of comparing the target to the middle item in the list

Boolean Expression: An expression that evaluates to true of false

C

Citizen Science: Crowdsourcing in scientific research

Cleaning Data: Making data uniform without changing its meaning

Computing Innovations: A new method, product, or idea that requires a computer

Creative Commons: A not-for-profit organization that has various forms of licenses that can be used to protect original work from being plagiarized

Crowdsourcing: The practice of obtaining input or information from a large number of people via the Internet

Cybersecurity: The protection of a system against unauthorized or criminal use of a system

D

Data: Anything stored, transmitted, or processed by computing systems in numerical forms

Data Abstraction: Filtering out specific details to focus on the information needed to process the data

Data Compression: A reduction in the size (number of bits) of data transmitted or stored

Data Types: A specified kind of information that is stored in a variable

Decimal: Numbers represented with base 10 digits

Decryption: The process of converting encrypted data into its original form

Digital Divide: The disparity between those who have access to technology and those who do not

Distributed computing: A model in which multiple devices run a program

E

Encryption: The process in which data is encoded to another form

F

Fault Tolerance: The ability of a network to find a different path between sender and receiver

G

Graphs: A visual representation of data used to give quick information on trends

H

Heuristic: An algorithm that finds an approximate solution rather than an exact solution

Hexadecimal: Numbers represented with base 16 digits

Hypertext Transfer Protocol (HTTP): A protocol used to interpret a web page

I

Information: See Data

Information Security: See Cybersecurity

Integer Overflow: The attempting to store a number that is too big for the data type

Integer Roundoff: Impression caused by limits in size of data type

Intellectual Property: A product that is protected from unauthorized use by others

Internet Protocol: Any protocol governing the Internet or other network

Iteration: The process in which a part of an algorithm repeats until it meets a condition or for a fixed number of times, either of which is selected by the programmer or user

L

Libraries: A collection of precompiled procedures that can be used by other programs

List: A data type that holds a collection of value

Loops: Sections of code statements that need to be repeated more than once

Lossless Compression: A reduction of the number of bits stored or transmitted that guarantees complete restoration of the original data

Lossy Compression: A significant reduction in the number of bits stored or transmitted that only allows for an approximation of the original data

M

Machine Learning: The ability of a computing system to train on data fed into software systems

Metadata: Data about data such as author, date created, usage, file size, etc.

O

Open Source: Software development that allows programmers and developers to access the source code and to modify and improve the code as they see the need

P

Parallel Computing: Breaking a program into smaller sequential operations using multiple processors

Path: A sequence of directly connected computing devices between two computing devices on a computer network

Patterns: Recognizable forms in sets of data

Personally Identifiable Information (PII): Information about a person that can uniquely identify them, such as educational, medical, financial, or employment information

Plagiarism: The copying of someone's work and passing it off as one's own

Precision: The number of significant figures or meaningful decimal places in measurement or calculation

Procedural Abstraction: The calling of a function with only concern for the end result rather than how the code functions

Procedures: A named group of programming code that performs a specific task

Protocol: An agreed upon set of rules that specify the behavior of a system

Pseudocode: A way of describing an algorithm that is not the specific code of any language

R

Random Number Generator: A program that picks a number at random from a range of values

Redundancy: Additional paths in a network to create fault tolerance

Route: See Path

Routing: The process of finding a path from sender to receiver

S

Scalability: The capacity for a system to change in size and scale to meet new demands

Selection: The use of a Boolean condition to evaluate which of two parts of an algorithm to use

Sequencing: The outlining of each step of an algorithm in a specific order to solve a problem

Sequential Computing: A process in which program instructions are processed one at a time

Simulation Models: Collections of computer software that respond to real-time input data to emulate a response that would resemble the real-world

String: A collection of characters

T

Transmission Control Protocol (TCP/IP): An Internet protocol in which packets are repeatedly sent until receipt is confirmed

Trends: General direction in which something is developing or changing over time

U

Undecidable Problem: A problem that cannot be solved using an algorithm

V

Variable: An abstraction inside a program that can hold a value

W

World Wide Web: A system of linked pages, programs, and files

Exam Reference
Sheet

Quick Reference

Instruction	Explanation
Assignment, Display, and Input	
Text: a ← expression Block: [a ⟵ expression]	Evaluates expression and then assigns a copy of the result to the variable a.
Text: DISPLAY(expression) Block: DISPLAY [expression]	Displays the value of expression, followed by a space.
Text: INPUT() Block: INPUT	Accepts a value from the user and returns the input value.
Arithmetic Operators and Numeric Procedures	
Text and Block: a + b a - b a * b a / b	The arithmetic operators +, -, *, and / are used to perform arithmetic on a and b. For example, 17 / 5 evaluates to 3.4. The order of operations used in mathematics applies when evaluating expressions.
Text and Block: a MOD b	Evaluates to the remainder when a is divided by b. Assume that a is an integer greater than or equal to 0 and b is an integer greater than 0. For example, 17 MOD 5 evaluates to 2. The MOD operator has the same precedence as the * and / operators.
Text: RANDOM(a, b) Block: RANDOM [a, b]	Generates and returns a random integer from a to b, including a and b. Each result is equally likely to occur. For example, RANDOM(1, 3) could return 1, 2, or 3.

Instruction	Explanation
Relational and Boolean Operators	

Instruction	Explanation
Text and Block: a = b a ≠ b a > b a < b a ≥ b a ≤ b	The relational operators =, ≠, >, <, ≤, and ≥ are used to test the relationship between two variables, expressions, or values. A comparison using relational operators evaluates to a Boolean value. For example, a = b evaluates to true if a and b are equal; otherwise it evaluates to false.
Text: NOT condition Block: NOT (condition)	Evaluates to true if condition is false; otherwise evaluates to false.
Text: condition1 AND condition2 Block: (condition1) AND (condition2)	Evaluates to true if both condition1 and condition2 are true; otherwise evaluates to false.
Text: condition1 OR condition2 Block: (condition1) OR (condition2)	Evaluates to true if condition1 is true or if condition2 is true or if both condition1 and condition2 are true; otherwise evaluates to false.
Selection	

Text:
 	
IF(condition)
{
<block of statements>
}
 	
Block:
 	
IF (condition)
  (block of statements)
	The code in block of statements is executed if the Boolean expression condition evaluates to true; no action is taken if condition evaluates to false.

Instruction	Explanation

Instruction	Explanation

Text:
 	
``
IF(condition)
{
<first block of statements>
}
ELSE
{
<second block of statements>
}
``
 	
Block:
 	
	The code in `first block of statements` is executed if the Boolean expression `condition` evaluates to `true`; otherwise the code in `second block of statements` is executed.

Instruction	Explanation

Text:
 	
``
REPEAT n TIMES
{
<block of statements>
}
``
 	
Block:
 	
	The code in `block of statements` is executed n times.

Text:
 	
``
REPEAT UNTIL(condition)
{
<block of statements>
}
``
 	
Block:
 	
	The code in `block of statements` is repeated until the Boolean expression `condition` evaluates to `true`.

Instruction	Explanation
List Operations	
For all list operations, if a list index is less than 1 or greater than the length of the list, an error message is produced and the program terminates.	

Text:
 	
`aList ← [value1, value2, value3, ...]`
 	
Block:
 	
`aList ◄── value1, value2, value3`
	Creates a new list that contains the values `value1`, `value2`, `value3`, and `...` at indices `1`, `2`, `3`, and `...` respectively and assigns it to `aList`.

Text:
 	
`aList ← []`
 	
Block:
 	
`aList ◄── []`
	Creates an empty list and assigns it to `aList`.

Text:
 	
`aList ← bList`
 	
Block:
 	
`aList ◄── bList`
	Assigns a copy of the list bList to the list `aList`.
	
	For example, if `bList` contains `[20, 40, 60]`, then `aList` will also contain `[20, 40, 60]` after the assignment.

Text:
 	
`aList[i]`
 	
Block:
 	
`aList i`
	Accesses the element of `aList` at index `i`. The first element of `aList` is at index `1` and is accessed using the notation `aList[1]`.

Text:
 	
`x ← aList[i]`
 	
Block:
 	
`x ◄── aList i`
	Assigns the value of `aList[i]` to the variable `x`.

Text:
 	
`aList[i] ← x`
 	
Block:
 	
`aList i ◄── x`
	Assigns the value of `x` to `aList[i]`.

Text:
 	
`aList[i] ← aList[j]`
 	
Block:
 	
`aList i ◄── aList j`
	Assigns the value of `aList[j]` to `aList[i]`.

Text:
 	
`INSERT(aList, i, value)`
 	
Block:
 	
`INSERT aList, i, value`
	Any values in `aList` at indices greater than or equal to `i` are shifted one position to the right. The length of the list is increased by 1, and `value` is placed at index `i` in `aList`.

Instruction	Explanation
List Operations—Continued	

Text:
 	
`APPEND(aList, value)`
 	
Block:
 	
`APPEND` `aList, value`
	The length of `aList` is increased by 1, and `value` is placed at the end of `aList`.

Text:
 	
`REMOVE(aList, i)`
 	
Block:
 	
`REMOVE` `aList, i`
	Removes the item at index `i` in `aList` and shifts to the left any values at indices greater than `i`. The length of `aList` is decreased by 1.

Text:
 	
`LENGTH(aList)`
 	
Block:
 	
`LENGTH` `aList`
	Evaluates to the number of elements in `aList`.

Text:
 	
`FOR EACH item IN aList`
`{`
`<block of statements>`
`}`
 	
Block:
 	
`FOR EACH item IN aList`
`block of statements`
	The variable `item` is assigned the value of each element of `aList` sequentially, in order, from the first element to the last element. The code in `block of statements` is executed once for each assignment of `item`.

Procedures and Procedure Calls	

Text:
 	
`PROCEDURE procName(parameter1,`
`              parameter2, ...)`
`{`
`<block of statements>`
`}`
 	
Block:
 	
`PROCEDURE procName` `parameter1,`
`parameter2, ...`
`block of statements`
	Defines `procName` as a procedure that takes zero or more arguments. The procedure contains `block of statements`.
	
	The procedure `procName` can be called using the following notation, where `arg1` is assigned to `parameter1`, `arg2` is assigned to `parameter2`, etc.:
	`procName(arg1, arg2, ...)`

Instruction	Explanation
Procedures and Procedure Calls—Continued	

Instruction	Explanation

Text:
``
PROCEDURE procName(parameter1,
                   parameter2, ...)
 	
{
<block of statements>
RETURN(expression)
 	
}
``
Block:
 	
``
PROCEDURE procName parameter1,
                    parameter2, ...
 	
    block of statements
    RETURN expression
``
	Defines `procName` as a procedure that takes zero or more arguments. The procedure contains `block of statements` and returns the value of `expression`. The RETURN statement may appear at any point inside the procedure and causes an immediate return from the procedure back to the calling statement.
	
	The value returned by the procedure `procName` can be assigned to the variable `result` using the following notation:
	`result ← procName(arg1, arg2, ...)`

Text:
`RETURN(expression)`
Block:
`RETURN expression`
	Returns the flow of control to the point where the procedure was called and returns the value of `expression`.

Robot	

If the robot attempts to move to a square that is not open or is beyond the edge of the grid, the robot will stay in its current location and the program will terminate.

Instruction	Explanation

Text:
`MOVE_FORWARD()`
Block:
`MOVE_FORWARD`
	The robot moves one square forward in the direction it is facing.

Text:
`ROTATE_LEFT()`
Block:
`ROTATE_LEFT`
	The robot rotates in place 90 degrees counterclockwise (i.e., makes an in-place left turn).

Text:
`ROTATE_RIGHT()`
Block:
`ROTATE_RIGHT`
	The robot rotates in place 90 degrees clockwise (i.e., makes an in-place right turn).

Text:
`CAN_MOVE(direction)`
Block:
`CAN_MOVE direction`
	Evaluates to `true` if there is an open square one square in the direction relative to where the robot is facing; otherwise evaluates to `false`. The value of `direction` can be `left`, `right`, `forward`, or `backward`.

Completely darken bubbles with a No. 2 pencil. If you make a mistake, be sure to erase mark completely. Erase all stray marks.

1.

YOUR NAME: _____
(Print)   Last   First   M.I.

SIGNATURE: _____ DATE: ___ / ___ / ___

HOME ADDRESS: _____
(Print)   Number and Street

_____
City   State   Zip Code

PHONE NO.: _____

IMPORTANT: Please fill in these boxes exactly as shown on the back cover of your test book.

5. YOUR NAME

First 4 letters of last name					FIRST INIT	MID INIT
Ⓐ	Ⓐ	Ⓐ	Ⓐ		Ⓐ	Ⓐ
Ⓑ	Ⓑ	Ⓑ	Ⓑ		Ⓑ	Ⓑ
Ⓒ	Ⓒ	Ⓒ	Ⓒ		Ⓒ	Ⓒ
Ⓓ	Ⓓ	Ⓓ	Ⓓ		Ⓓ	Ⓓ
Ⓔ	Ⓔ	Ⓔ	Ⓔ		Ⓔ	Ⓔ
Ⓕ	Ⓕ	Ⓕ	Ⓕ		Ⓕ	Ⓕ
Ⓖ	Ⓖ	Ⓖ	Ⓖ		Ⓖ	Ⓖ
Ⓗ	Ⓗ	Ⓗ	Ⓗ		Ⓗ	Ⓗ
Ⓘ	Ⓘ	Ⓘ	Ⓘ		Ⓘ	Ⓘ
Ⓙ	Ⓙ	Ⓙ	Ⓙ		Ⓙ	Ⓙ
Ⓚ	Ⓚ	Ⓚ	Ⓚ		Ⓚ	Ⓚ
Ⓛ	Ⓛ	Ⓛ	Ⓛ		Ⓛ	Ⓛ
Ⓜ	Ⓜ	Ⓜ	Ⓜ		Ⓜ	Ⓜ
Ⓝ	Ⓝ	Ⓝ	Ⓝ		Ⓝ	Ⓝ
Ⓞ	Ⓞ	Ⓞ	Ⓞ		Ⓞ	Ⓞ
Ⓟ	Ⓟ	Ⓟ	Ⓟ		Ⓟ	Ⓟ
Ⓠ	Ⓠ	Ⓠ	Ⓠ		Ⓠ	Ⓠ
Ⓡ	Ⓡ	Ⓡ	Ⓡ		Ⓡ	Ⓡ
Ⓢ	Ⓢ	Ⓢ	Ⓢ		Ⓢ	Ⓢ
Ⓣ	Ⓣ	Ⓣ	Ⓣ		Ⓣ	Ⓣ
Ⓤ	Ⓤ	Ⓤ	Ⓤ		Ⓤ	Ⓤ
Ⓥ	Ⓥ	Ⓥ	Ⓥ		Ⓥ	Ⓥ
Ⓦ	Ⓦ	Ⓦ	Ⓦ		Ⓦ	Ⓦ
Ⓧ	Ⓧ	Ⓧ	Ⓧ		Ⓧ	Ⓧ
Ⓨ	Ⓨ	Ⓨ	Ⓨ		Ⓨ	Ⓨ
Ⓩ	Ⓩ	Ⓩ	Ⓩ		Ⓩ	Ⓩ

2. TEST FORM

3. TEST CODE

4. REGISTRATION NUMBER

⓪	Ⓐ	Ⓙ	⓪	⓪	⓪	⓪	⓪	⓪	⓪	⓪
①	Ⓑ	Ⓚ	①	①	①	①	①	①	①	①
②	Ⓒ	Ⓛ	②	②	②	②	②	②	②	②
③	Ⓓ	Ⓜ	③	③	③	③	③	③	③	③
④	Ⓔ	Ⓝ	④	④	④	④	④	④	④	④
⑤	Ⓕ	Ⓞ	⑤	⑤	⑤	⑤	⑤	⑤	⑤	⑤
⑥	Ⓖ	Ⓟ	⑥	⑥	⑥	⑥	⑥	⑥	⑥	⑥
⑦	Ⓗ	Ⓠ	⑦	⑦	⑦	⑦	⑦	⑦	⑦	⑦
⑧	Ⓘ	Ⓡ	⑧	⑧	⑧	⑧	⑧	⑧	⑧	⑧
⑨			⑨	⑨	⑨	⑨	⑨	⑨	⑨	⑨

6. DATE OF BIRTH

Month	Day		Year	
◯ JAN				
◯ FEB	⓪	⓪	⓪	⓪
◯ MAR	①	①	①	①
◯ APR	②	②	②	②
◯ MAY	③	③	③	③
◯ JUN		④	④	④
◯ JUL		⑤	⑤	⑤
◯ AUG		⑥	⑥	⑥
◯ SEP		⑦	⑦	⑦
◯ OCT		⑧	⑧	⑧
◯ NOV		⑨	⑨	⑨
◯ DEC				

7. GENDER
◯ MALE
◯ FEMALE

1. Ⓐ Ⓑ Ⓒ Ⓓ
2. Ⓐ Ⓑ Ⓒ Ⓓ
3. Ⓐ Ⓑ Ⓒ Ⓓ
4. Ⓐ Ⓑ Ⓒ Ⓓ
5. Ⓐ Ⓑ Ⓒ Ⓓ
6. Ⓐ Ⓑ Ⓒ Ⓓ
7. Ⓐ Ⓑ Ⓒ Ⓓ
8. Ⓐ Ⓑ Ⓒ Ⓓ
9. Ⓐ Ⓑ Ⓒ Ⓓ
10. Ⓐ Ⓑ Ⓒ Ⓓ
11. Ⓐ Ⓑ Ⓒ Ⓓ
12. Ⓐ Ⓑ Ⓒ Ⓓ
13. Ⓐ Ⓑ Ⓒ Ⓓ
14. Ⓐ Ⓑ Ⓒ Ⓓ

15. Ⓐ Ⓑ Ⓒ Ⓓ
16. Ⓐ Ⓑ Ⓒ Ⓓ
17. Ⓐ Ⓑ Ⓒ Ⓓ
18. Ⓐ Ⓑ Ⓒ Ⓓ
19. Ⓐ Ⓑ Ⓒ Ⓓ
20. Ⓐ Ⓑ Ⓒ Ⓓ
21. Ⓐ Ⓑ Ⓒ Ⓓ
22. Ⓐ Ⓑ Ⓒ Ⓓ
23. Ⓐ Ⓑ Ⓒ Ⓓ
24. Ⓐ Ⓑ Ⓒ Ⓓ
25. Ⓐ Ⓑ Ⓒ Ⓓ
26. Ⓐ Ⓑ Ⓒ Ⓓ
27. Ⓐ Ⓑ Ⓒ Ⓓ
28. Ⓐ Ⓑ Ⓒ Ⓓ

29. Ⓐ Ⓑ Ⓒ Ⓓ
30. Ⓐ Ⓑ Ⓒ Ⓓ
31. Ⓐ Ⓑ Ⓒ Ⓓ
32. Ⓐ Ⓑ Ⓒ Ⓓ
33. Ⓐ Ⓑ Ⓒ Ⓓ
34. Ⓐ Ⓑ Ⓒ Ⓓ
35. Ⓐ Ⓑ Ⓒ Ⓓ
36. Ⓐ Ⓑ Ⓒ Ⓓ
37. Ⓐ Ⓑ Ⓒ Ⓓ
38. Ⓐ Ⓑ Ⓒ Ⓓ
39. Ⓐ Ⓑ Ⓒ Ⓓ
40. Ⓐ Ⓑ Ⓒ Ⓓ
41. Ⓐ Ⓑ Ⓒ Ⓓ
42. Ⓐ Ⓑ Ⓒ Ⓓ

43. Ⓐ Ⓑ Ⓒ Ⓓ
44. Ⓐ Ⓑ Ⓒ Ⓓ
45. Ⓐ Ⓑ Ⓒ Ⓓ
46. Ⓐ Ⓑ Ⓒ Ⓓ
47. Ⓐ Ⓑ Ⓒ Ⓓ
48. Ⓐ Ⓑ Ⓒ Ⓓ
49. Ⓐ Ⓑ Ⓒ Ⓓ
50. Ⓐ Ⓑ Ⓒ Ⓓ
51. Ⓐ Ⓑ Ⓒ Ⓓ
52. Ⓐ Ⓑ Ⓒ Ⓓ
53. Ⓐ Ⓑ Ⓒ Ⓓ
54. Ⓐ Ⓑ Ⓒ Ⓓ
55. Ⓐ Ⓑ Ⓒ Ⓓ
56. Ⓐ Ⓑ Ⓒ Ⓓ

57. Ⓐ Ⓑ Ⓒ Ⓓ
58. Ⓐ Ⓑ Ⓒ Ⓓ
59. Ⓐ Ⓑ Ⓒ Ⓓ
60. Ⓐ Ⓑ Ⓒ Ⓓ
61. Ⓐ Ⓑ Ⓒ Ⓓ
62. Ⓐ Ⓑ Ⓒ Ⓓ
63. Ⓐ Ⓑ Ⓒ Ⓓ
64. Ⓐ Ⓑ Ⓒ Ⓓ
65. Ⓐ Ⓑ Ⓒ Ⓓ
66. Ⓐ Ⓑ Ⓒ Ⓓ
67. Ⓐ Ⓑ Ⓒ Ⓓ
68. Ⓐ Ⓑ Ⓒ Ⓓ
69. Ⓐ Ⓑ Ⓒ Ⓓ
70. Ⓐ Ⓑ Ⓒ Ⓓ

Completely darken bubbles with a No. 2 pencil. If you make a mistake, be sure to erase mark completely. Erase all stray marks.

1.

YOUR NAME: _____
(Print)   Last   First   M.I.

SIGNATURE: _____   DATE: ___ / ___ / ___

HOME ADDRESS: _____
(Print)   Number and Street

_____
City   State   Zip Code

PHONE NO.: _____

IMPORTANT: Please fill in these boxes exactly as shown on the back cover of your test book.

2. TEST FORM

3. TEST CODE

4. REGISTRATION NUMBER

5. YOUR NAME

First 4 letters of last name				FIRST INIT	MID INIT
Ⓐ	Ⓐ	Ⓐ	Ⓐ	Ⓐ	Ⓐ
Ⓑ	Ⓑ	Ⓑ	Ⓑ	Ⓑ	Ⓑ
Ⓒ	Ⓒ	Ⓒ	Ⓒ	Ⓒ	Ⓒ
Ⓓ	Ⓓ	Ⓓ	Ⓓ	Ⓓ	Ⓓ
Ⓔ	Ⓔ	Ⓔ	Ⓔ	Ⓔ	Ⓔ
Ⓕ	Ⓕ	Ⓕ	Ⓕ	Ⓕ	Ⓕ
Ⓖ	Ⓖ	Ⓖ	Ⓖ	Ⓖ	Ⓖ
Ⓗ	Ⓗ	Ⓗ	Ⓗ	Ⓗ	Ⓗ
Ⓘ	Ⓘ	Ⓘ	Ⓘ	Ⓘ	Ⓘ
Ⓙ	Ⓙ	Ⓙ	Ⓙ	Ⓙ	Ⓙ
Ⓚ	Ⓚ	Ⓚ	Ⓚ	Ⓚ	Ⓚ
Ⓛ	Ⓛ	Ⓛ	Ⓛ	Ⓛ	Ⓛ
Ⓜ	Ⓜ	Ⓜ	Ⓜ	Ⓜ	Ⓜ
Ⓝ	Ⓝ	Ⓝ	Ⓝ	Ⓝ	Ⓝ
Ⓞ	Ⓞ	Ⓞ	Ⓞ	Ⓞ	Ⓞ
Ⓟ	Ⓟ	Ⓟ	Ⓟ	Ⓟ	Ⓟ
Ⓠ	Ⓠ	Ⓠ	Ⓠ	Ⓠ	Ⓠ
Ⓡ	Ⓡ	Ⓡ	Ⓡ	Ⓡ	Ⓡ
Ⓢ	Ⓢ	Ⓢ	Ⓢ	Ⓢ	Ⓢ
Ⓣ	Ⓣ	Ⓣ	Ⓣ	Ⓣ	Ⓣ
Ⓤ	Ⓤ	Ⓤ	Ⓤ	Ⓤ	Ⓤ
Ⓥ	Ⓥ	Ⓥ	Ⓥ	Ⓥ	Ⓥ
Ⓦ	Ⓦ	Ⓦ	Ⓦ	Ⓦ	Ⓦ
Ⓧ	Ⓧ	Ⓧ	Ⓧ	Ⓧ	Ⓧ
Ⓨ	Ⓨ	Ⓨ	Ⓨ	Ⓨ	Ⓨ
Ⓩ	Ⓩ	Ⓩ	Ⓩ	Ⓩ	Ⓩ

TEST CODE bubbles:
⓪ Ⓐ Ⓙ
① Ⓑ Ⓚ
② Ⓒ Ⓛ
③ Ⓓ Ⓜ
④ Ⓔ Ⓝ
⑤ Ⓕ Ⓞ
⑥ Ⓖ Ⓟ
⑦ Ⓗ Ⓠ
⑧ Ⓘ Ⓡ
⑨

REGISTRATION NUMBER and digit columns: 0 1 2 3 4 5 6 7 8 9

6. DATE OF BIRTH

Month		Day		Year	
○ JAN					
○ FEB	⓪	⓪	⓪	⓪
○ MAR	①	①	①	①
○ APR	②	②	②	②
○ MAY	③	③	③	③
○ JUN		④	④	④
○ JUL		⑤	⑤	⑤
○ AUG		⑥	⑥	⑥
○ SEP		⑦	⑦	⑦
○ OCT		⑧	⑧	⑧
○ NOV		⑨	⑨	⑨
○ DEC				

7. GENDER
○ MALE
○ FEMALE

1. Ⓐ Ⓑ Ⓒ Ⓓ
2. Ⓐ Ⓑ Ⓒ Ⓓ
3. Ⓐ Ⓑ Ⓒ Ⓓ
4. Ⓐ Ⓑ Ⓒ Ⓓ
5. Ⓐ Ⓑ Ⓒ Ⓓ
6. Ⓐ Ⓑ Ⓒ Ⓓ
7. Ⓐ Ⓑ Ⓒ Ⓓ
8. Ⓐ Ⓑ Ⓒ Ⓓ
9. Ⓐ Ⓑ Ⓒ Ⓓ
10. Ⓐ Ⓑ Ⓒ Ⓓ
11. Ⓐ Ⓑ Ⓒ Ⓓ
12. Ⓐ Ⓑ Ⓒ Ⓓ
13. Ⓐ Ⓑ Ⓒ Ⓓ
14. Ⓐ Ⓑ Ⓒ Ⓓ

15. Ⓐ Ⓑ Ⓒ Ⓓ
16. Ⓐ Ⓑ Ⓒ Ⓓ
17. Ⓐ Ⓑ Ⓒ Ⓓ
18. Ⓐ Ⓑ Ⓒ Ⓓ
19. Ⓐ Ⓑ Ⓒ Ⓓ
20. Ⓐ Ⓑ Ⓒ Ⓓ
21. Ⓐ Ⓑ Ⓒ Ⓓ
22. Ⓐ Ⓑ Ⓒ Ⓓ
23. Ⓐ Ⓑ Ⓒ Ⓓ
24. Ⓐ Ⓑ Ⓒ Ⓓ
25. Ⓐ Ⓑ Ⓒ Ⓓ
26. Ⓐ Ⓑ Ⓒ Ⓓ
27. Ⓐ Ⓑ Ⓒ Ⓓ
28. Ⓐ Ⓑ Ⓒ Ⓓ

29. Ⓐ Ⓑ Ⓒ Ⓓ
30. Ⓐ Ⓑ Ⓒ Ⓓ
31. Ⓐ Ⓑ Ⓒ Ⓓ
32. Ⓐ Ⓑ Ⓒ Ⓓ
33. Ⓐ Ⓑ Ⓒ Ⓓ
34. Ⓐ Ⓑ Ⓒ Ⓓ
35. Ⓐ Ⓑ Ⓒ Ⓓ
36. Ⓐ Ⓑ Ⓒ Ⓓ
37. Ⓐ Ⓑ Ⓒ Ⓓ
38. Ⓐ Ⓑ Ⓒ Ⓓ
39. Ⓐ Ⓑ Ⓒ Ⓓ
40. Ⓐ Ⓑ Ⓒ Ⓓ
41. Ⓐ Ⓑ Ⓒ Ⓓ
42. Ⓐ Ⓑ Ⓒ Ⓓ

43. Ⓐ Ⓑ Ⓒ Ⓓ
44. Ⓐ Ⓑ Ⓒ Ⓓ
45. Ⓐ Ⓑ Ⓒ Ⓓ
46. Ⓐ Ⓑ Ⓒ Ⓓ
47. Ⓐ Ⓑ Ⓒ Ⓓ
48. Ⓐ Ⓑ Ⓒ Ⓓ
49. Ⓐ Ⓑ Ⓒ Ⓓ
50. Ⓐ Ⓑ Ⓒ Ⓓ
51. Ⓐ Ⓑ Ⓒ Ⓓ
52. Ⓐ Ⓑ Ⓒ Ⓓ
53. Ⓐ Ⓑ Ⓒ Ⓓ
54. Ⓐ Ⓑ Ⓒ Ⓓ
55. Ⓐ Ⓑ Ⓒ Ⓓ
56. Ⓐ Ⓑ Ⓒ Ⓓ

57. Ⓐ Ⓑ Ⓒ Ⓓ
58. Ⓐ Ⓑ Ⓒ Ⓓ
59. Ⓐ Ⓑ Ⓒ Ⓓ
60. Ⓐ Ⓑ Ⓒ Ⓓ
61. Ⓐ Ⓑ Ⓒ Ⓓ
62. Ⓐ Ⓑ Ⓒ Ⓓ
63. Ⓐ Ⓑ Ⓒ Ⓓ
64. Ⓐ Ⓑ Ⓒ Ⓓ
65. Ⓐ Ⓑ Ⓒ Ⓓ
66. Ⓐ Ⓑ Ⓒ Ⓓ
67. Ⓐ Ⓑ Ⓒ Ⓓ
68. Ⓐ Ⓑ Ⓒ Ⓓ
69. Ⓐ Ⓑ Ⓒ Ⓓ
70. Ⓐ Ⓑ Ⓒ Ⓓ

Completely darken bubbles with a No. 2 pencil. If you make a mistake, be sure to erase mark completely. Erase all stray marks.

1.

YOUR NAME: _____
(Print)   Last   First   M.I.

SIGNATURE: _____ DATE: ___/___/___

HOME ADDRESS: _____
(Print)   Number and Street

_____
City   State   Zip Code

PHONE NO.: _____

IMPORTANT: Please fill in these boxes exactly as shown on the back cover of your test book.

2. TEST FORM

_____

3. TEST CODE

4. REGISTRATION NUMBER

⓪	Ⓐ	Ⓙ	⓪	⓪	⓪	⓪	⓪	⓪	⓪	⓪	⓪
①	Ⓑ	Ⓚ	①	①	①	①	①	①	①	①	①
②	Ⓒ	Ⓛ	②	②	②	②	②	②	②	②	②
③	Ⓓ	Ⓜ	③	③	③	③	③	③	③	③	③
④	Ⓔ	Ⓝ	④	④	④	④	④	④	④	④	④
⑤	Ⓕ	Ⓞ	⑤	⑤	⑤	⑤	⑤	⑤	⑤	⑤	⑤
⑥	Ⓖ	Ⓟ	⑥	⑥	⑥	⑥	⑥	⑥	⑥	⑥	⑥
⑦	Ⓗ	Ⓠ	⑦	⑦	⑦	⑦	⑦	⑦	⑦	⑦	⑦
⑧	Ⓘ	Ⓡ	⑧	⑧	⑧	⑧	⑧	⑧	⑧	⑧	⑧
⑨			⑨	⑨	⑨	⑨	⑨	⑨	⑨	⑨	⑨

5. YOUR NAME

First 4 letters of last name				FIRST INIT	MID INIT
Ⓐ	Ⓐ	Ⓐ	Ⓐ	Ⓐ	Ⓐ
Ⓑ	Ⓑ	Ⓑ	Ⓑ	Ⓑ	Ⓑ
Ⓒ	Ⓒ	Ⓒ	Ⓒ	Ⓒ	Ⓒ
Ⓓ	Ⓓ	Ⓓ	Ⓓ	Ⓓ	Ⓓ
Ⓔ	Ⓔ	Ⓔ	Ⓔ	Ⓔ	Ⓔ
Ⓕ	Ⓕ	Ⓕ	Ⓕ	Ⓕ	Ⓕ
Ⓖ	Ⓖ	Ⓖ	Ⓖ	Ⓖ	Ⓖ
Ⓗ	Ⓗ	Ⓗ	Ⓗ	Ⓗ	Ⓗ
Ⓘ	Ⓘ	Ⓘ	Ⓘ	Ⓘ	Ⓘ
Ⓙ	Ⓙ	Ⓙ	Ⓙ	Ⓙ	Ⓙ
Ⓚ	Ⓚ	Ⓚ	Ⓚ	Ⓚ	Ⓚ
Ⓛ	Ⓛ	Ⓛ	Ⓛ	Ⓛ	Ⓛ
Ⓜ	Ⓜ	Ⓜ	Ⓜ	Ⓜ	Ⓜ
Ⓝ	Ⓝ	Ⓝ	Ⓝ	Ⓝ	Ⓝ
Ⓞ	Ⓞ	Ⓞ	Ⓞ	Ⓞ	Ⓞ
Ⓟ	Ⓟ	Ⓟ	Ⓟ	Ⓟ	Ⓟ
Ⓠ	Ⓠ	Ⓠ	Ⓠ	Ⓠ	Ⓠ
Ⓡ	Ⓡ	Ⓡ	Ⓡ	Ⓡ	Ⓡ
Ⓢ	Ⓢ	Ⓢ	Ⓢ	Ⓢ	Ⓢ
Ⓣ	Ⓣ	Ⓣ	Ⓣ	Ⓣ	Ⓣ
Ⓤ	Ⓤ	Ⓤ	Ⓤ	Ⓤ	Ⓤ
Ⓥ	Ⓥ	Ⓥ	Ⓥ	Ⓥ	Ⓥ
Ⓦ	Ⓦ	Ⓦ	Ⓦ	Ⓦ	Ⓦ
Ⓧ	Ⓧ	Ⓧ	Ⓧ	Ⓧ	Ⓧ
Ⓨ	Ⓨ	Ⓨ	Ⓨ	Ⓨ	Ⓨ
Ⓩ	Ⓩ	Ⓩ	Ⓩ	Ⓩ	Ⓩ

6. DATE OF BIRTH

Month	Day		Year	
◯ JAN				
◯ FEB	⓪	⓪	⓪	⓪
◯ MAR	①	①	①	①
◯ APR	②	②	②	②
◯ MAY	③	③	③	③
◯ JUN		④	④	④
◯ JUL		⑤	⑤	⑤
◯ AUG		⑥	⑥	⑥
◯ SEP		⑦	⑦	⑦
◯ OCT		⑧	⑧	⑧
◯ NOV		⑨	⑨	⑨
◯ DEC				

7. GENDER
◯ MALE
◯ FEMALE

The Princeton Review®

1. Ⓐ Ⓑ Ⓒ Ⓓ
2. Ⓐ Ⓑ Ⓒ Ⓓ
3. Ⓐ Ⓑ Ⓒ Ⓓ
4. Ⓐ Ⓑ Ⓒ Ⓓ
5. Ⓐ Ⓑ Ⓒ Ⓓ
6. Ⓐ Ⓑ Ⓒ Ⓓ
7. Ⓐ Ⓑ Ⓒ Ⓓ
8. Ⓐ Ⓑ Ⓒ Ⓓ
9. Ⓐ Ⓑ Ⓒ Ⓓ
10. Ⓐ Ⓑ Ⓒ Ⓓ
11. Ⓐ Ⓑ Ⓒ Ⓓ
12. Ⓐ Ⓑ Ⓒ Ⓓ
13. Ⓐ Ⓑ Ⓒ Ⓓ
14. Ⓐ Ⓑ Ⓒ Ⓓ

15. Ⓐ Ⓑ Ⓒ Ⓓ
16. Ⓐ Ⓑ Ⓒ Ⓓ
17. Ⓐ Ⓑ Ⓒ Ⓓ
18. Ⓐ Ⓑ Ⓒ Ⓓ
19. Ⓐ Ⓑ Ⓒ Ⓓ
20. Ⓐ Ⓑ Ⓒ Ⓓ
21. Ⓐ Ⓑ Ⓒ Ⓓ
22. Ⓐ Ⓑ Ⓒ Ⓓ
23. Ⓐ Ⓑ Ⓒ Ⓓ
24. Ⓐ Ⓑ Ⓒ Ⓓ
25. Ⓐ Ⓑ Ⓒ Ⓓ
26. Ⓐ Ⓑ Ⓒ Ⓓ
27. Ⓐ Ⓑ Ⓒ Ⓓ
28. Ⓐ Ⓑ Ⓒ Ⓓ

29. Ⓐ Ⓑ Ⓒ Ⓓ
30. Ⓐ Ⓑ Ⓒ Ⓓ
31. Ⓐ Ⓑ Ⓒ Ⓓ
32. Ⓐ Ⓑ Ⓒ Ⓓ
33. Ⓐ Ⓑ Ⓒ Ⓓ
34. Ⓐ Ⓑ Ⓒ Ⓓ
35. Ⓐ Ⓑ Ⓒ Ⓓ
36. Ⓐ Ⓑ Ⓒ Ⓓ
37. Ⓐ Ⓑ Ⓒ Ⓓ
38. Ⓐ Ⓑ Ⓒ Ⓓ
39. Ⓐ Ⓑ Ⓒ Ⓓ
40. Ⓐ Ⓑ Ⓒ Ⓓ
41. Ⓐ Ⓑ Ⓒ Ⓓ
42. Ⓐ Ⓑ Ⓒ Ⓓ

43. Ⓐ Ⓑ Ⓒ Ⓓ
44. Ⓐ Ⓑ Ⓒ Ⓓ
45. Ⓐ Ⓑ Ⓒ Ⓓ
46. Ⓐ Ⓑ Ⓒ Ⓓ
47. Ⓐ Ⓑ Ⓒ Ⓓ
48. Ⓐ Ⓑ Ⓒ Ⓓ
49. Ⓐ Ⓑ Ⓒ Ⓓ
50. Ⓐ Ⓑ Ⓒ Ⓓ
51. Ⓐ Ⓑ Ⓒ Ⓓ
52. Ⓐ Ⓑ Ⓒ Ⓓ
53. Ⓐ Ⓑ Ⓒ Ⓓ
54. Ⓐ Ⓑ Ⓒ Ⓓ
55. Ⓐ Ⓑ Ⓒ Ⓓ
56. Ⓐ Ⓑ Ⓒ Ⓓ

57. Ⓐ Ⓑ Ⓒ Ⓓ
58. Ⓐ Ⓑ Ⓒ Ⓓ
59. Ⓐ Ⓑ Ⓒ Ⓓ
60. Ⓐ Ⓑ Ⓒ Ⓓ
61. Ⓐ Ⓑ Ⓒ Ⓓ
62. Ⓐ Ⓑ Ⓒ Ⓓ
63. Ⓐ Ⓑ Ⓒ Ⓓ
64. Ⓐ Ⓑ Ⓒ Ⓓ
65. Ⓐ Ⓑ Ⓒ Ⓓ
66. Ⓐ Ⓑ Ⓒ Ⓓ
67. Ⓐ Ⓑ Ⓒ Ⓓ
68. Ⓐ Ⓑ Ⓒ Ⓓ
69. Ⓐ Ⓑ Ⓒ Ⓓ
70. Ⓐ Ⓑ Ⓒ Ⓓ